Drafting the Irish Free Sta ......

Manchester University Press

Drafting the Irish Free State Constitution

Laura Cahillane

Manchester University Press

Published by Manchester University Press
Altrincham Street, Manchester M1 7JA

www.manchesteruniversitypress.co.uk

British Library Cataloguing-in-Publication Data
A catalogue record for this book is available from the British Library

Library of Congress Cataloging-in-Publication Data applied for

ISBN 978 1 5261 0057 3 hardback

ISBN 978 1 7849 9511 9 paperback

First published 2016

Typeset in 10/12 Times New Roman
by Servis Filmsetting Ltd, Stockport, Cheshire
Printed in Great Britain
by CPI Group (UK) Ltd, Croydon CR0 4YY

The Arthur Cox Foundation

Arthur Cox, solicitor, classical scholar and former president of the Incorporated Law Society of Ireland, was associated with the setting up of many Irish companies, not least the ESB. He was a specialist in company law and was a member of the Company Law Reform Committee which sat from 1951 and reported to the government in 1958, ultimately giving rise to the Companies Act 1963. When he decided to retire from practice as a solicitor in 1961 a number of his clients, professional colleagues and other friends, in recognition of his outstanding contribution to Ireland and his profession, thought that a fund should be established as a tribute to him, which fund would be used to encourage the writing and publication of legal textbooks. There was a generous response to this appeal.

After his retirement Arthur Cox studied for the priesthood and was ordained in 1963. He went to Zambia to do missionary work. He died there in 1965 as a result of a car accident.

The Foundation was established to honour Arthur Cox and was for many years administered by Mr Justice John Kenny in conjunction with the Law Society. John Kenny was the encouraging force behind the publication of a number of Irish legal textbooks. Without his quiet drive and enthusiasm there would have been no Foundation. To both Arthur Cox and John Kenny we pay tribute.

The Foundation's funds have been used to assist the writing and publication of Irish legal textbooks and the development of electronic databases of Irish legal materials. The Foundation has recently inaugurated an annual prize for the best overall results in the business and corporate law modules of the Law Society's Professional Practice Courses.

The Law Society, as the continuing trustee of the Foundation, is pleased to have been able to assist in the publication of this book.

Simon J. Murphy
President
Law Society of Ireland

Contents

Acknowledgments

I would like to extend my thanks to various people who helped me in different ways on this project: First, to the Arthur Cox Foundation, who provided generous sponsorship which enabled publication of the project; also to the Irish Research Council, who funded the PhD research on which this book is based; to the many academics and historians who kindly gave of their time to discuss aspects of the project and to comment on the work; to Professor David Gwynn Morgan and Dr Conor O'Mahony, who supervised my PhD thesis in University College Cork, and to the Law School at the University of Limerick for their support. A special thank you to Mr Justice Gerard Hogan for his guidance, help and inspiration and for kindly agreeing to write the foreword.

Finally, I would like to thank my family for their patience, encouragement and support.

Some of the material in this book formed part of a journal article and has been reprinted with permission from the *American Journal of Legal History*. See Laura Cahillane, 'An Insight into the Irish Free State Constitution' (2014) 54 (1) *American Journal of Legal History* 1. The material in Chapter 8 was originally published as an article in the *Dublin University Law Journal*: see Laura Cahillane, 'Anti-Party Politics and the Irish Free State Constitution' (2012) 35 *Dublin University Law Journal* 34.

Laura Cahillane

Foreword

The Constitution of the Irish Free State lasted just over 15 years from 6 December 1922 until its ultimate demise on 29 December 1937 when the Constitution of Ireland took effect. For all of its (relatively) short life the Constitution was dogged by at least three fundamental weaknesses. First, it was linked with the terms of the Anglo-Irish Treaty of 1921. Section 2 of the Irish Free State (Saorstát Éireann) Act 1922 provided that the Treaty would have the force of law and that the Oireachtas was absolutely debarred from enacting any legislation inconsistent therewith. All of this meant that, as the 1922 Constitution was bound up with a treaty which had paved the way for civil war, the Constitution was deprived of a degree of popular acceptance from the start. Second, the Constitution could be amended by ordinary legislation for an eight-year period (save where this would conflict with the terms of the Treaty) and this period was itself extended by the Constitution (Amendment No. 19) Act 1928 for a further eight years: there was no period during the currency of the 1922 Constitution when it could not have been amended by ordinary legislation. Third, this paved the way for the doctrine of 'implicit amendment' when the courts simply assumed that, where legislation was inconsistent with the Constitution, it had the effect *pro tanto* of amending the Constitution in this implicit and oblique fashion.

These defects fatally flawed the 1922 Constitution almost from birth. The (comparative) success and longevity of the 1937 Constitution is due in no small measure to the fact that the drafters learnt from these drafting oversights so that the legal supremacy of the Constitution is put beyond question (see, e.g., Article 15.4.1) and, once the three-year transitional period (which could not itself be extended by ordinary legislation) had expired, the Constitution can be amended only by means of referendum: see Article 46 and Article 51.

These drafting difficulties notwithstanding, the Constitution of 1922 contained much that was of value and even today remains of intrinsic interest. In some ways the finest tribute to it was paid by its implacable political opponents, since so much of that document is reflected in the present Constitution. For my part, one of the most interesting features of the 1922 Constitution was the extent to which the drafters consciously sought to borrow from the non-British legal tradition. Not only was the existence of a system of fundamental rights and judicial review of legislation conspicuously novel, but many of those fundamental rights provisions themselves were borrowed – in some cases, almost by means of a direct translation – from the (then avant-garde) interwar continental constitutions, most notably from the much admired Weimar Constitution of 1919. It provides another example of how the nation builders of the 1920s sought to emulate the best of other countries and to set for themselves and the country high standards of governance.

The present book offers the first comprehensive analysis of the drafting of the 1922 Constitution and its aftermath. It is elegantly written by one of the finest constitutional scholars of her generation, Dr Laura Cahillane. Dr Cahillane's work is sure to be the definitive account of a fascinating and hugely important period in Irish constitutional history. Every page of this book shows the meticulous scholarship and measured insights of a constitutional lawyer and historian of the highest possible standing. We all owe Dr Cahillane a huge debt of gratitude for providing us with such an engaging and impressive work which will make a further enormous contribution to our understanding of contemporary constitutional law and history.

Gerard Hogan
Court of Appeal Building
Four Courts
Dublin 7
14 August 2015

The 1922 Constitution Committee (image courtesy of the National Library of Ireland)

Introduction

The modern Irish state was born in 1922 with the promulgation of the Irish Free State Constitution. It was at this moment that many aspects of our legal and political system were created. This momentous but relatively unexplored moment of Ireland's constitutional history has been overshadowed in popular memory by the 1916 Rising, the convocation of the first Dáil in 1919 and specifically by the present Irish Constitution of 1937. These topics have been written about extensively, and recent scholarship has shed light on the circumstances in which the 1937 Constitution came about. However, the circumstances leading to the creation of the 1922 Constitution remain somewhat obscure. This Constitution also gained a bad reputation as a working entity; it was the subject of controversy, misinformation, myth and half-truth. These in turn have each promoted a certain air of contempt or even derision towards what was no less than one of independent Ireland's basic democratic foundations.

This book addresses these issues; it examines the 1922 Constitution, with the benefit of hindsight, and provides a picture of both the document itself and the circumstances surrounding its creation and ultimate demise. It examines the manner in which the Constitution was drafted and, in doing so, elucidates the original intentions of those who drafted the document and examines the reasons why the results did not turn out as anticipated.

Many accounts of the Irish Free State Constitution are quite negative, and the dominant portrayal of the Constitution is that it was a failure; this book explores whether this portrayal perhaps fails to give sufficient credit to the vision of the drafters and the contribution that the Constitution has made to our current legal and political system.

Although many readers will already be familiar with this period in Irish history, for those who may be unaware of the events which led to the drafting of the

1

1922 Irish Free State Constitution, the following contextual information may be useful.[1]

The creation of the Irish Free State Constitution was made possible only following the signing of the Anglo-Irish Treaty on 6 December 1921 by Irish and British representatives.[2] This Treaty was the outcome of a truce which brought an end to centuries of revolutionary struggle in Ireland. The agreement provided for the creation of a new Irish state, which would remain within the British Commonwealth but would have internal autonomy. Previous to this, Ireland had been part of the United Kingdom, a position violently resisted by many Irish. In 1916, a revolutionary group within the state had initiated a rising,[3] which eventually led to a war of independence which lasted from 1919 until the truce in 1921.

However, the Treaty agreement was a controversial one and was not universally accepted in Ireland. Many of those who had fought in the War of Independence believed that a free Irish republic could have been achieved and so they were unwilling to accept anything less than that position. In particular, they refused to take an oath to the British King, something which had been specified in the Treaty. The Treaty agreement eventually led to a split amongst Irish nationalists; Eamon de Valera, then President of Dáil Éireann,[4] and his supporters disapproved of the agreement and refused to recognise the authority of the new Irish state which had been created.[5] However, the Treaty was approved by a majority of the Dáil, and those who were prepared to accept its terms then undertook the task of creating the Irish Free State and writing its first constitution. This task was undertaken by Michael Collins, who became Chairman of the Provisional Government, and Arthur Griffith, who became President of the Dáil.

---

[1] This is intended as general background information only for those who may be unfamiliar with the context.

[2] For an account of the circumstances surrounding the signing of the Treaty and the discussions which led to that point, see Frank Pakenham, *Peace by Ordeal: An Account from First-Hand Sources of the Negotiation and Signature of the Anglo-Irish Treaty 1921* (3rd edn, London, 1962).

[3] The 1916 Easter Rising. This was a small and unsuccessful rising organised by the Irish Republican Brotherhood. It was an event which had little support and inspired little sympathy or respect, until the brutal actions of the British gave it a retrospective grandeur: leaders were shot following trials by field general court martial, in clandestine circumstances, and buried in a mass grave at Arbour Hill. For more, see Adrian Hardiman, 'Shot in Cold Blood: Military Law and Irish Perceptions in the Suppression of the 1916 Rebellion' in Doherty, Gabriel, and Keogh, Dermot (eds), *1916: The Long Revolution* (Cork, 2007), 225

[4] The Irish Parliament which had been created in 1919.

[5] De Valera had not been involved in negotiating the terms of the agreement.

1

The Constitution Committee and the beginning of the drafting process

I do not think I ever worked on a Committee where there was more good fellowship, and where it was possible to have strong differences of opinion without any personal feeling whatsoever. I doubt if a better Committee from the point of view of character and good-will ever attempted to draft a Constitution in any country.[1]

The Constitution Committee

On a cold, sleety day in January 1922, when the newspapers carried stories of the success of the Collins–Craig Agreement, Michael Collins himself was addressing a modest gathering in the Mansion House. Seven men sat in front of him and the anticipation in the room was palpable. These men had been given the immense task of constructing a new constitution for the embryonic Irish state. Outside, Ireland teetered on the brink of civil war and this constitution would represent a chance to finally bring peace to a battered nation. It would need to be not only a document which would appease the Provisional Government and the British authorities but also one which would satisfy the Southern Unionists and would entice the moderate anti-treaty leaders back in from the cold. In essence, these men were being asked to prevent both a civil war and a return to hostilities between the fragile Irish state and Britain. The significance of their task would not have been lost on these men.

Following the signing of the Anglo-Irish Treaty on 6 December 1921, it had been decided to establish a Constitution Committee to draw up a suitable constitution which would be based on the Treaty. Collins had appointed himself chairman of this Constitution Committee but, owing to his many other commitments, he attended only one further meeting and so, guided by his instructions,

---

[1] Letter from James Douglas to L. Hollingsworth Wood, 9 March 1922, in Brian Farrell, 'The Drafting of the Irish Free State Constitution II' (1970) 5 *Irish Jurist* 343, 347.

the committee worked otherwise independently. Because of the magnitude of their task, it was of the utmost importance that the Committee, chosen by Collins and Arthur Griffith, should comprise accomplished, intelligent, politically neutral members.[2] The Committee was an interesting mix of nine very different characters.

Darrell Figgis was appointed acting chairman and, in the absence of Collins, effectively directed the proceedings of the Committee. He was a renowned literary figure in Ireland and had been an active member of the Irish Volunteers. Akenson and Fallin have described his appointment as a 'most curious choice'[3] as he was very unpopular. While Figgis was friendly with Griffith, a rift had occurred between himself and Collins but, despite this, he was, as Farrell notes, 'a major influence on the shaping of the Constitution, both in his daily attendance at the Committee and in the subsequent debate in the Constituent Assembly'.[4] Figgis was a hard worker in terms of his studies of constitutions and he was particularly impressed with the German Weimar Constitution. Having written a book on the ancient Gaelic state,[5] he was anxious, as were the others, that aspects of this ancient heritage be reflected in the new Constitution.

Hugh Kennedy was a distinguished lawyer and would later become the first Chief Justice of the Irish Free State. Kennedy was a constitutional nationalist and he saw Dominion status as a way to establish new Irish institutions of the state, which he believed were necessary in order to ensure the legitimacy of the state. He was devoted to the work of the Constitution Committee and accompanied almost every delegation for negotiations with the British government. He played a major role both in the preliminary drafting and the legal phrasing of the document. He was the only member of the drafting Committee who was present at the discussions of the Irish government and subsequently he assumed the leading role in the constitutional negotiations and redrafting in London.

James Douglas was a Quaker and close friend of Collins. He was a pacifist and was involved with the Irish Conference Committee in 1917 which sought full Dominion status for Ireland on the Canadian model. He may have been chosen

---

[2] The exact basis on which members of the Committee were chosen is unclear. It appears Thomas Johnson of the Labour Party was asked but did not accept a position on the Committee. See letter from Figgis to Collins, 9 March 1922, National Archives of Ireland (NAI), S8952.Various other people were proposed; Griffith suggested Michael Francis Doyle, an American lawyer who was unable to attend (Hugh Kennedy Papers, University College Dublin Archives, P4/317). Figgis suggested Ernest Henry Alton of Trinity College Dublin but subsequently withdrew that recommendation but also proposed Lord Justice James O'Connor. See NAI, S8952. It seems members of the clergy were also approached but none was inclined to join the Committee. See NAI, Cabinet minutes PG1, 17 and 28 January 1922.

[3] D.H. Akenson & F.P. Fallin, 'The Irish Civil War and the Drafting of the Irish Constitution' (1970) V (1) *Éire-Ireland* 10, 13.

[4] Brian Farrell, 'The Drafting of the Irish Free State Constitution I' (1970) 5 *Irish Jurist* 115, 117.

[5] Darrell Figgis, *The Gaelic State in the Past and Future* (Dublin, 1917).

because of his work with the Irish White Cross;[6] Collins felt that Douglas's membership of the Committee was imperative as, besides the fact that he was experienced, conscientious and nonpartisan, he had also earned the trust of all varieties of Irish nationalists. Douglas reported regularly to Collins on the progress of the Committee.

Clement J. France, a lawyer from Seattle, Washington State, was an outspoken champion of workers' rights. He came to Ireland in 1922 as a representative of the American Committee for Relief in Ireland. It was at this time that he met Douglas. The latter was impressed by France's contribution to the success of the White Cross organisation and he proposed that France might be a useful addition to the Committee considering both his transatlantic experience and his legal capability. Later, however, Douglas was to doubt whether this was a sound decision. He received a letter from John Ryan, a New York correspondent who warned Douglas about France, saying France was claiming he had a special place in Irish governmental circles and that he was not to be taken as representative of Irish-American opinion.[7] Douglas duly passed on the letter to Collins, while noting that France had been a great help to the work of the Committee. However, more letters were received within a few weeks which convinced Douglas that 'the face value of the correspondence makes France look a pure adventurer'.[8] Despite this, it appears France did make a valuable contribution to the work of the Committee. He was particularly concerned with the idea of complete economic freedom for Ireland and the protection of the natural endowments of the state.

Timothy James McNeill, brother of the nationalist revolutionary Eoin MacNeill,[9] had served as a high-ranking civil servant in the Raj Civil Service in Calcutta before returning to Ireland. He had been active in a number of nationalist movements and became chairman of Dublin County Council. After serving on the Constitution Committee, McNeill was appointed as Irish High Commissioner in London and later as Governor-General. McNeill, like Douglas and France, was also involved in the White Cross.

James Murnaghan was a lawyer and an academic. He was appointed to the Supreme Court in 1925. He does not appear to have been involved in any way with Sinn Féin or any other nationalist organisation. Unfortunately, there is little

---

[6] A civilian relief organisation, set up to raise funds in the United States in order to supply relief to people whose property had been devastated by the Crown forces in reprisals for IRA activity.

[7] See Farrell, 'Drafting II', 351. Ryan commented that they were unaware of France's views so they could not say if these were an accurate representation of Irish-American opinion. However, he also commented that France's brother had lately come from Russia with obviously communist opinions which shocked the great majority of thinking Americans.

[8] *Ibid.*, 352.

[9] Famous Irish scholar, nationalist, revolutionary and politician. He co-founded the Gaelic League and also established the Irish Volunteers. He was also professor of early Irish history at University College Dublin.

information available on Murnaghan and, because he missed so many meetings due to illness, he does not seem to have had as great an influence as some of the others on the Committee, although he did work on the judicial provisions with John O'Byrne.[10]

John O'Byrne worked in the Civil Service in London for a few years before returning to Ireland to work in the Irish Land Commission. He later became a Supreme Court judge. While it seems O'Byrne was a regular attender, besides his work on the judicial provisions, there is little evidence of his influence on the Drafts.

While not involved in the original meetings, Alfred O'Rahilly was later invited to join the Constitution Committee. He was Professor of Mathematical Physics in University College Cork, a deeply religious Catholic, and was well known for his writings supporting the politics of Sinn Féin. He had very specific views on how the new Constitution should be structured as he had spent a number of years forming opinions on the subject, particularly while in prison on Bere Island. He favoured the use of the Swiss Constitution as a model.

Kevin O'Shiel was also a late addition to the Committee. He is credited with being largely responsible for the success of the Dáil Land Courts. As well as his work for the Committee in 1922, he acted as Assistant Legal Adviser to the Provisional Government and, because of his volume of work, he was unable to attend many meetings.

There were also three civil servants appointed as secretaries; E.M. Stephens[11] was the principal secretary and he was joined by R.J.P. Mortished[12] and P.A. O'Toole.[13]

In total, there were five lawyers on the Committee and four lay persons, including a professor, a businessman, a writer and a former British civil servant. The absence of any women on the Committee is notable, although it would not have been considered unusual. All were pro-Treaty nationalists.[14] At least four members[15] had also been involved in the Irish White Cross, which indicates that this organisation was seen as a neutral one whose members would be acceptable

---

[10] See Document 29, Papers of E.M. Stephens, MSS 4234–41, Trinity College Dublin Archives.

[11] He later became secretary to the Boundary Commission.

[12] Later he was an Irish representative at the International Labour Office at Geneva.

[13] He was requested by the Committee during a meeting on 30 January. He worked for the Public Record Office.

[14] Donal O'Sullivan has written that the absence of any anti-Treaty members was 'regrettable' but it was also 'inevitable' since the Constitution was to be based on the Treaty. Donal O'Sullivan, *The Irish Free State and Its Senate: A Study in Contemporary Politics* (London, 1940), 70.

[15] Figgis, Douglas, McNeill and France. O'Rahilly may also have had some involvement as a document entitled 'constitution for the Irish White Cross' was found among his papers. See Alfred O'Rahilly Papers, Special Collections, University College Cork. Mortished was also involved in the organisation.

to all sides.[16] It seems that Figgis, Douglas and Kennedy were the most influential members of the Committee, with O'Shiel and Murnaghan contributing least, due to their absences. O'Rahilly was also quite productive but his opinions were often too uncompromising for the others.

The work of the Committee

Beginnings

The Committee had an extremely short time within which to complete its drafting work: the Provisional Government had specified one month. One of the princi-pal reasons for this short period was that the Provisional Government wished to attend the 'Geneva Conference'[17] in order to be recognised internationally as a new state. The British had agreed that, if the Constitution was in draft by March, then they would have no technical objection to the attendance of Irish Free State representatives at the Conference. Apart from the initial meeting, all Committee gatherings were held in the Shelbourne Hotel in what came to be known as the Constitution Room. The Committee sat almost every day for a month, and the drafting stage was completed by 7 March 1922 after twenty-seven meetings and members had considered a total of over fifty documents.[18]

Collins had outlined what he wanted from the drafting Committee at their initial meeting on 24 January. He told them not to be 'bound up by legal formalities' but to draft 'a constitution of a Free State' and the Provisional Government would fight to have it accepted. He pointed out that what was needed was 'a true democratic constitution' and he stressed that they were 'to bear in mind not the legalities of the past but the practicalities of the future'.[19] Subsequently in correspondence to Douglas, Collins also specified that he wanted 'a constitution that would be short, simple, easy to alter as the final stages of complete freedom were achieved and only contain what was necessary to establish constitutional machinery to govern Ireland'. He also made the point that it should omit everything already covered in the treaty and should rest solely upon authority derived from the Irish people.[20]

The only specific requirements given to the Committee by Collins were that Articles 3, 4 and 6 of the Treaty (these dealt with the King and Governor-General) should certainly be left out of the Constitution[21] and that a bi-cameral legislature

---

[16] In fact, Akenson & Fallin have written that it was their activity in the White Cross which brought them to the attention of Collins. See Akenson & Fallin, 'The Irish Civil War and the Drafting of the Irish Constitution', 16.

[17] The League of Nations Council, eighteenth session, May 1922.

[18] See Farrell, 'Drafting I', 120.

[19] J. Alfred Gaughan (ed.), *Memoirs of Senator James G. Douglas (1887–1954): Concerned Citizen* (Dublin, 1998), 163–4.

[20] *Ibid.*

[21] Minutes of the first meeting in Hugh Kennedy Papers, University College Dublin Archives, P4.

would be necessary in order to please the Southern Unionists.[22] Collins did not intend to provoke the British by leaving out any mention of the Crown;[23] rather he felt that, if these provisions were already covered in the Treaty, there was no sense in repeating them in the Constitution itself, particularly when the Treaty would be included as an annexe to the Constitution. Furthermore, de Valera and his supporters might be more likely to relent if they saw that the Constitution did not contain any British references.

Members of the Committee were content with Collins's terms, particularly the dropping of certain Treaty provisions. In fact, O'Rahilly accepted Collins's invitation to join the Committee only on the understanding that he did not recognise the Treaty as constitutionally binding and he would not agree to any mention of the King in the Constitution. Other members were a little worried as to how this could be done and Douglas questioned Collins on how the oath could possibly be left out of the new document.[24] However, Kennedy decided that, legally, the Treaty did not require the inclusion of the oath in the Constitution. Collins agreed and made the point that, if it were put in, it would look as if the Irish wanted it.[25]

Collins also told Douglas that he wished Ireland's Constitution to be one which would provide the country with equality not simply within the British Empire but among all nations of the world.[26] As Akenson and Fallin have noted, it is clear that Collins was pressing for a radical and highly independent constitution.[27] Griffith told the Committee that he wanted as little as possible of the Canadian Constitution in that of the Irish Free State.[28] In other words, it was to be uniquely Irish.

Apart from Collins's aspirations and his instructions on the legislature, the Committee was given relative freedom within which to draft the document. Kennedy later explained that:

---

[22] Griffith had met with the Southern Unionists on 16 November 1921, when he agreed that an upper House would form part of the legislature and that the Southern Unionists would be consulted as to the specific details of the House. Apparently the Cabinet approved this agreement and on 6 December, following the signing of the Treaty, Griffith again met with the Unionists to guarantee that their interests would be safeguarded.

[23] Although the British assumed that was exactly what he was trying to do and when they saw the Draft Constitution, they claimed it was a subterfuge. See Chapter 4. s

[24] See Stephens's Notebook, Papers of E.M. Stephens, MSS 4235, Trinity College Dublin Archives.

[25] See Gaughan, *Memoirs of James Douglas*, 87.

[26] Letter from Collins to Douglas, 28 January 1922 in Papers of James Douglas (in the possession of Harold Douglas, Dublin) as cited by Akenson & Fallin, *The Irish Civil War*, 24.

[27] Akenson & Fallin, *The Irish Civil War*, 24.

[28] Joseph M. Curran, *The Birth of the Irish Free State 1921–1923* (Alabama, 1980), 208.

[The Committee's] work was given coherent direction by unity of purpose to make secure the full measure of sovereign statehood and political liberty won by the sufferings and sacrifice of their countrymen and crystallised in the Treaty of 1921, and by unity of principle in the simple instruction given them by Griffith and Collins, namely, to draft a democratic constitution. The Committee was happily free from any obligation to accept existing British or Dominion models, and could, on the one hand, respond to the guidance of Irish history and existing Irish conditions and, on the other hand, borrow of the experience of the constituted democracies of the world.[29]

Naturally, the constitutional experience of the members was limited. The system with which they were most familiar was, of course, that of the British. However, they were all in agreement that much of this system would be unsuitable as a model for the new Irish system. On this point, Kohn has explained that 'theoretical inclination and republican outlook alike led the framers of the Irish Constitution to seek inspiration from Continental models, however experimental, rather than from the empirical framework of the British Constitution'.[30]

One of the principal limitations of the British system was that the unwritten constitution was framed around the Crown, whereas the Committee was unanimous in the decision that, under the new Irish Constitution, the people would be sovereign. The Committee was even less enamoured with the British mode of election and their style of government. The most obvious written constitution to which they might have turned was the United States Constitution. They would have had France's expertise in this area as well as the fact that O'Shiel had written a book on the framing of that document.[31] However, again there were elements of that Constitution which made it an unsuitable candidate; mostly the fact that it was federal in character.[32] It was not dismissed completely, however, and much of it was examined by the Committee.[33]

Different members were influenced in turn by various other constitutions. O'Rahilly had made an intense study of the Swiss Constitution and was impressed by many of the provisions which he felt could be translated into the Irish situation. He was shocked that some of the others had no knowledge of it at all and even lent his copy to Kennedy.[34] Figgis, on the other hand, was greatly impressed by the German (Weimar) Constitution. All members seemed impressed by the spirit and tone of the postwar constitutions. As well as these sources, the Committee was obliged to study the Canadian system because the Treaty specified Canada as

---

[29] Kennedy in the foreword to Leo Kohn, *Constitution of the Irish Free State* (London, 1932), xi.

[30] Kohn, *ibid.*, 78.

[31] Kevin O'Shiel, *The Making of a Republic* (Dublin, 1920).

[32] Although Canada was also a federation and the Swiss Constitution, which was also a major inspiration, was also federal.

[33] The American experience may have inspired the judicial review provisions. See Chapter 9.

[34] Akenson & Fallin, 'The Irish Civil War', 26.

a model for the new Irish system.[35] Thomas Towey has described how Kennedy realised early on the potential in being tied to Canada. Kennedy felt that Canada 'had outgrown her colonial status as well as her constitution and in the gradual evolution of law, practice and constitutional usage had reached national stature and exhibited marks of national sovereignty'.[36] Because of this, the Committee, but especially Kennedy, commenced an intense study of Canadian practice in order to decide how Ireland could benefit from it.

In fact, the Committee became familiar with a vast number of foreign constitutions as at the beginning of its sessions it sought and received a number of constitutions from around the world together with historical introductions on each. These proved very useful to the Committee in drafting various parts of the Constitution and the documents were also made available to members of the Constituent Assembly for comparison purposes during the debates on the Constitution.[37] As well as constitutional documents, the Committee also requested many copies of books on the British Commonwealth in order for the members to familiarise themselves with the Dominion structures.

A short time into proceedings of the Committee Figgis distributed a memorandum which gave details of a drafting strategy and the approach they were to take. Farrell has observed that this document was remarkably similar to a document in the memoirs of Douglas which is described as 'suggestions' of Michael Collins.[38] In fact, that document was written by Douglas and it appears that it was drawn up as a result of questions put to Collins by Douglas rather than something which Collins deliberately circulated to the members.[39] Nevertheless, these 'suggestions' obviously had an effect as the document disseminated by Figgis directed the future drafting work. Essentially, the document comprised seven chapters:

1. A preamble which would also briefly enunciate the rights of the people.
2. A general chapter dealing with matters such as the flag, citizenship and right of free assembly etc.
3. The National Assembly.
4. Executive government.
5. The King's representative.
6. The judicature.
7. Finance.

---

[35] Although, as noted earlier, Griffith instructed the Committee to use as little as possible of the Canadian Constitution, the Committee discovered that it could use it to its advantage by concentrating on practice rather than the letter of the law.

[36] Thomas Towey, 'Hugh Kennedy and the Constitutional Development of the Irish Free State, 1922–1923' (1977) 12 *Irish Jurist* 355.

[37] These documents were later made into a book: *Select Constitutions of the World* (Dublin, 1922).

[38] Farrell, 'Drafting I', 122.

[39] Murnaghan had never heard of this document. See Farrell, 'Drafting I', 122.

These are quite general, but Figgis suggested that various other sections could be added to deal with unspecified matters and that these would fall naturally into place if the order of approach could be agreed.[40]

The early meetings were mainly concerned with issues such as citizenship and naturalisation. The idea of initiation of legislation was also proposed quite early on.[41] Many suggestions were made which were ruled out at later stages, such as the proposal for a constitutional court or the proposal to have an external relations committee as part of the executive. Experts were also brought in to advise the Committee on certain financial and electoral issues. In particular, the records mention Professors Bastable and Oldham, Mr Waterfield of the British Treasury in Ireland and Mr Humphreys of the PR Society of Britain in connection with proportional representation.[42] Douglas has described the meetings as 'all most friendly with frank discussion'.[43] However, while most of the Committee meetings may have been congenial, it is clear that certain difficulties did arise between members, most notably between Figgis and Douglas and between O'Rahilly and many of the others. There had already been some tension between Douglas and Figgis; the latter apparently blamed Douglas for his own failure to be appointed secretary of the Irish White Cross.[44] In late February, Figgis accused Douglas of secretly meeting with Erskine Childers to discuss constitutional matters. Douglas responded that since the Committee began its work he had seen Childers once 'for two minutes on a tram'. O'Rahilly also caused what Farrell refers to as 'personality problems'. O'Rahilly had hoped to involve members of the Catholic hierarchy in the drafting process, a move resisted by the others. Later, following frequent absences, he wrote to the Committee outlining his disagreement with 'practically every section' of the draft which had been sent to him. After that, he decided to pursue his own draft.[45]

Talking points: a second Chamber

The Committee found agreement in relation to most constitutional matters. However, there were one or two major disagreements. The Senate became a talking point among members almost immediately. On 30 January, the Committee discussed the question of the second House and, although it was stated that the question of whether or not the provision of a second House was a good idea was outside of their terms of reference, the members were each given a chance to air their opinion on the matter.

---

[40] Farrell, 'Drafting I', 127.
[41] Stephens's Notebook, MSS 4235, Trinity College Dublin Archives. See also Chapter 7.
[42] *Ibid.*
[43] Gaughan, *Memoirs of James Douglas*, 81.
[44] Akenson & Fallin, 'The Irish Civil War', 14.
[45] O'Rahilly began his own project on 21 February. Farrell has provided a detailed account of these problems. See Farrell, 'Drafting II'.

Figgis did not hesitate to express his opinion that 'a good one cannot operate and a bad one is worse than useless'.[46] He believed that if they were to have a second Chamber it should be protected; it should have definite rights and limited franchise. He also suggested vocation as a means of citizen representation. Douglas and O'Byrne agreed that a nominated House was pointless but disagreed with Figgis's ideas on election, with Douglas instead favouring proportional representation by members of the lower House and citizens who had special qualifications. Douglas strongly resisted the idea of special representation, especially for the Southern Unionists. Kennedy generally concurred with the ideas of Douglas, particularly the strategy of having a college of electors drawn from the lower House with powers to appoint the members of the upper House. He also questioned whether it would be advisable to permit the inclusion of clergy members in the upper Chamber. On the other hand, O'Byrne favoured the representation of different interests; he felt that membership of the House should be small with large electoral constituencies and a fixed term of 10 years.[47]

Murnaghan and McNeill spoke out against the idea of a House whose main function was delay of legislation and Murnaghan proposed the idea of joint sittings of both Houses in cases of conflict, which O'Byrne agreed with. Douglas believed that the upper House should have powers to initiate and revise legislation but only limited powers of delay. France warned against the possibility of small local interests taking precedence over more important issues and suggested a membership of 25.[48]

Farrell notes that the secretaries also gave their opinions and details their contribution:

> Mortished said that a functional chamber was impossible: opposed giving the senate power to initiate legislation and thought there should be 'technical qualifications' for members. Stephens argued the advantage of a functional upper house but gives no details of his case in his notes on the meetings. O'Toole opposed the functional idea; he thought that technical knowledge could easily be supplied; he favoured larger constituencies but held that the senate should not be allowed to rival the lower house – no financial bills and 'the fate of the ministry should not be decided in the upper house'.[49]

Figgis summarised all of the arguments and eventually the Committee decided that the Senate would have powers of delay and revision but not a veto and that it could initiate legislation but not financial bills.[50] However, the Committee was unable to reach agreement on the mode of election for senators and by late February there were four alternative proposals before the Committee: a Senate elected by the Dáil, one elected partly by the Dáil and partly by the people,

---

[46] Stephens's Notebook, MSS 4235, Trinity College Dublin Archives.
[47] *Ibid.*
[48] *Ibid.*
[49] Farrell, 'Drafting I', 129.
[50] *Ibid.*

direct election by the people with the whole country forming one single constituency or direct election by large constituencies.[51] Although the Senate continued to be a controversial topic (and it remains controversial today) and indeed the provision was the main candidate for amendment during 1922 to 1937, the Committee did agree on general recommendations to submit to the Provisional Government, although slightly different versions were eventually presented when the Committee later split into three groups.[52]

Disagreements: the executive

The Committee did not always find ways to resolve their differences of opinion and one of the principal sources of conflict was the form of the executive which should be adopted. Although there were a number of different disagreements related to this topic, including the responsibility of ministers, dissolution of the Dáil and the powers of the President,[53] the biggest source of contention was an idea which had come from Douglas; he envisaged a separate group of administrative ministers who would be expert outsiders[54] and who would take charge of certain departments. This was the original idea behind the external ministers strategy which was eventually implemented. Douglas's plan was that these ministers would be subject to collective responsibility but a defeat of one of the ministers would not affect the government. He felt they should be elected by the Dáil and should serve for a ten-year period. France supported the scheme, noting that there was a need for stability and that ministerial positions required technical knowledge which could not be earned if the position was to change with each change of government. However, Kennedy initially disagreed with France's line of reasoning, pointing out that instead of stability, it could lead to stagnation. Murnaghan also opposed the scheme.[55]

All of the members were agreed that they wanted to distance themselves from the British system[56] but some were more insistent than others on the distance

---

[51] See Farrell, 'Drafting II', 345.

[52] See below.

[53] The word 'president' was used by the Committee but it was a prime ministerial role which was envisaged, not a presidential one.

[54] This may have been an attempt to include personalities like de Valera and Childers who insisted they would not take an oath of allegiance and therefore would not sit in Parliament. However, it is more likely that this was a happy coincidence rather than the main motivation for the scheme.

[55] See Stephens's Notebook, MSS 4235, Trinity College Dublin Archives.

[56] There were a few reasons for this besides a wish to move away from all things British, including the fact that the Committee was quite insistent on the idea of sovereignty of the people rather than Parliament or Crown. In addition, the Committee was not impressed with the British party system which led to petty party politics and, because they had decided on the system of proportional representation, they felt this would not work well with the British system as they anticipated this mode of election would lead to numerous small political parties. See Chapter 8.

required. Eventually, three separate executive schemes emerged. Figgis outlined an alternative scheme in a memorandum called 'Proposal for the Creation of an Executive'. His scheme involved the idea of legislative control of the executive. He felt the executive itself should comprise only five to ten members elected by the Dáil by Proportional Representation. Once elected, the ministers would set up councils representing their function. He proposed that ministers would sit in the Dáil but not vote.

However, O'Rahilly was completely disenchanted with the British system and had other ideas. Farrell has described his proposal as follows:

> This provided for an Executive Council consisting of President, Vice-President and Minister of External Affairs and not more than seven other ministers chosen 'from among all the Irish citizens eligible for Dáil Éireann' but requiring the three named ministers to be members of the Dáil; the President, when elected by the Dáil, would appoint the other two but there was to be no extension of executive power of influence.[57]

The scheme also provided that, if elected to the Council, a member would have to vacate his seat in Parliament. It appears as though this model was too radical for some of the members and some of these provisions were revised.

At this stage, the Committee was able to reach a compromise between these three positions and in their first complete draft of the Constitution, which is referred to as Document 28,[58] the provisions on the executive were 'neutral but open'.[59] When it came to the ultimate decision on these matters, however, the Committee did not come to a decision so easily. O'Rahilly now proceeded to draw up his own 'Minority Report' and the external ministers scheme was still being considered as an alternative to Document 28. At this stage, it was clear the Committee was not going to come up with one composite draft and so they applied for a time extension. However, the time limit was still too short and so the Committee divided into three factions and decided to submit separate documents.

Draft A was the work of Figgis, McNeill and O'Byrne. Draft B, which was essentially the same draft but with a different section on the executive, was endorsed by Douglas, Kennedy and France. O'Rahilly had missed quite a few meetings and was unhappy with the direction the other drafts had taken so he also decided to draw up an alternative draft. This document was quite removed from the others and was by far the most radical. Murnaghan, who had also missed many of the meetings, decided to endorse O'Rahilly's Draft C. O'Shiel declined to sign any of the Drafts citing lack of qualification due to his frequent absences.

---

[57] Farrell, 'Drafting II', 343.

[58] In relation to the numbering of documents, these seem to have been numbered consecutively rather than categorically by Stephens in his files. Memoranda, drafts and letters are all simply given consecutive numbers.

[59] Farrell, 'Drafting I', 133. However, it is unclear whether O'Rahilly ever endorsed this document as he had already decided to draft his own document at this stage.

Conclusion

While there may have been disappointment among Committee members that they could not produce one draft upon which there was unanimous agreement, their achievement was still remarkable. In the space of about six weeks and after only 27 meetings, they had come up with the plans for the 1922 and, essentially, the 1937 Constitutions. The Committee was prolific in its study of foreign constitutions and legal systems, and lengthy, in-depth discussions were held on the suitability of many of the provisions. Each of the Drafts was well thought out and expressly suited to Irish conditions and, even though some ideas and various provisions were dropped at different stages from April to December 1922, many of these reappeared again in 1937. Furthermore, while they may have had differences of opinion on certain points, all members wished to provide a sovereign, democratic and uniquely Irish document which would inspire the trust of the people in the new state.

2

The Drafts

Introduction

February and early March 1922 were a busy time for the Provisional Government. On the two occasions the Dáil sat in March, the government had to deal with numerous questions on issues such as unemployment, the ownership of evacuated land, the setting up of a police force, the future of the Dáil courts and still many debates descended into arguments on the Treaty.[1] Furthermore, on 22 February, a decision had been made at the Sinn Féin Árd Fheis that the coming election[2] would not be held within the next three months but, when it was to be held, the Constitution would 'be placed before the people in its final form'.[3] Thus the Provisional Government had about 12 weeks to decide on an appropriate draft Constitution and obtain the approval of the British authorities before presenting it to the Irish people.[4]

On 7 March, the day Griffith and Collins launched their election campaign with meetings in College Green, all three Drafts prepared by the Committee were submitted to the Provisional Government for consideration. While all of the Drafts share similarities in structure and form, there were significant differences between them in relation to detail. Draft B was eventually chosen by the Provisional Government, for reasons which will be explored below, and was presented, with amendments, to the British authorities. Because of this, it is quite similar in structure to the eventual Irish Free State Constitution of December 1922. The same terms were maintained as well as many of the ideas. Draft A is quite similar to Draft B in many respects, especially in relation to terminology, and most of the provisions are the same. In fact, if it were not for the disagreements in relation to the executive, it is likely that O'Rahilly's Draft C would

---

[1] See *Dáil Debates*, vol 2, cols 144ff, 1 March 1922, col 224ff, 2 March 1922.
[2] See Chapter 4.
[3] *Irish Times*, 'Events during 1922', 1 January 1923.
[4] On the decision to submit the draft to the British authorities, see Chapter 3, 45.

have been the sole minority draft. Draft C appears dissimilar as it uses American terminology for the legislative provisions, the structure is slightly different and it contains some substantial differences in detail. Given that these documents are not generally known, and have not previously been examined in any great detail, all three are worth examining in depth here.[5] Since Draft B was the document which was eventually accepted it is useful to consider this first and to compare the differences in the other two Drafts.

The three Drafts

Preamble and preliminary Articles

Draft B begins with a preamble[6] which acknowledges that all authority comes from God and makes purposeful statements, including the words 'free people' which are intended to convey the magnitude of the new status of the country. The preamble concludes with the phrase: 'that Ireland may take her rightful place among the Nations of the earth'. Already, the tone has been set and Section I[7] follows in the same manner, with Article 1 directly proclaiming the nation's sovereignty and Article 2 clarifying that all powers of government are derived from the people. In fact, these declarations contained in Article 1 are quoted directly from a declaration of sovereignty written by Pádraig Pearse and also contained in the Democratic Programme of 1919. (This was one of three documents adopted by the first Dáil on 21 January 1919. The other two documents were the Dáil Constitution and the Declaration of Independence.)

Draft A is similar and uses the same terms in the preamble but it is longer and sounds even more philosophical, as it speaks of taking 'control of our destiny' and developing the 'spiritual aspirations of our people'.[8] The preliminary Articles which follow mirror Draft B.

Draft C contains a similar preamble,[9] again asserting that political authority

---

5 While copies of the Drafts were published by Farrell and by Akenson & Fallin, they have not previously been analysed or examined in any detail.

6 'We, the people of Ireland, acknowledging that all authority comes from God, and in the exercise of our right as a free people, do hereby create Saorstát Éireann and give it this Constitution. Through it we shall endeavour to re-establish our national life and unity that Ireland may take her rightful place among the Nations of the earth.'

7 Note the word 'section' is used in the Drafts to refer to chapters or blocks of Articles, unlike Bunreacht na hÉireann where a section is a smaller part of an Article. These sections were included simply for the purposes of clarity and were deleted later.

8 'We, the people of Ireland, in our resolve to renew and re-establish our State and to found it on principles of freedom and justice, take control of our destiny in order that Ireland may take her place among the Nations of the world as a free democratic State. In the exercise of our sovereign right as a free people and to promote the welfare and to preserve and develop the heritage and the spiritual aspirations of our people, we hereby declare Saorstát Éireann established and give it this Constitution.'

9 'We, the Irish people, acknowledging that political authority comes from God to the

comes from God to the people and it goes on to declare: 'our natural right to national independence and unity ...'. The preambles of Drafts A and C both declare a wish to develop the state on the principles of justice and liberty/freedom. Unlike Drafts B and A, Draft C does not elaborate on sovereignty, perhaps because it was felt the preamble was sufficient as a declaration of sovereignty, but it does state in Article 1 that legislative power resides directly in the people of Ireland. The reference to unity in Draft C is also worthy of note. The theme of popular sovereignty introduced here is evident throughout the Drafts with further provisions designed to strengthen the power of the people.[10]

Fundamental rights

Following the preamble, Draft B contains a section on fundamental rights. Through this section, and in fact throughout the whole document, evidence can be found of France's views on public ownership of land and the natural resources of the state. The very first Article declares that 'all right to private property is subordinated to the public right and welfare of the nation'. Articles 11, 12, 41 and 42 on the natural resources of the state also deal with this topic, and it appears that the authors purposely placed a great emphasis on this point, to the detriment of the right to hold private property, which is never mentioned. Presumably, the memory of the Land Wars was still quite fresh and acted as a deterrent to the inclusion of a right to private property.[11]

Conversely, Draft C specifically guarantees the right to hold private property and specifies that 'expropriation of private property may be effected only by legislation for the benefit of the community, and with compensation'.[12] However, Draft C does not neglect the natural resources of the state, affirming that their exploitation by private individuals or associations shall be permitted only under State supervision'.[13] These provisions contain a left-wing tone, something which can be seen, to varying degrees, in places throughout all three Drafts.[14]

Draft B guarantees the right to liberty,[15] inviolability of the dwelling,[16] free

people, asserting our natural right to national independence and unity, and in pursuance of our claim to determine freely the forms of Irish Government, hereby vote and confirm this Constitution in the Constituent Assembly of the Irish Free State, in order to base the organisation and development of our country on the principles of justice and liberty.'

[10] See Chapter 7.
[11] See Chapter 6, 88–9.
[12] Art 62, Draft C.
[13] Art 65, Draft C.
[14] This is considered further below.
[15] Art 6, Draft B.
[16] Art 7, Draft B.

exercise of religion,[17] freedom of expression[18] and free primary education,[19] and, while there is no general equality provision, Article 3, which contains the citizenship provision, also provides that all 'men and women have as citizens the same rights' and in Article 5 there is a prohibition on titles of honour. The Committee felt strongly about this last provision and it appears that, at the time, equality between the various strata of society was of more pressing interest than equality between the sexes[20] (although, as we will see below, Draft C covers both areas).

In this section also, the Irish language is proclaimed to be the national language, with English being equally recognised. Although English was declared to be equal, the declaration of Irish as the national language constituted a statement about the status Irish was to have in the new state. In contrast, Draft C declares that the Irish and English languages are equal.[21]

In the fundamental rights section, Draft A is almost word for word the same as Draft B, apart from some slight differences in the phraseology of Articles 11 and 12.

Draft C is more detailed with respect to the rights provisions. Interestingly, rather than having the fundamental rights provisions at the beginning of the document, like Drafts A and B, Draft C locates this section at the end with only amendment of the Constitution to follow. This structure is rather like that adopted in 1937. Also, in Draft C, there are separate sections, which do not feature in the other Drafts, dealing with 'Individual Rights and Duties', 'Family, Education and Religion' and 'Economic Life'. It is worth considering these separately.

Individual rights and duties in Draft C

The first section deals with citizenship. It contains an equality provision in Article 46 which provides that 'all citizens are equal before the law, independently of birth, sex, status or rank'. It also specifies that titles of nobility will no longer be conferred or received. Article 47 subsection 1 authorises a limited freedom of expression while subsection 2 details the limits involved. Articles 49 and 50 give the right of assembly and the right to form unions and associations. Articles 51 and 52 deal with the military and seem out of place in this section but deal with important matters nonetheless, as Article 52 subsection 2 declares that all 'proclamations of so-called martial law shall be null and void'.

There is also a provision which is not located in this section but rather among the judicial provisions in Article 43, which states that 'Limitations of liberty, personal or domiciliary, are admitted only in cases provided for by law ...'. Despite

---

[17] Art 8, Draft B.
[18] Art 9, Draft B.
[19] Art 10, Draft B.
[20] Interview with Professor Tom Garvin, University College Dublin, 13 July 2010. Garvin noted that the women's time had simply not yet arrived. Also women were not sufficiently organised to campaign for equality rights. Also see Chapter 6, 90–2.
[21] Art 26 (2), Draft C.

the three separate sections of rights in this document, the right to liberty is never mentioned except in the form provided in this Article.

Family, education and religion in Draft C

The second section goes into details which are not found in Drafts A or B. A strong emphasis is placed on marriage and it is given the 'special protection' of the State. Article 53 provides:

> (1) Marriage, as the basis of family life and national well-being, is under the special protection of the State; and all attacks on the purity, health and sacredness of family life shall be forbidden. (2) The Irish State shall recognise, as heretofore, the inviolable sanctity of the marital bond. (3) The civil validity of religiously solemnised marriages shall be recognised, provided that the details of registration prescribed by legislation are duly complied with.[22]

Maternity also receives this protection in a separate Article, as do young people, who are protected from exploitation in that the employment of under-14s was forbidden and industrial night work by women was also forbidden. Article 55 reads:

> (1) Maternity shall be under the special protection of the law. (2) Young people shall be protected against exploitation and against moral, intellectual or bodily neglect. (3) The employment of children under fourteen in wage-earning occupations, work of adolescents in injurious trades, and industrial night work of women shall be forbidden by law.[23]

It is strange that the maternity provision was located separately from the marriage provision. This, possibly, could open the argument that maternity was meant to include mothers outside of wedlock also. However, given the stigma of this situation (and the religious leanings of O'Rahilly) it is unlikely that this is what was intended.

While the purpose of subsection (3) of the provision is obvious, the second part could pose a problem in that it interferes with a woman's right to work. Of course,

---

[22] There are obvious similarities here between this provision and the original Article 41.3 of the 1937 Constitution. In fact, Keogh and McCarthy have written in relation to this provision that 'In their initial October draft, de Valera and Hearne drew on O'Rahilly's work'. See Dermot Keogh & Andrew McCarthy, *The Making of the Irish Constitution 1937* (Cork, 2007), 112. In addition, the other submissions which inspired the final provisions in 1937, such as those from Fr Cahill, the Jesuits and Archbishop McQuaid, were all influenced by Leo XIII's Encyclical *Rerum Novarum*, which was also an influence on O'Rahilly.

[23] There are hints of the sentiments included in this provision in Article 41.2 of the 1937 Constitution. See above. This provision (as well as certain other provisions from Draft C) is also reminiscent of Article 45 of the 1937 Constitution, which contains the Directive Principles of Social Policy. However, Keogh & McCarthy have written in relation to Article 45 that in drafting his submission for this Article (which was quite close to the final version) McQuaid stated that he had read O'Rahilly's Draft but was 'politely dismissive of it'. See Keogh & McCarthy, *The Making of the Irish Constitution*, 120.

this would not have been as obvious at a time when women generally did not have (or seek) such rights.

Article 54 provides that it is parents who have the right and duty to educate their children until they have completed their fourteenth year but the state has the power of supervision. Article 56 creates the Council of Education which would run the educational system under state supervision and also provides that there would be no state monopoly of education. The idea of a Council of Education sounds very interesting and there is no equivalent in the other Drafts. However, it is simply mentioned in the provision with no guidance as to how it would have functioned. It is also referred to in Article 37 which provides for 'functional autonomy for the different branches of social service and economic life'. That Article also specifies that 'legislation shall determine the advisory, supervisory, and administrative capacity of such Councils'. We are not provided with any more information on how such councils would operate.

Article 57 provides that the teaching of religion in schools was to be obligatory but Article 59 states that there was to be no state-endowed church[24] and guarantees free practice of religion 'in so far as public order or morality is not thereby affected'.

Economic life (and property) in Draft C

The third section, on 'Economic Life' (which also has no equivalent in Drafts A or B), begins with some aspirational-sounding duties for citizens involving the use of their mental and physical powers for the welfare of the community.[25] Citizens are also given a right to 'leisure and conditions necessary for spiritual interests, social obligations and political rights' and, strangely, the next subsection declares that 'all transactions opposed to morality and all usurious contracts shall be regarded as null and void'.

As mentioned above, Article 62 contains the provisions on private property. Article 63 provides that the natural resources of Ireland are under the 'special supervision and control' of the state and private property must not be allowed to interfere with conservation which is for the wellbeing of the community. Any unappropriated resources are then claimed by the state. Article 64 contains a strange provision in relation to land: 'The landholder is bound, in duty to the community, to secure a reasonably efficient working or utilisation of the land.'[26] Article 67, which concludes the sections on rights, contains another rather unusual provision:

---

[24] Perhaps this was intended to avoid the British situation of a state-established church as well as ensuring compliance with the Treaty requirements.

[25] It was common in the postwar constitutions to include duties as well as rights. See generally Agnes Headlam-Morley, *The New Democratic Constitutions of Europe: A Comparative Study of Post-War European Constitutions with Special Reference to Germany, Czechoslovakia, Poland, Finland, The Kingdom of the Serbs, Croats & Slovenes and the Baltic States* (Oxford, 1928).

[26] Art 64 (2), Draft C.

It shall be the aim of social legislation to promote the association of employees with employers in the management and control of industry, to favour the diffusion of property, and to encourage co-operative ownership and organisation, and to facilitate the formation and functioning of professional guilds.

These provisions seem to have almost Marxist undertones. As previously mentioned, Draft C is not alone in this aspect, however, as Drafts A and B also contain left-leaning provisions. Article 1 from both Drafts (mentioned above) was taken from the Democratic Programme of the First Dáil and contains phrases written by Pearse:

The Nation's sovereignty extends not only to all men and women of the nation, but to all the material possessions of the nation, the nation's soil and all its resources and all the wealth and wealth-producing processes within the nation; and all right to private property is subordinated to the public right and welfare of the nation. It is the duty of every man and woman to give allegiance and service to the commonwealth, and it is the duty of the nation to ensure that every citizen shall have opportunity to spend his or her strength and faculties in the service of the people. In return for willing service it is the right of every citizen to receive an adequate share of the produce of the nation's labour.[27]

This left-wing thread runs through other provisions also, such as the aforementioned Articles 11, 12, 41 and 42 of Draft B which deal with public ownership of natural resources. It seems as though the Committee was very impressed by a memorandum drawn up by France on this subject.[28] France was conscious of the danger that these ideas might be seen as socialist and therefore would be rejected and so he made sure to stress, in his memorandum, that public control of the natural resources would in fact promote free private enterprise. It was no surprise that France was aware of being seen as left-wing as it was known that his brother had recently been in Russia and had returned with 'obviously communist opinions which shocked the great majority of thinking Americans'.[29]

Even though these provisions were eventually toned down and some of them were removed before bringing the eventual amended Draft B to London, the British were shocked at the 'Soviet character of these articles'.[30] Winston Churchill also

---

[27] Article 1 of Drafts A and B.
[28] Document 24 is a 12-page memorandum by France on Natural Endowments in which he warns against alienating the natural resources of a sovereign state to private individuals or corporations and cites examples from New York, Boston, Philadelphia and Baltimore to illustrate his case. He describes natural resources as being 'gifts of the Creator and belong therefore, by natural right to promote the happiness prosperity and wellbeing of all the people in that state'. He says there are 4 classes of these: 'harbours, resources of power, land and fisheries'. Papers of E.M. Stephens, MSS 4236, Box III, Trinity College Dublin Archives.
[29] The American journalist John D. Ryan in a letter to Douglas, see in Brian Farrell, 'The Drafting of the Irish Free State Constitution II' (1970) 5 *Irish Jurist* 343, 351.
[30] British National Archives, CAB21/257.

remarked on the 'Bolshevik character' of the draft Irish Constitution.[31] However, these provisions were influenced by the ancient Gaelic state and the writings of older Irish patriots and land agitators and were not intended by the Committee to be Communist.[32]

The legislature

Returning to Draft B, following the rights section is Section II – 'Legislative Provisions'. Much of this section was used in the final document and in the 1937 Constitution so its provisions, by now, may seem quite straightforward. The legislative assembly called the Oireachtas is created, consisting of two Houses – Dáil Éireann (the Chamber of Deputies) and Seanad Éireann (the Senate).[33] The power of law-making is, subject to certain limitations including the powers of the Seanad, vested in the Dáil[34] and all citizens of 20 years and over are eligible to vote for members of the Oireachtas.[35] Article 17 states that no person can be a member of both Houses. Article 18 provides that members are privileged from arrest coming to, going from or within either House and Article 19 makes all reports, publications and utterances made in either House privileged. Most of the remaining Articles are standard, dealing mostly with sittings.[36]

These provisions are the same in Draft A.

At first glance, Draft C appears to differ radically from Draft B but in fact this is due, for the most part, to the American terminology used. The Oireachtas is referred to as Congress and each House as the House of Representatives and Senate. However, the same general provisions are included as regards sittings and membership etc.

The lower House

All Drafts deal with the lower Chamber first and none of the Drafts contains anything radical in this section. In each Draft, election is to be by proportional representation with not less than one member elected for every thirty thousand of

---

[31] Farrell 'Drafting II', 351.
[32] See Chapter 6.
[33] Art 13, Draft B.
[34] Art 13, Draft B.
[35] Art 15, Draft B.
[36] Article 20 provided that each House would make its own rules and standing orders; Article 21 provided that each House would elect its own Chairman and Deputy Chairman; Article 22 provided that all questions could be decided by a majority of votes of present members; Article 23 provided that the Oireachtas could make provision for payment of members and for travelling expenses; Article 24 provided that the Oireachtas would hold at least one session a year and Article 25 provided that sittings should be public but that in cases of special emergency either House could hold a private meeting. It seems that so much time was spent discussing the Senate that there was very little time to discuss much else involving the legislature and the Committee had no disagreements on the other provisions.

the population.[37] The Dáil sits for a maximum of four years in Drafts B and A and three years in Draft C.[38] Perhaps O'Rahilly was attempting to be more democratic in this regard but the reality is that having a general election every three years would not have appealed to the Provisional Government, who believed that what was needed at the time was stability.

Powers of legislative inquiry

Draft C also provides that the House may appoint 'Committees of Inquiry'[39] and various other committees such as a Finance Committee and a Committee for External Affairs which would have special powers akin to those of a Committee of Inquiry.[40]

The debate on powers of inquiry has been a controversial one and has recently been taken up again. In 2002, the *Maguire v. Ardagh*[41] case considered the scope of the investigative powers of the Oireachtas and in 2011 a referendum was held, proposing to amend the Constitution in order to reverse the effect of that case but the measure did not pass.[42]

It is interesting that this provision was specifically included in Article 15 of Draft C when there is no mention of any sort of inquiry in the other Drafts. It is possible that the architects of Drafts A and B simply disagreed with the idea that elected representatives should have powers of investigation. Notably, this provision was not included in the 1922 Constitution itself, or its successor. As Justice Geoghegan (who was speaking about the 1937 Constitution but his words are relevant nonetheless) stated in the *Maguire* case:

> If a power of inquiry of the kind contended for in this case was to be vested in the Oireachtas, one would have expected the Constitution would have expressly said so and that it would then either have been expressly provided that certain appropriate powers of enforcing attendance of witnesses and penalising those who did not would be included, or at the very least, that there would be provisions in the Constitution expressly contemplating legislation to establish compellability and enforceability powers.[43]

---

[37] In order to be eligible for election, Drafts B and A specify that a candidate must have reached the age of 20 years, whereas in Draft C candidates must have completed their twenty-first year.

[38] Art 14, Draft C.

[39] Art 15, Draft C.

[40] Art 16, Draft C.

[41] [2002] 1 IR 385. The case concerned the procedures to be applied by a parliamentary inquiry into an incident in which a member of the Garda Síochána shot dead a civilian, John Carthy. The Supreme Court held that the conducting of an inquiry, capable of leading to adverse findings of fact and conclusions as to the personal culpability of an individual not a member of the Oireachtas, was *ultra vires* in that the holding of such an inquiry was not within the inherent powers of the Houses of the Oireachtas.

[42] The amendment would have allowed the Oireachtas to conduct inquiries and make findings which could attribute personal culpability to identifiable individuals.

[43] [2002] 1 IR 385, 711.

Following this line of reasoning it would seem that the others must have disagreed with O'Rahilly on the suitability of this type of provision for the legislature. After all, O'Rahilly had been inspired in this respect by the Weimar Constitution, which contains a similar provision,[44] and this particular Constitution had been a model for Figgis in many other respects. However, it is also possible that the architects of Drafts A and B agreed with the provision but felt it was not necessary to specifically include it. The French Constitution of the time, like many others, had nothing to say on the topic of legislative inquiries but they were, as O'Dowd has noted, 'undoubtedly an established feature of constitutional law and practice in 1922'.[45] In addition, Chief Justice Keane, dissenting, commented in the *Maguire* case:

> In that context, the absence of any reference to committees of inquiry from the text of the Constitution – or of the Constitution of the Irish Free State, 1922 – is, in my view, of little significance. Such committees were, as we shall see, an established feature of a parliamentary tradition which, in so many of its aspects, we inherited from the United Kingdom ...[46]

Whether they disagreed with the provision or felt it was too obvious to include in the Constitution, the Provisional Government agreed with the decision taken in Drafts A and B not to include any such provision in the final Draft.[47]

The upper House

The Drafts differ considerably with regard to the detail here. In general, the Committee wished to avoid replicating the lower House and so the main features were long periods of representation and smaller membership.

Draft B details that the Seanad will be composed of 40 members.[48] A senator's term of office would be 12 years and 10 members would be elected every three years.[49] Before an election, the Dáil would nominate twice the number of candidates needed, and for the election the whole country would form one constituency. The candidates nominated by the Dáil would be 'citizens who have done honour to the Nation by reason of useful public service or who because of special

---

[44] Article 34 of the Weimar Constitution provided: 'The Reichstag has the right and, on proposal of one fifth of its members, the duty to appoint committees of investigation. These committees, in public sittings, inquire into the evidence which they, or the proponents, consider necessary.' See Benegal Shiva Rao (ed.), *Select Constitutions of the World* (Madras, 1934), 214.

[45] See John O'Dowd, 'Knowing How Way Leads on to Way: Some Reflections on the Abbylara Decision' (2003) 38 *Irish Jurist* 162, 177.

[46] [2002] IR 385, 504.

[47] For more on this area, see O'Dowd, 'Knowing How Way Leads on to Way'.

[48] Eligible candidates will have reached the age of 30 years. Art 30, Draft B.

[49] Art 31, Draft B. In order for this to work, the Senators of the first Seanad were to have been divided up into four classes who would serve for 12, nine, six and three years so that once this period was up there would be an election for a quarter of the Seanad every three years.

qualifications or attainments represent important aspects of the Nation's life'.[50] This is the only detail given besides Article 81, which deals with the procedure for the constitution of the first Seanad.[51]

The provisions in Draft A are mostly the same.[52]

There are only two Articles dealing with the Senate in Draft C. In contrast to A and B, all senators are chosen by the lower House. Senators serve for a period of 10 years and five senators retire every year. This is achieved by dividing the members into 10 consecutive classes. Article 17 states that this House shall comprise 'fifty persons of national achievement, merit or eminence'.[53]

The idea of having personalities of a 'senatorial' character to make up the upper House is shared by the Drafts, but Draft C noticeably excludes the possibility of the electorate being involved in the appointment process. O'Rahilly explained his reasons for not having a direct election, by the people, of the Senate, arguing that to do otherwise would increase antagonism between the Senate and the House of Representatives, each claiming to be the direct exponent of the people's will, but also that it would possibly exclude desirable senators, such as bishops or scholars who might not put themselves forward for election. He also believed that 'if there is to be a Senate at all, we do not believe in making it merely ornamental. Hence we assign to it real power e.g. the power in certain cases of calling a referendum.'[54]

The Seanad's power of delay is something which occupied some time during the Committee's discussions[55] and it is treated in slightly different ways in each

---

50 Art 29, Draft B. It is possible that this provision was intended to provide for functional representation, something which was discussed in detail by the Committee. In a document entitled 'Document 15' Figgis states that since writing *The Gaelic State* he did not think 'functional representation is at present practicable. The only functions sufficiently organised to form colleges of electors are the legal and medical functions.' But he felt that the Senate should be devised so that this method of election would be possible in the future when the various functions would be better organised. (In fact, there is a similar provision contained in Article 19 in Bunreacht na hÉireann providing for representation of vocational or other groups.) Despite the intention, the idea was never realised under the 1922 Constitution (or under the present one) perhaps because the possibility for functional representation was also alternatively envisaged as part of the executive. See Figgis, *The Gaelic State* (Dublin, 1917). See also Chapter 8 on functional representation.

51 Here, 30 members were to have been elected by the Dáil and 10 nominated by the Uachtarán, who was to have special regard to providing representation for groups or parties not then adequately represented in the Dáil. The members would then be grouped into four classes of 10; the first group (those nominated by the Uachtarán) were to hold office for 10 years, the second for nine years, the third for six years and the fourth for three years.

52 Except for the constitution of the first Seanad whereby members were to be elected 'from duly qualified persons by the members of Dáil Éireann'.

53 Article 18 declares that citizens who have reached the age of 35 years are eligible.

54 O'Rahilly's letter to the Provisional Government, file 4, Papers of E.M. Stephens, MSS 4234, Trinity College Dublin Archives.

55 Perhaps this is because of what was happening in Westminster at the time. The Parliament Act 1911 had been passed, which asserted the supremacy of the House of

Draft. In Draft B, the Seanad may not delay a money bill, but may delay a bill which does not impose taxation or appropriate revenues or moneys for not longer than 180 days.[56] Draft A provides that, if the bill is a money bill, it may not be suspended for a longer period than one calendar month; otherwise the situation is the same as in Draft B.[57] Draft C provides that if the Senate has not expressed disapproval after one month of the bill being sent for consideration this shall be held to constitute approval.[58]

The executive

Again, the Drafts differ in relation to the structure of the executive but here it is not only Drafts B and C which differ but A contains substantial differences in these provisions also.

In Draft B, the Cabinet is referred to as the Aireacht. This is a council of 12 Ministers (Airidhe) who will be responsible to the Dáil.[59] At least four of these will be members of the Dáil, including the Uachtarán,[60] the Tánaiste, a Minister for External Affairs and a Minister for Finance. These four alone are responsible for matters relating to external affairs.[61] The remaining eight ministers (referred to as extern or external ministers) will not be members of the Oireachtas (though they must be eligible for election to the Dáil). They will be nominated with due regard to their suitability for office by a committee of members of the Dáil, which will be proportionally and impartially representative of the Dáil. Each of these ministers will be the responsible head of an executive department and will serve for a term of four years.[62] They will not necessarily be affected by a dissolution of the Dáil and may only be removed for 'malfeasance'.[63] While there seems to be a

Commons by limiting the suspensory veto powers of the House of Lords. Provided the provisions of the Act were met, legislation could have been passed without the approval of the House of Lords. The Act was a reaction to the behaviour of the Lords who had already stalled the second Home Rule Bill 1893 and then they threw out the Liberal Government's budget in 1909. The Act imposed a maximum legislative delay of one month for 'money bills' and two years for other types of bill. The Act was amended to further curb the powers of the upper House in 1949.

[56] Art 37, Draft B.
[57] Arts 37 and 39, Draft A.
[58] Art 33 (1), Draft C.
[59] Art 53, Draft B.
[60] This figure is referred to at times as President of Saorstát Éireann but it is in fact a prime ministerial role.
[61] Art 56, Draft B.
[62] Art 55, Draft B.
[63] This aspect of Draft B was criticised by Figgis because it makes it practically impossible to remove these ministers. However, in his letter to the Provisional Government, Douglas states that, even if there is a dissolution, when the new Dáil is elected it can always choose to remove the old external ministers. However, it is unclear how this is possible seeing as the only removal provision contained in the Draft is the one abovementioned.

divide between the 'big four' and the remaining eight ministers, Article 56 states that the Aireacht (meaning the full 12) shall meet and act as a single authority.[64]

This provision was originally based on and influenced by the Swiss system[65] whereby it would allow the possibility of having people, not necessarily politicians, who are experts in a particular area to run a department in that area and they would not have to be members of Parliament. However, a useful side effect of this provision is that it would also allow members of the opposition to participate in government without having to give up their beliefs because, at this stage, only members of the Oireachtas were required to take the oath. So, the provision would permit the appointment of de Valera or any of his followers as external ministers. They would be responsible for a particular department and would be involved in government but at the same time would have no power in relation to international affairs, which was the responsibility of the inner core of ministers.

It is very likely that the Provisional Government was attracted by this possibility. Collins was involved in negotiating the election Pact[66] at the time and he was still hopeful that an agreement could be reached between pro- and anti-Treaty sides and that de Valera would come into government with him. Because of this, the executive provisions in Draft B would have been extremely appealing.

The remaining provisions on the executive are conventional, involving the budget, summoning and dissolving the House and the seal of the Uachtarán. One further Article of interest here is Article 59, which provides that a minister's salary shall not be diminished during his term of office.[67]

The same terminology is used in Draft A but Figgis was against the idea of external ministers and, because of this disagreement, this Draft differs considerably from B. In Draft A, the Aireacht comprises the Uachtarán and between four and nine other ministers. According to Article 53, the Dáil elects the Uachtarán, who then appoints the ministers 'with the assent of the Dáil'. The ministers may be members of the Dáil. However, according to Article 55, it also seems that persons who are not or have never been in the Dáil could also be ministers.[68] This was not an attempt to include senators as they are specifically excluded. It looks like an attempt by Figgis to reconcile his views with those of the architects of

---

[64] The difficulties involved in such an arrangement do not appear to have been discussed at this stage.

[65] It is well documented in Stephens's notes that this plan was taken from the Swiss-style executive where, under Article 96 of that Constitution, seven people would be elected to the Federal Council for three years by the Parliament. None of the members of the Council would be members of Parliament.

[66] See Chapter 4, 47–9.

[67] The recent controversies on judicial pay and the pay cuts taken by ministers illustrate just how unusual and ill-advised this provision was.

[68] Art 55 of Draft A specifies that if an Aire is a member of the Seanad at the time of his appointment, he must resign his seat immediately. There is no similar provision in relation to the Dáil but Article 55 states that an Aire who is not a member of the Dáil may still speak in that House where given leave, which implies that the minister does not have to be a member of the Dáil.

Draft B, possibly because he knew the strength of the consequences of Draft B's executive plan. Nevertheless, it was intended in Draft A that ministers should be chosen from within the Dáil. Figgis believed that it would be wise to leave these provisions as open as possible.[69] This is the principal difference between Drafts A and B.

The executive is referred to as the Executive Council in Draft C and consists of a President, a Vice-President, a Minister of External Affairs and seven other ministers who serve for a term of three years.[70] The external minister idea is taken up again here, in a more extreme form, as, while the three named ministers are also members of the House of Representatives and elected by that House, the remaining seven may not be members of either Chamber and indeed must resign their seat if that is the case.[71] In electing these ministers, the House is to have regard to 'personal fitness but also of the desirability of assuring the representation of the different regions ...'.[72] Like Draft B, Draft C specifies that the external ministers have only a consultative voice when it comes to international affairs but that all decisions emanate from the Executive Council as a single authority.[73] Article 23 declares that the Executive Council will have the power of appointment, control, supervision and dismissal of all officers and officials and it may call in the aid of experts for special matters.

While the executive provisions in Drafts B and C are similar, it may be useful to elucidate the differences. In Draft C, ministers who are not members of the Chamber are to be elected *en bloc* on principles of proportional representation by the Chamber, whereas in Draft B these ministers are elected for particular posts by the Chamber following nomination by a Committee selected to represent the Chamber proportionately and impartially. The architects of Draft B maintained that each minister should be elected on the basis of his fitness to the specific department. Under Draft C, the external ministers are elected for three years, are not removable and their term is coterminous with each Dáil. Under Draft B, the term is four years and will generally have the same term as the Dáil but, in the case of a dissolution, the ministers need not necessarily resign with the Dáil but can afterwards be removed by the new Dáil. Individual ministers can also be removed upon recommendation of a specialised committee.[74]

Noticeably, there is no mention of the King or Crown in relation to the legislative or executive provisions in any of the three Drafts.

---

[69] Letter from Figgis to the Provisional Government, file 2, Papers of E.M. Stephens, MSS 4235, Trinity College Dublin Archives.
[70] Art 19, Draft C. The English terms are used and the Irish translations are given in parentheses.
[71] They will simply be citizens who are eligible for election to the lower Chamber.
[72] Art 19 (3), Draft C.
[73] Art 22, Draft C.
[74] See letter from signatories of Draft B, file 2, Papers of E.M. Stephens, MSS 4235, Trinity College Dublin Archives.

The judiciary

There was more agreement in relation to the judicial provisions. Draft B provides that new courts will be established by the Oireachtas. These will comprise courts of first instance, one of which, known as the Cúirt Náisiúnta (National Court), will exercise 'full original jurisdiction in and power to determine all matters and questions ... in the territorial jurisdiction of Saorstát Éireann', and a final court of appeal to be called the Árd-Chúirt (the High Court of Appeal).[75] The Árd-Chúirt was to have appellate jurisdiction from all decisions of the Cúirt Náisiúnta and these decisions were to be final and conclusive and not capable of being reviewed by any other person, court or tribunal whatsoever.[76] This was clearly in violation of what the British had in mind in terms of appeal to the Judicial Committee of the Privy Council. The Árd-Chúirt was also given the power of judicial review of legislation in Article 70, which provides that the power of the court 'shall extend to the question of the validity of any law having regard to the provisions of the Constitution and to the interpretation of treaties'.

This section also provides that the judges of the Árd-Chúirt and Cúirt Náisiúnta will be appointed by the Aireacht and removable only for stated misbehaviour or incapacity, their remuneration is not to be diminished during their terms of office and the appointment of all other judges is to be prescribed by law. All judges are to be 'independent in the exercise of their functions and subject only to the law'.[77] In addition, Article 74 declares that the jurisdiction of courts martial shall not be extended to or exercised over the civil population save in times of war and Article 76 specifies that the penalty of death should not be attached to any offence,[78] a view espoused by Collins.[79]

There is another interesting provision (which also appears in the other Drafts)[80] in Article 77 of Draft B which, anticipating *Byrne v. Ireland*,[81] states that: 'Proceedings may be instituted against the Irish Free State in such manner as

---

[75] Art 68, Draft B.

[76] Art 69, Draft B.

[77] Art 73, Draft B.

[78] This provision, which had not appeared in the other Drafts, was eventually dropped. See NAI, PG22. George O'Brien had commented that, while he agreed with the sentiment, he felt that it was something better left to legislation. For more on O'Brien's analysis see Chapter 3, 39–43.

[79] Apparently Collins had shared the wish of Douglas that this provision be included, saying 'we've had enough executions in Ireland ... it would be a good thing to see the end of them'. See J. Alfred Gaughan (ed.), *Memoirs of Senator James G. Douglas, (1887–1954): Concerned Citizen* (Dublin, 1998), 87. Douglas had prepared a memorandum on this topic, giving instances of capital punishment provisions in seventeen different countries. See Document 53, Papers of E.M. Stephens, MSS 4236, Trinity College Dublin Archives.

[80] This is also found in Article 78 of Draft A and Article 42 of Draft C.

[81] [1972] IR 241. In this case it was held that the State had no sovereign immunity from suit.

may be determined by law'. This appears to rule out one of the Crown's powers of prerogative for the fledgling state.[82]

There are some slight differences in Draft A, mostly only in terms of terminology. Article 65 declares that the judicial power of the state shall be vested in and exercised by the Árd-Chúirt (High Court) and the Iar-Chúirt Eilimh (Court of Final Appeal) and by inferior courts which were to be established by law. Article 67 provides that decisions of the Iar-Chúirt Eilimh will be final and conclusive and not be reviewed by any person, court or tribunal. The judges of these courts are to be appointed by the Aireacht and they are to be independent and pledge themselves to abide by the law. Article 72 specifies that, subject to exceptions, the law is to be administered in public, a provision which does not appear in Draft B. The remaining provisions in this section – judicial review, jurisdiction of courts martial etc. – mirror those of Draft B save for wording differences.

This section is much longer in Draft C, which provides that the new court system would be made up of a Supreme Court and inferior courts. However, despite the number of provisions, many matters are still left to be decided afterwards by law. For example, in Article 38, it is specified that:

> (3) Congress shall by law determine the original and appellate jurisdiction of the Supreme Court; and in particular may assign thereto original jurisdiction in matters relating to (a) this Constitution and its interpretation, (b) admiralty and maritime jurisdiction, (c) the competency of subordinate parliaments, (d) the validity of elections to the House of Representatives. (4) Judges shall in adjudicating have the right to inquire into the validity of an executive decree; but save as aforesaid they shall not be competent to question the validity of a duly promulgated law.

This last part is quite interesting in that it precludes any power of judicial review of legislation. The reason for this is that O'Rahilly wished to abide by the Swiss theory that the people were the ultimate interpreter of the Constitution. This would function concurrently with the machinery of the referendum and initiative.[83]

Draft C also ignores the Judicial Committee of the Privy Council in that Article 39 declares that the decisions of the appellate division of the Supreme Court will be final and not subject to review by any other person, court or tribunal whatsoever. Interestingly, while the judges of the Supreme Court are to be appointed by the Executive Council with the consent of the Senate, all other judges are to be appointed by the judges of the Supreme Court. This plan, had it been adopted, would have been a new departure in relation to appointment of the judiciary and presumably one in which it was attempted to avoid any claims of executive bias or 'legal patronage'.[84]

---

[82] The Crown had a power of immunity from suit as part of prerogative. See Laura Cahillane, 'The Prerogative and Its Survival in Ireland: Dusty Antique or Positively Useful?' (2010) 1 (2) *Irish Journal of Legal Studies* 1.

[83] See below.

[84] This term was used by O'Rahilly in his letter to the provisional Government explaining his proposals. See file 4, Papers of E.M. Stephens, MSS 4234, Trinity College Dublin Archives.

Amendment, referendum and initiative

Draft B contains a section entitled 'Referendum and Initiative', dealing with ordinary legislation as well as constitutional amendment, which appears to have been inspired by the Swiss idea[85] of complete sovereignty of the people and direct democracy whereby the people are directly involved in legislating. In relation to constitutional amendment, any amendment would have to be submitted to a referendum of the people (after passing through the Oireachtas) and passed only if either a majority of voters on the register vote in favour or if two-thirds of the actual voters are in favour.[86] Article 47 provides for a procedure for suspension of new laws which can then be submitted to the people, if demanded by a petition signed by at least thirty thousand voters on the register.

Article 48 provides for the possibility of the initiative whereby the people may propose laws or constitutional amendments after five years from the date of adoption of the Constitution. Article 49 also provides that the state shall not declare or enter into a war save with the assent of a majority of voters on the register.

Again, this section is replicated in Draft A.

Section 10 of Draft C is concerned with amendment. Article 68 is the principal provision here but is drafted in a confusing and seemingly contradictory manner:

> This Constitution may at any time be amended through the forms required for ordinary legislation. But, except as provided in the following article, every repeal or modification of, or addition to an article of the Constitution, or insertion of a new article therein, must be approved by a majority of the House and of the Senate and must be submitted separately to the decision of the people, voting yes or no, and must be accepted by a majority of those who take part in the vote thereon.

There is also provision made for questions on whether to undertake a general or partial revision of the Constitution,[87] in that not only is it possible to make specific amendments to the Constitution but the people may also demand an entire revision. Article 70 also provides for a procedure whereby a hundred thousand voters may demand the addition of a new Article or repeal or modification of any existing Articles.

Although ordinary legislation is not mentioned in this section of Draft C, there is an equivalent to Draft B's initiative in the earlier section on legislation; Article 29 provides that eighty thousand voters may demand the passing of a specific law

---

[85] During the meetings of the Constitution Committee and the debates in the Constituent Assembly, references are made to the 'Swiss idea' or 'Swiss theory' of direct democracy and popular sovereignty. This is not any particular academic theory which is being referred to but rather the general idea behind the devices included in the Swiss Constitution to strengthen popular sovereignty. For a modern discussion of the Swiss version of popular sovereignty, see G.A. Fossedal, *Direct Democracy in Switzerland* (New Brunswick, 2002).

[86] Art 50, Draft B.

[87] Arts 69 and 71, Draft C.

or in Article 30 they may present a demand in the form of a completely drafted bill.

Decentralisation and subordinate legislatures

In Draft C, among the provisions for the referendum, it is declared in Article 27 that the state 'shall foster the ideal of decentralisation and regional autonomy' and Congress is given the authority to 'transmit to local representative assemblies such derivative authority in legislative, administrative, cultural and economic affairs, as is compatible with the unity and integrity of Ireland'. It is further stated that Congress may delegate the right to make ordinances (in relation to a specified class of subjects) to local parliaments. A similar but less weighty provision is also included in Drafts B and A where Articles 43 and 44 respectively state that the Oireachtas may create subordinate legislatures. The idea, as O'Rahilly explained in his letter to the Provisional Government, is to provide for the possibility of the creation of a federal state whereby more power could be given to local county councils or the Northern Parliament.[88] The reference to subordinate legislatures is vital in that it is the only way in which Northern Ireland could have been included in the embryonic Irish state. The inclusion of a provision providing for subordinate legislatures had been specifically requested by Collins.[89]

External relations

Drafts B and A both contain a short identical section containing one article on external relations. This Article[90] states that Ireland will continue to be 'in association with the Community of Nations known as the British Commonwealth of Nations'.[91] The remainder of the Article provides that the Treaty will have the force of law and the representative of George V will 'be styled Commissioner of the British Commonwealth, and shall be appointed only with the previous assent of the Aireacht of Saorstát Éireann'. He may also sign Acts which have been passed by the Oireachtas 'to signify the assent of His Majesty the King'. Presumably, the name 'Commissioner' rather than Governor-General was intended to play down the possible significance of this figure. Historically, High

---

[88] Here it seems as though O'Rahilly has conflated the two concepts of local government and federalism. Of course they are two entirely different things, the key difference being that, generally, federalism involves the union of various different legal or political systems under a central federal authority. Power is divided between the central authority and the constituent political units. Local government simply involves a measure of devolution in that county councils are given a certain amount of autonomy on local matters. O'Rahilly does not elaborate on this point and so, unfortunately, we do not know whether he has confused the two concepts or whether there was a certain reasoning behind this.

[89] See Gaughan, *Memoirs of James Douglas*, 81.

[90] Art 79 in Draft B and Art 78 in Draft A.

[91] This is reminiscent of de Valera's famous 'Document No. 2'.

Commissioners were envoys of the Imperial government appointed to manage protectorates or groups of territories not fully under the sovereignty of the British Crown, e.g. Cyprus. Evidently, the Irish wished to distance themselves further from the Crown colonies, which were administered by a Governor-General, in order to show that the Irish Free State was a sovereign state of itself.

Notably, references to the Crown and the King's representative were completely left out of Draft C and given only a brief mention at the end of Drafts A and B, and the oath was ignored in all Drafts. The jurisdiction of the Judicial Committee of the Privy Council was also specifically ruled out in all Drafts where the decisions of the highest court in each Draft were said to be final, conclusive and not reviewable by any other court or body. Furthermore, nowhere in any of the Drafts does it say that the Treaty is supreme or that the Constitution is subordinate to the Treaty. It appears that the Committee wanted to avoid any mention of these controversial areas but it is also clear that they felt it was not necessary to include any detail on the Treaty provisions in the actual Constitution when they were already set out in the Treaty.

Conclusion

Overall, the Drafts are an accurate representation of Collins's original aspirations for a new Constitution. They are all short, uncomplicated, general rather than too detailed and they avoid important references to British authority.

All of the Drafts were insistent on sovereignty of the people. This was important as most Irish people were opposed to the English idea of sovereignty of Parliament or Crown. The architects' dedication to this principle can be seen in the provisions relating to legislation, referendum and initiative as well as the general provisions on sovereignty. In order to try and bring some stability to the new state, it was imperative that the people felt that not only they were included but that they had a powerful voice. In fact this was the one area in which the Irish delegates stubbornly refused to back down during negotiations in London,[92] despite pressure from the British. The Drafts were also united in their desire to provide a more democratic form of government and a break from the British system.

Thus the Committee had achieved what it had set out to achieve, despite failing to produce a unanimous draft. Farrell has noted similarly that despite their differences,

> [the Drafts] shared a common desire to break with the rigid disciplined parties of the existing British model of cabinet government. They all, in some measure, were ready to deviate from the established structure with the common purpose of making

---

[92] See Thomas Mohr, 'British Involvement in the Creation of the Constitution of the Irish Free State' (2008) 30 (1) *Dublin University Law Journal* 166, 170, and Chapter 4.

the executive more responsive to the people than to the exigencies of party demand. All were in this sense radically democratic, experimental and open to an independent economic policy ... The drafts offered were, in short, typical of the optimism about constitutional engineering which was briefly and deceptively recaptured after the first World War.[93]

---

[93] Farrell, 'Drafting II', 355.

3

Consideration by the government of the three Drafts

Introduction

On presenting the Drafts to the Provisional Government for consideration, Figgis also included an accompanying covering letter. In the letter, he explained that the Committee had heard witnesses in relation to electoral practice, financial administration and the differences between the British and French systems. He thanked Professors Bastable and Oldham, Mr Waterfield of the British Treasury in Ireland and Mr Humphreys of the PR Society of Britain for their help with these matters. He also thanked Risteard Ó Foghludha, Tadg Ó Donnchadha, An tAthair Ó Duinnín and Padhraic Ó Domhnalláin for their expertise in translating and attributing Irish titles and other words. He also included some short explanations of the differences between the three Drafts.[1]

However, the architects of Draft B decided to send in their own letter to present the case for Draft B. While the original letter, written by Figgis, had been neutral in tone and had the simple intention of providing some basic information on the Drafts, the letter on Draft B was an attempt to persuade the government to choose that Draft. Figgis and the others were unaware of this and it caused some tension between Committee members when it emerged that Kennedy, Douglas and France had done this.

Letter on Draft B

The letter, written by Douglas, pointed out that the principal difference between A and B was the executive and also claimed that the architects of Draft C would prefer the executive in Draft B to that of A, since their Draft contained 'practically

---

[1] See letter to the Provisional Government to accompany the Drafts, file 2, Papers of E.M. Stephens, MSS 4235, Trinity College Dublin Archives.

the same plan'.[2] They argued that the net result of their analysis of the three Drafts demonstrated that six members of the Committee – Figgis, O'Byrne, McNeill, Kennedy, Douglas and France – were in substantial agreement both as to form and wording on the whole Constitution, except the executive section. The architects of Draft B argued that the executive in Draft A was the same as the British system with the one difference that ministers who did not obtain seats in the House could still be appointed. They claimed that Draft B, on the other hand, was a variation of the Swiss system which would preserve unity on Irish ideals. It was argued in the letter that, if this opportunity to make a break with the past was not seized, then Dáil Éireann would simply continue in the British party style. In addressing the claim that the proposals on the executive in Draft A were more open and therefore easier to change where necessary, they argued that it should not be left open because that would not lead to stability whereas the system in B would allow for stability and also provide an opportunity to include the opposition in government.

The letter also explained the differences between Drafts B and C. It was argued that the executive in Draft C was unsuitable as external ministers were to be elected *en bloc* rather than because of personal expertise. Also in Draft C, senators would be elected by the lower Chamber voting on proportional representation and the Senate would be given power of veto on legislation, something not included in Drafts A or B. Overall, the architects of Draft B contended that Draft C lacked legal precision. The letter also emphasised the importance of public ownership of land and natural resources which, it was claimed, was given the greatest protection in Draft B.[3]

Letter on Draft A

When it emerged some time later that Douglas's letter had been sent to the Provisional Government, the authors of the two alternative Drafts decided to follow suit. Figgis began his letter as follows:

> As signatories of Draft A of the Constitution it had not been our original intention to submit any separate covering letter. It was our belief that the difference between the three Drafts would be sufficiently apparent to you. Learning that the signatories of Draft B have put their point of view before you in an independent covering letter, it occurs to us that you might find it helpful if we were also to do the same.[4]

He identified the executive section as the chief difference between Drafts A and B and, as a rebuttal to remarks made in the letter by Douglas, referred to a remark

---

[2] Letter from signatories of Draft B, file 2, Papers of E.M. Stephens, MSS 4235, Trinity College Dublin Archives.

[3] *Ibid.*

[4] Letter from Figgis to Provisional Government, file 2, Papers of E.M. Stephens, MSS 4234, Trinity College Dublin Archives.

made by O'Rahilly during the Committee stage that if 'Alternative C' were not to be accepted, 'he would prefer to see Alternative A accepted, inasmuch as A being very simple and allowing of development, would permit of the subsequent development of C if circumstances warranted such development'.[5] Figgis pointed out the merits in an open and flexible provision on the executive and remarked that 'it has always been proved that rigid constitutions prove irritating and obstructive of development'. He criticised the plan in Draft B, arguing that it was impossible 'at this moment to say that any distinct form of Executive will best suit the national character'. He felt that it was imperative that the executive 'should not be fixed in a rigid and unalterable mould' and particularly not 'in a cumbersome and unwieldy form'.[6]

A number of pages follow, which analyse the provisions of Draft B in detail and contain stinging criticism of that Draft. Figgis also made the case for his own executive proposal, distancing it from the British system by saying it was like provisions found in most countries of the world and that practice in these countries often varied from British practice 'so we would have every reason to believe it would vary as widely in Ireland'. Figgis concluded his criticism of Draft B with the following comment:

> One of the chief arguments in favour of 'B' given in Committee by its signatories was that it would lead to unity in the present divided state of the country. In answer to this we would first of all say that it is no business for a Constitution, which is devised as the fundamental law of a State, to take cognisance of such considerations. These are the concerns of politics not of Constitutions; and a Constitution should be drafted on such broad lines as to permit the inclusion of many divergent policies from time to time.[7]

He also noted that Kennedy originally criticised the proposals which subsequently took shape in Executive B, with the remark that they would 'lead to stagnation'.

Letter on Draft C

In O'Rahilly's letter, he explained that, while he was unable to consult with his colleague Professor Murnaghan, he felt it advisable to write a few brief notes in order to explain his position.[8] He clarified that he did not intend to criticise either Draft A or B and he then proceeded to go through his Draft, explaining his choices. He justified his executive as an adaptation of the Swiss system, which he believed was itself an improvement of the American system, to Irish conditions. He elucidated that in writing the provisions on the executive, they 'took into

---

[5] *Ibid.*
[6] *Ibid.*
[7] *Ibid.*
[8] Letter from O'Rahilly to Provisional Government, file 4, Papers of E.M. Stephens, MSS 4234, Trinity College Dublin Archives.

account the abnormal condition of Ireland as regards its external relations and also the evils of a purely party system'. All authority was to be 'collegiate'. He also stated that he was opposed to direct appointment by the House of individual ministers to individual offices.

He noted that, in his Draft, power was given for gradually transforming Ireland into a federal state, by increasing the power of the county councils or by acknowledging the Northern Parliament. However, as already noted, this possibility was included in each of the Drafts.

Significantly, O'Rahilly pointed out that in his plan, 'legal patronage of the executive' was to be abolished. Instead, judges should be appointed by the executive only with the consent of the Senate, with lower judges being appointed by the Supreme Court. He also explained his reasons for excluding judicial review, opting for the Swiss theory whereby the people are the ultimate interpreters of the Constitution. In addition, he noted that his Chapter 8 on rights, including provisions on marriage and protection of women and children, was distinctive and embodied Christian ideals. O'Rahilly finished his letter by stating that he must be explicit concerning some delicate matters and so he wished to state that he had assumed the following:

> (1) Partition is not regarded as legal and valid from the purely Irish juristic standpoint.
> (2) The Treaty, though obligatory, is not constitutional; it is through ordinary legislation that the obligations which it imposes on us must be carried out, just as England is carrying out her treaty obligations by ordinary legislation ... The Constitution is, after all, merely a special collection of legislative principles and enactments which we accept for ourselves and on the amendment of which we voluntarily impose certain restrictions. The inclusion therein of treaty provisions is not only unusual but in no way adds to the international obligation which they already involve.

Criticisms

While it seems the government was leaning towards Draft B,[9] it decided it needed some advice on the matter and so it enlisted the help of T.M. Healy[10] and Dr George O'Brien,[11] who produced two memoranda on the Drafts.

---

[9] Kennedy's support of Draft B would have been very influential as he was in essence, although not yet officially, the Attorney General. There is also evidence that the government had already chosen Draft B. See Brian Farrell, 'The Drafting of the Irish Free State Constitution IV' (1971) 6 *Irish Jurist* 345, 347–8.

[10] Originally a passionate supporter and ally of Parnell, he later became his most severe critic and the chief author of his downfall. He continued the Home Rule struggle until the aftermath of 1916 when he realised his struggle was pointless and turned his sympathies to the Sinn Féin leaders. He was one of the few King's Counsel to support Sinn Féin. He was later to become the first Governor-General.

[11] He was a lawyer and an economist and became a Professor of Political Economy and National Economics in University College Dublin.

Professor Culverwell,[12] Eoin MacNeill[13] and Lord Midleton[14] also submitted memoranda.[15]

Healy's analysis of the Drafts was unhelpful and boorish. He refers to the Drafts as 'raumaush'[16] and 'pure fudge, which must make us a laughing stock'.[17] Farrell notes that the 'essence of Healy's argument was total opposition to the attempt to define precisely the character of the new state'.[18] But, in fact, the Drafts had been very ambiguous in relation to this point. Farrell has quoted Healy's remarks:

> What is wanted is dry unassailable technique, which can't be quarrelled with by either Carson or de Valera, but which by its generality imports and attracts the utmost sovereignty without saying so. This can be done more effectively by vagueness than by assertion. Not definition but looseness is what is needed, provided the looseness favors [sic] Irish construction, or interpretation hereafter ... We need vagueness instead of definition, but above all not the definition of Tir-na-nOg or Noah's Ark ... Leave no loophole for attack or cramp. Banish sentiment. Imitate the style of a Bill of Costs. Cherish the acorn and keep away from transplanting oaks. Have one eye on Carson and the other on de Valera.[19]

He went on to propose his own version of a draft which would give supremacy to the new Irish Parliament, promise absolute religious liberty and ensure that the Treaty was a fundamental part of the Constitution. It appears that neither the government nor the Committee was pleased with Healy's critique.

---

[12] Professor of Education, Trinity College Dublin.

[13] Brother of James McNeill, Eoin was co-founder of the Gaelic League and founder of the Irish Volunteers.

[14] Former member of the Irish Unionist Alliance, representative of the Southern Unionists. The Desmond Fitzgerald Papers, University College Dublin Archives, P80/668, contain an undated memo from Lord Midleton. The memo called for the same power for the Governor-General as in Canada, a democratic lower House and a complicated scheme for the Senate. The memo was concluded as follows: 'It should be put in record that in the Irish convention in 1918 a practically unanimous decision was arrived at by a body of 96 Irishmen that a strong senate was an absolute necessity, and the composition of it was less democratic than that which is now suggested.'

[15] It was originally envisaged to have a criticising committee but, perhaps because of time constraints, this never came about. There were a number of suggestions as to who would be asked to become a member of this committee. Tom Johnson of the Labour Party, Professor Magennis and Gerald Fitzgibbon were all mentioned but it was subsequently decided not to include TDs. Figgis suggested Charles Murphy, Secretary of State for Canada. and a priest, Father Cronin, was also mentioned. It is unclear as to why this was not followed up. See NAI, PG1, 38, S8952 Letter from Figgis to Collins, 29 January 1922.

[16] Ráiméis is the Irish for rubbish.

[17] Letter from Healy to E.J. Duggan, 21 March 1922, Papers of E.M. Stephens, MSS 4236, Trinity College Dublin Archives.

[18] Farrell, 'Drafting IV', 348.

[19] *Ibid.*

In contrast, the government was impressed with the criticisms of Dr O'Brien. He took Draft B as the principal document: 'If I am not mistaken, what the Provisional Government required was that I should direct my attention primarily and principally to draft B. The other drafts were sent to me, as I understand it, not for criticism, but simply as documents which would be of assistance in criticising draft B.'[20] So, while accepting B as the primary document, he set about writing provisions he thought should be included as well as certain alternative provisions, deleting unnecessary provisions and seeking out provisions which could cause difficulties.

He began his criticism by noting that it was a sound maxim that a constitution should be as short as possible and 'should fetter as little as possible the freedom of the legislative body which it creates'. He then suggested the omission of various provisions 'which appear to me to deal with matters which could be more satisfactorily dealt with by ordinary legislation'.[21] He also felt that 'the name Dáil Éireann had acquired such a high place in the national sentiment that it may be unwise to apply it to a single chamber of the legislature'[22] and favoured, instead, O'Rahilly's version. In fact, O'Brien favoured quite a few of O'Rahilly's provisions:

> [He] shared with O'Rahilly a suspicion about the state's right to intervene in the lives of individual citizens. It was a doubt that had both a liberal and a conservative effect. On the suggested religious provision he suggested the Committee had not gone far enough in ensuring equality; on the promise of free education he feared an incursion into family rights ... He recommended the substitution of Article 59 in draft C.[23]

He felt it was necessary to include the phrase 'free practice of religion' as Draft B ensured only the right to believe in religion.[24] Although the Committee disagreed with his suggestion, the government ultimately agreed and the provision was amended.

As is evident from the above quotation, O'Brien also agreed with O'Rahilly in relation to the education provision. He suggested a cautious approach in relation to state intervention. He felt it was necessary to emphasise that the duty of the state to provide for education arises only where the parents have failed to do so. He felt that O'Rahilly's provision in Draft C, whereby the primary duty of the state is one of supervision, was much more suitable.

---

[20] Letter from George O'Brien to Provisional Government, Papers of E.M. Stephens, MSS 4235, Trinity College Dublin Archives.

[21] *Ibid.*

[22] *Ibid.*

[23] Farrell, 'Drafting IV', 350.

[24] What Draft B actually provided in terms of religious freedom was contained in Article 8, which provided: 'The free exercise and profession of conscience in respect of religious faith is an inviolable right of every citizen, and no law may be made either directly or indirectly to endow any religion, or to give any preference, or to impose any disability on account of belief.'

He was more critical of the left-leaning provisions on public property and natural resources and expressed the opinion that Article 12 was 'not only unnecessary but objectionable ... because it is likely to misconstruction [*sic*] and might frighten a certain section of the electorate'.[25] He felt Articles 41 and 42[26] also on natural resources were unnecessary.

He also seemed to suggest that any court should be able to determine the validity of any legal question which comes before them. This is in contrast to Drafts A and B where only the superior courts had such jurisdiction. O'Brien believed his view must prevail; otherwise, he believed, all other courts would be limited in relation to the cases they could and could not hear. He suggested all appeals could then lie to the Árd-Chúirt.

The Committee met again in April in order to consider the criticisms of Healy and O'Brien and the final version of the chosen Draft B. It did not take them long to dismiss Healy's criticisms and, in response to his claim that it was too long, they noted that the Draft would fit on one page of a newspaper. They spent longer on O'Brien's proposals but disagreed with many of them. The Committee seems to have been insulted by the criticism in relation to the provisions on public ownership of resources, and Douglas remarked that he felt these articles should have been examined by someone 'friendly to the idea'. The Committee also specifically disagreed with his views on judicial review. The sensible view of the Committee was that it would be undesirable for inferior courts to call into question the validity of a law.[27]

Following consideration of the criticisms, Figgis wrote to the Provisional Government indicating that the Committee was going to stand over Articles 11, 12, 41 and 42. However, the government decided to follow O'Brien's advice on these points and Articles 11 and 12 were reduced to one, less radical provision and Articles 41 and 42 were deleted.

Other prominent figures may also have been asked to venture opinions and criticisms. The archives of George Gavan Duffy[28] contain a letter written by him to Collins in which he noted that he had read through the Drafts and felt that they needed little alteration in substance although he opined they did require a lot of 'cutting down'.[29]

---

[25] Letter from George O'Brien, Papers of E.M. Stephens, MSS 4235, Trinity College Dublin Archives.

[26] These were almost extensions of Articles 11 and 12, although located in the legislative section. They related to remainders, reversions, rights, titles and interests in land and natural resources and also the utilisation of water power and electricity.

[27] Stephens's Notebook, Papers of E.M. Stephens, MSS 4235, Trinity College Dublin Archives.

[28] He was a member of pro-Treaty Sinn Féin and Minister for Foreign Affairs but resigned from the government in July 1922. He acted almost as opposition during the debates in the Constituent Assembly. He was also a signatory of the Treaty.

[29] He suggested to Collins: 'If you have not had this done already and if the draft showing suggested cuts in red ink would be of any use to you, I would be very glad to do this and send it along.' Collins replied to this letter and indicated to Gavan

Eoin MacNeill also submitted a memorandum in which he suggested that Draft C was largely a statement of national and social principles, which would have great value but should not form part of a constitution. He felt it should be separately considered and adopted, if approved. He criticised the provision which gave the Treaty force of law in the Constitution; he believed the effect was to convert the Treaty into an Irish statute 'more binding in every word than any ordinary statute since it is backed by the Constitution'.[30] He suggested that the clause should state that 'The said Treaty shall be valid as regards the relations of Saorstát Éireann to the aforesaid Community of Nations'. He also questioned whether the Dominions should not also ratify the Treaty.[31]

MacNeill's view on giving the Treaty force of law in the Constitution was one shared by many. Gavan Duffy complained that it made the Treaty 'a part of the Constitution and it seems to make the Constitution derive its force from the Treaty'.[32] O'Rahilly also criticised the fact that the Treaty was included in the Constitution, something which he noted was done contrary to the advice of the members of the Constitution Committee who, he added, were all supporters of the Treaty.[33]

Final decision of the government

The Provisional Government considered these matters during May 1922. Figgis and Douglas were invited to attend the meetings during which the executive provisions were to be discussed. The Committee then held a final meeting on 24 May, the same day as the government began its final consideration of the Drafts. During this meeting Kennedy declared that Draft B had been decided upon and the Committee was now asked to revise that Draft. The Committee felt this was impossible and indicated as such to the government. However, the Committee did carry out some revision after all, and the section on external relations was amended as per Eoin MacNeill's memorandum.

Thus, an amended Draft B was chosen as the successful model. In some ways this choice was obvious; Kennedy was already legal adviser and soon to be

Duffy that his view on how to cut down the Drafts would be useful. Collins wrote that he was sure he had made clear his belief that all of the Drafts were too long and detailed. He suggested applying the cutting down process to Draft B, while making a memorandum of any extractions from Draft A. Thus, it is obvious that the Provisional Government had already chosen its preferred Draft. See George Gavan Duffy Papers, University College Dublin Archives, P152, letter to Collins on 6 April 1922. Unfortunately, the draft with amendments in red ink was not included in the archives.
30 Hugh Kennedy Papers, P4/339, University College Dublin Archives.
31 *Ibid.*
32 Letter to Collins, 14 June 1922. George Gavan Duffy Papers, P152, University College Dublin Archives.
33 Alfred O'Rahilly Papers, P178/57, University College Dublin Archives.

Attorney General and his opinion was bound to have had a heavy influence. As well as this, the executive in Draft B was most certainly attractive to Collins, who was still in negotiations with de Valera and would have hoped that the external ministers scheme would ease the latter's criticisms of the Treaty and the proposed Constitution and might even coax him to re-enter government. However, in one respect the choice is a little surprising in that it contained some socialist or left-leaning provisions; it was experimental and would not have appealed to the conservative, property-owning class as it was. The Provisional Government wanted stability more than anything else and so it would have suited it to bring in a conservative document which would not contain any drastic changes to the system and would put the minds of the wealthy conservatives (whose help they needed to stabilise the economy) at ease. The fact is that the Provisional Government was very short of money, as the Irish Free State had to meet its expenditure out of its own revenue and it also had to bear much of the cost of the extensive damage done during the War of Independence.[34] This is why most of Cumann na nGaedheal's reign consisted of exercises in balancing the books and this is why it is surprising the Provisional Government did not opt for a more conservative draft. At the same time, it is clear that Collins (rather than Griffith) had a more radical document in mind. Thus it is clear that, despite the quality of all three Drafts, Draft B would have been the most attractive to the Provisional Government.

The Draft which was brought to London

The Draft which was decided upon was essentially Draft B with some alterations. There were some minor changes made but also some obvious and major changes. First, a new preamble was agreed upon, which was closer to O'Rahilly's version, although even this was later removed for fear of aggravating the British. Articles 1, 2 and 3 were simplified to state that Ireland is a free and sovereign nation, all powers of government are derived from the people and the sovereignty of the nation extends to all the possessions and resources of the country. Article 11 was amended to read: 'All citizens have the right to free elementary education.' Article 12 contained the less radical combined version of Draft B's Articles 11 and 12. The voting age was raised to 21. There were slight changes to the detail on the Seanad and the provisions on the executive were amended to include that 'the Dáil *may* from time to time on the motion of the President determine that a particular minister or ministers not exceeding three, may be members of the Oireachtas in addition to the four members of the Dáil above mentioned'.[35] In addition, the positions of the Ministers for Finance and External Affairs were no longer specified to be portfolios only for the internal ministers. There were

---

[34] See Donal Corcoran, *The Irish Free State 1922–32: Government and Administration* (Unpublished Thesis, University College Cork, 2009), 17.

[35] Emphasis added.

changes in relation to the titles of the judiciary and courts, the provision abolishing the death penalty was deleted and two additional articles were included in the External Affairs section.

Although it caused controversy among the Irish politicians, the Provisional Government decided to take the Draft to London before showing it to the Dáil or the Irish people. When the issue was raised later in the Constituent Assembly during the debates on the Constitution, Kevin O'Higgins explained that the reason the document was sent to the British first was essentially that the Irish were not quite sure how much they could get away with:

> Someone told me, when I was young, I do not know whether it is strictly true or not, that the cat measures with his whiskers whether the hole is big enough for it to pass through; the whiskers report back to the cat the hole is too small. That is pretty well what we did. We went over and we tried whether a certain passage was big enough, and we found it was not. We are reporting that back to this Dáil, and if this Dáil thinks we are wrong it can try the passage, and we only hope that it does not get stuck half-way through and land itself in a mess.[36]

In hindsight, it was probably a wise course of action, considering the reaction of the British to the Draft Constitution. It seems Gavan Duffy was one of the few who anticipated the magnitude of the British reaction. In a letter to Collins he wrote:

> I don't think that our friends, who have gone across to London, (with the exception of Kennedy), realise in the least that the English Government will find the Constitution a very much tougher proposition to swallow than your agreement with de Valera. I may be quite wrong, but my impression is that their anxiety about the agreement will become quite a secondary issue once they have seen the Constitution because they will be horribly frightened by the bad example that the Constitution gives to independent elements of the Dominions; I am sure that they will make desperate efforts to get the Oath into the Constitution on the ground that they have stuck it into the Acts creating Dominion Governments in Canada, Australia and Africa.[37]

He goes on to say they should not concede this point about the inclusion of the oath as it is within their rights to leave it to standing orders. He also notes that he is apprehensive of the concessions which the Irish may be forced to make upon the Constitution. Although Gavan Duffy refers to the possible reaction as 'idiotic British sentiment', he correctly predicted what would happen in London.

---

[36] *Dáil Debates*, vol 1, col 1009, 29 September 1922.
[37] Letter to Collins, 26 May 1922, George Gavan Duffy Papers, P152, University College Dublin Archives.

Conclusion

Considering the length of time they were given within which to draft a constitution for a new state, it is notable that the Committee managed to come up with three Drafts of such quality and strength. Draft B may have been the obvious choice for the Provisional Government at that time, but all of the Drafts contained a strong basic structure for the running of the state and emphasised the important aspects of popular sovereignty and various democratic devices as well as the need to move away from British-style party politics. The Draft which was produced following governmental consideration was a remarkably strong document and it drew together all of the different sources of inspiration in a unique way. The conservative members of society might have been pleased with the constitutionalism and the traditional parliamentary structures. The socialists might have pointed to the echoes of the Democratic Programme of 1919. The people might have been impressed that the ultimate power in the state was given to them. It was a document which might have pleased even the anti-Treaty radicals as it contained the famous words of Pearse, the experiment of external ministers, as well as declarations of sovereignty and public ownership of land and resources. Significantly, it looked like the Constitution of an independent republic. However, it was this very fact which ensured that the British would be furious with the document.

4

British reaction to the Draft Constitution

The draft Constitution presented to the British by the Provisional Government was noteworthy for its emphasis on democratic ideals and popular sovereignty. It was not content to slavishly follow British models and contained a number of striking innovations.[1]

Introduction: the Collins–de Valera Pact

During the period of the drafting of the Constitution, there were discussions as to when the general election required by Article 17 of the Treaty would take place. Collins had made an agreement with de Valera in February to postpone the election for three months but the British were getting impatient and wished the Provisional Government to make the necessary arrangements. However, there were disagreements among pro- and anti-Treaty sides as to the validity of the election. This was partly because it was proposed to use an unrevised register for the election in order to save time. The result of the disagreements was that many election registers around the country were stolen by those opposed to the proposed election in the hope of preventing the election.[2]

In order to combat the difficulties, Collins met with de Valera in order to negotiate a compromise. The result of these discussions was the Collins–de Valera Pact which was announced on 20 May 1922. Among the provisions of the Pact were that existing pro- and anti-Treaty Dáil representation would provide the basis for candidates (i.e. Sinn Féin would put forward a panel of candidates – 68

---

[1] Thomas Mohr, *The Irish Free State and the Legal Implications of Dominion Status* (Unpublished PhD Thesis, University College Dublin, 2007), 36.

[2] During the negotiations, Griffith told Churchill that the election would have been invalidated by the destruction of the polling booths. The British were told that the purpose of the Pact was simply to carry out the election without turmoil and they were told that in Kerry and south Limerick around 40 or 50 registers had already been seized. See British National Archives Cabinet Office Files (hereinafter CAB) 43/7, 100.

nominated from the pro-Treaty side and 58 from the anti-Treaty side) and that the Treaty would not be an issue in the election. Other parties were 'graciously permitted to enter the contest'.[3]

The effect of the agreement would be that the resulting Cabinet would consist of 'the President, elected as formerly;[4] the Minister of Defence, representing the Army; and nine other Ministries – five from the majority party and four from the minority, each party to choose its own nominees'.[5] This would mean that the four minority members would become external ministers; the fact that the new Cabinet was to consist of members of both parties, together with the proposals in relation to the external ministers, meant that anti-Treaty politicians could effectively enter the government without taking the oath of allegiance or signing the Treaty, as was required by Article 17 of the Treaty.

The idea of external ministers and the fact that they would not be required to take the oath, by virtue of their being non-Parliamentarians, was important in relation to the Pact but, as we shall see, it caused some consternation during discussions with the British. The original idea was devised to allow experts to run certain departments. Therefore, the question of whether or not these ministers would take the oath should not technically have had any impact on the external ministers scheme. However, the scheme was marketed to Collins by Kennedy as one which would 'allow unity on all internal affairs' in that it would be possible to 'invite Dev & Co to come in in important internal ministries without taking any responsibility as to external affairs'.[6] Thus, it was important in order to allow for the possibility of involvement of the anti-Treaty side that these ministers would not have to take the oath.

Commentators have given mixed opinions on the infamous election Pact. Dorothy Macardle has pointed out the advantages of the agreement in that the Treaty issue could be postponed until the area could be examined and clarified; in the meantime, the Draft Constitution would be published and examined, and the coalition government which would be returned would be committed to national unity.[7] However, Joseph Curran and Joe Lee have argued that the Pact was simply clever tactics by Collins, with Curran writing that Collins would have lost little no matter which way it went,[8] and Lee commenting that 'Collins's behaviour did smack of the "too clever by half" variety at this stage'.[9]

Whatever the view of recent academics, the British government of the time was extremely suspicious of this Pact and many of the discussions on the expected Constitution turned to the question of the election. Leo Kohn has observed that the

---

[3] Joe Lee, *Ireland 1912–1985: Politics and Society* (Cambridge, 1989), 58.
[4] The President was elected by the Assembly.
[5] Collins–de Valera Pact, CAB43/7, 8.
[6] Hugh Kennedy Papers, P4/308, University College Dublin Archives.
[7] Dorothy Macardle, *The Irish Republic* (Dublin, 1999), 709–13.
[8] Joseph M. Curran, *The Birth of the Irish Free State 1921–1923* (Alabama, 1980), 189.
[9] Lee, *Ireland 1912–1985*, 59.

Pact 'had undoubtedly stiffened British insistence on the maintenance of the strict formalism of the Dominion Constitutions despite its conclusive abrogation by the interpretative clauses of the Treaty'.[10]

Fear arose amongst the British politicians that Collins was 'in the hands of de Valera'.[11] During a meeting of the British Signatories[12] on 23 May 1922, Lloyd George expressed the view that 'the Free Staters would slide into accommodation with the Republicans'.[13] Winston Churchill[14] stated that if 'the proposed election [had] been a bona fide one they could have put pressure on us to stretch the Constitution to suit them. As no election of value is contemplated we are in a position to be much more searching in our examination of the Constitution.'[15] Lloyd George later commented that the British were 'drifting into a position of either having to abandon or re-conquer Ireland'. He also stated: 'We may have to face re-conquest. But before that we should make clear to the civilised world that the present position is not our fault.'[16] This was the attitude and position of the British before they received the Draft Constitution. It was hardly an atmosphere conducive to cordial negotiation.

The conference on Ireland[17]

The negotiations between British and Irish representatives on the Draft Irish Constitution lasted from 26 May until 15 June.[18] The main Irish party arrived in London on Thursday 25 May. It consisted of Griffith, Eamonn Duggan,[19] Kevin O'Higgins,[20] Kennedy and Diarmuid O'Hegarty.[21] Collins and W.T. Cosgrave[22] arrived on Friday evening.

---

[10] Leo Kohn, *The Constitution of the Irish Free State* (London, 1932), 79.

[11] CAB43/7, 16.

[12] It appears that the British signatories of the Treaty constituted the negotiating committee for the Irish Constitution also. The phrase 'British Signatories' is used without explanation in the British documents.

[13] CAB43/7, 9.

[14] Secretary of State for the Colonies. As part of this position, Churchill was also responsible for the supervision of the transfer of power in Ireland as Chairman of the Provisional Government of Ireland Committee of the Cabinet.

[15] CAB43/7, 12.

[16] CAB43/7, 19–20.

[17] This is the name given by the British to the negotiations on the Draft Constitution.

[18] These discussions comprised more than just the negotiations on the Draft Constitution. In particular, many meetings centred on the disturbances in Ulster and the violence in the areas of Pettigo and Beleek. In addition, the British held private meetings about the possibility of a return to military action in Ireland.

[19] Minister for Home Affairs.

[20] Minister for Economic Affairs.

[21] Secretary.

[22] Cosgrave was Minister for local government at the time but later became President of the Executive Council.

On 26 May, before the British had received the Draft and before the official discussions were to take place, Churchill met with Griffith,[23] Duggan, O'Higgins and Kennedy. Churchill questioned Griffith about the election arrangements and the powers of the resulting provisional Parliament. He also expressed trepidation about the validity of the election and the Pact which had been agreed. This resulted in a long discussion during which the Irish attempted to explain the purpose of the Pact to the still dubious Churchill and to assure him that the pro-Treaty side were sincere in their claims that they would abide by the Treaty.[24]

Churchill then brought up the external ministers provision and stated that he believed it would be held to be a breach of the Treaty. Griffith countered with the argument that, during the war, the British government had had a war Cabinet containing only five or six ministers while there were other ministers outside of that Cabinet. Following a final attempt by Griffith to explain the level of instability in Ireland and the possibility of peace that the Pact had brought, the meeting was terminated.[25]

The British signatories met later to discuss what Churchill had learned from the meeting. There were concerns over whether action should be taken on foot of the election Pact. Churchill stated that until they knew the details of the Constitution they should not decide what line to take; 'whether they should put the most favourable construction on the manoeuvres of the Irish politicians to conform with the Treaty on the one hand, whilst on the other maintaining the scheme of a republic'.[26] He maintained that this was what was actually happening: 'Their [the Irish leaders'] whole procedure had been to leave intact the republican conception whilst at the same time establishing the organisation of the Provisional Government.'[27]

It was decided that the British government had to consider what its position would be if a farcical election were held. This was discussed for some time in an attempt to decide whether to say that they did not endorse the election or allow it to proceed but make a statement that they would not recognise any election which was not a bona fide one. Lloyd George questioned whether they were really ready to take a decision. He stressed that, if it was necessary to 'break',[28] a clear issue would be required on which the British government could carry with them not only the British people in Britain but the people of the Dominions also. He did not think a clear issue at present existed. If the Draft which they were to receive the next day was that of a republican Constitution and if it were a clear breach of the Treaty, 'there would be something for them to go on'.[29]

---

[23] Griffith had actually met with Churchill earlier that morning at the Colonial Office but no record of the discussion exists.

[24] CAB43/7, 17ff.

[25] CAB43/7, 34–5. See also 43.

[26] CAB43/7, 36.

[27] *Ibid.*

[28] Lloyd George used this word to signify calling off negotiations and returning to hostilities.

[29] CAB43/7, 36.

This did not bode well for the republican-leaning Draft Constitution which had been approved by the Provisional Government.

The British receive the Draft

On Saturday 27 May, British Law Officers Sir Ernest Pollock and Sir Leslie Scott examined the Draft together with Sir Frederick Liddell,[30] Sir Francis Greer,[31] John Risley,[32] Alfred Cope[33] and Lionel Curtis.[34] Later, Lloyd George, Chamberlain[35] and Churchill met with Griffith and Collins in order to discuss the Draft. Needless to say, the British were not pleased. Lloyd George accused Griffith and Collins of creating 'a republic in disguise' which 'stripped the monarchy of any influence or prestige and made it ridiculous'.[36] He said he had only just seen it and so he would mention only three or four points. These were: the attitude towards the monarchy, the absence of the Appeal to the Judicial Committee of the Privy Council, the treaty-making power and the oath. Griffith admitted that the Constitution had been drawn up in a hurry but that they believed it did conform to the Treaty and, if it did not, he was ready to consider any points put before him but he would like specific instances. The British then stated that they needed to consult with their legal advisers.[37]

When both parties met again later, the Irish were told that all on the British side were in agreement that the document was a complete evasion of the Treaty and that they would be given a document detailing the complaints on Monday.

On 28 May Lord Chief Justice Hewart conferred with the Law Officers and drew up a memorandum on the Draft which was considered by the British signatories when they met again the next day. The memo was deemed to be satisfactory but it was agreed that the language needed amending so as not to mislead the Canadians into taking the Irish side. Public opinion in Britain and the Dominions was always on the minds of the British negotiators. Curran has explained how, in its original form, the memorandum was simply a legal document with no account of existing constitutional practice and, because citizens in the Dominions had much more regard for practice than law, the document had to be adjusted to give greater emphasis to Canadian constitutional practice.[38] The amendments were effected by Sir Edward Grigg and Lionel Curtis before the memorandum was given to the Irish.[39]

The document reiterated the Irish position under the Treaty and stated that the

---

[30] First Parliamentary Counsel.
[31] Parliamentary Draftsman in the Irish office.
[32] Principal Legal Adviser in the Colonial Office.
[33] Assistant Under-secretary at Dublin Castle.
[34] Secretary.
[35] Lord Privy Seal.
[36] Curran, *Birth of the Irish Free State*, 204.
[37] CAB43/7, 55.
[38] Curran, *Birth of the Irish Free State*, 206.
[39] CAB43/7, 76–7.

Constitution must be in accordance with that agreement. The memorandum then proceeded to describe the fundamental principles of the Canadian Constitution in order to demonstrate how these had been ignored. It was noted that, until Article 74, the draft Constitution was that of an independent republic in that the Crown did not feature at all. Even Articles 74 and 75, which were the Articles dealing with the relationship of the Irish Free State to Britain, were unsatisfactory. It was pointed out that the Constitution omitted any mention of the specific restrictions and obligations imposed by the Treaty. In particular, the British were adamant that the oath be included in the Constitution.[40]

Of course, this reaction had been predicted by Gavan Duffy[41] and could not have been a surprise to the Irish delegation, especially since the British were essentially correct; in reading the draft Constitution, until Article 74 one could have assumed it was a constitution for an independent republic.

Deadlock and Kennedy's letter

After much to-ing and fro-ing,[42] Kennedy and Lord Chief Justice Hewart met to discuss a redraft. It seems agreement proved impossible at that time, with Kennedy adamant to retain the Irish interpretation of the Treaty provisions. The Irish maintained that there was nothing in the Treaty which required them to include the Appeal to the Privy Council, nor was there any provision specifying the inclusion of the oath in the Constitution itself. However, the British insisted that these were necessary for membership of the Commonwealth. Kennedy then prepared a document entitled 'Observations on the Criticisms of the British Government on the Draft Irish Constitution'. This document was an attempt to help the British understand the unique position of Ireland. It highlighted the fact that Ireland had not been a British colony like the other Dominions and the English common law had been imposed by statute and was therefore alien to the country. It pointed out that, following the Treaty signing:

> [G]lowing speeches were made by leading English statesmen, expounding as the inspiration of new hopes that the Irish people would, with freedom from English interference or influence, get themselves to build up a constitution for the government of their own country which constitution would be wholly of their creation and in accordance with their own wishes and views of their needs, with full play for Irish traditions and Irish thought to give colour and lend vitality to the framing and building up of institutions which the Irish people could honour as their own.[43]

It noted that the Crown's involvement in the executive was a subject of particular concern; while the British might associate the symbol of the Crown with popular

---

[40] CAB23/30, 152–62.
[41] See Chapter 3, 45.
[42] A number of meetings took place between 29 and 31 May. Not all of them centred on the Constitution. See n. 18 above.
[43] CAB23/30, 149.

sovereignty, in Ireland it was a 'symbol of tyranny'.[44] Finally, the document emphasised that the Irish Constitution had been framed to meet Irish conditions. It was an attempt to explain why the Draft did not contain the symbols which were considered so important by the British and why, according to the Irish interpretation, these symbols could be left out without offending the Treaty. This attempt was made in vain a number of times during the negotiations.

A critical stage and Lloyd George's letter

On 31 May, Churchill made the following statement in the House of Commons, in the presence of Griffith and Collins: 'I have been asked to give assurances that we will not tolerate the setting up of a Republic. I have given those assurances. In the event of such a Republic it will be the intention of the Government to hold Dublin as one of the preliminary essential steps to military operations.'[45] The situation at this stage was extremely fragile. A note was sent to the Irish asking them whether they meant to honour their signatures to the Treaty.[46] At the same time, Tom Jones[47] was sent to see Griffith and Collins to make sure they understood how grave a view the British government took of Kennedy's declaration. Jones reported back that he had made it clear that war was the alternative to agreement.[48]

On 1 June, at a Cabinet meeting, Lloyd George enunciated the points on which the Draft did not carry out the Treaty. He pointed out that the document was 'purely republican in character and but thinly veiled'.[49] In response to a remark made by the First Commissioner of Works,[50] the Prime Minister agreed that the Irish draftsmen must have acted under instructions from the politicians.[51] It was agreed that the British signatories together with Lord Balfour should draft a document containing the views of the British government. The document, which was later approved by the Cabinet, insisted on definite answers to six questions:

1. Was the Irish Free State to be within the Empire on the basis of common citizenship or merely associated with it?

---

[44] Curran, *Birth of the Irish Free State*, 210.
[45] CAB43/7, 80.
[46] CAB43/7, 82.
[47] Principal Assistant Secretary to Lloyd George. Both men were Welsh and had a close relationship.
[48] Thomas Jones, *Whitehall Diary: Vol III Ireland 1918–1925* (London, 1971), 208. Lloyd George had asked, during a Cabinet meeting, whether the Irish realised how close to a break they were.
[49] CAB23/30, 128.
[50] David Alexander Edward Lindsay, 27th Earl of Crawford and 10th Earl of Balcarres.
[51] CAB23/30, 131. This is perhaps in response to the fact that the Irish had always made a point of the fact that the Constitution Committee responsible for the Draft comprised only Treaty supporters and the only instruction given to them had been to draft a constitution along the lines of the Treaty.

2. Was the position of the Crown in Ireland to be the same as in the other Dominions?
3. Was the treaty-making power of the Free State to be the same as that of Canada?
4. Were the Free State Courts to stand in the same relation to the King in Council [the Judicial Committee of the Privy Council] as did the other Dominions?
5. Was the Treaty oath of allegiance to be incorporated in the Free State Constitution as the oath required of members of Parliament?
6. Would all members of the Irish Provisional Government be required to sign the declaration of acceptance of the Treaty as stipulated in Article 17 of the Treaty?[52]

The Cabinet then discussed the possible military action which could be taken in the event of an unsatisfactory answer from the Irish side. [53]

Lloyd George also met with Griffith and Collins privately that evening. This meeting resulted in many arguments during which Griffith and Collins attempted to explain the conception of the symbol of the Crown in Ireland. Collins tried to convey the abhorrence which the Irish people had for the Royal symbols.[54] He complained that the British government was requiring execution of the letter of the Treaty in 'Shylock spirit'. He also accused the British of trying to force the English common law upon Ireland[55] and demanded safeguards which Ireland needed since it did not have the distance of Canada from Britain. Protests were made about the Privy Council and fear was expressed in relation to the possibility of Carson and his allies sitting in judgment on Irish cases. When Lloyd George began to describe Ireland's international position under the Treaty, Collins retorted that Ireland had to get its own house in order first.[56]

In general, the Irish leaders attempted to explain that it was because of Irish fears and different perceptions that it was difficult to find a balance between the

---

[52] The six questions have been paraphrased from 'Letter from the Prime Minister to Mr A Griffith' in CAB24/137, 67–9.

[53] It was agreed to convene a joint meeting of the Provisional Government of Ireland Committee and the Subcommittee on Ireland of the Committee of Imperial Defence, with a view to determining the administrative and military action which might be taken in the event of a rupture of the negotiations. During the meeting, Churchill impressed on all present the need for the most scrupulous secrecy. The meeting addressed the possibilities of cutting of revenue to Ireland, occupation of Custom Houses, diversion of merchant vessels and possible areas of refuge for the loyal population. A subcommittee was formed to produce a report. See CAB23/30, 139.

[54] This must have had some effect on Lloyd George as later, at a Cabinet meeting, he remarked that the Irish were 'fed up with the Crown this, and the Crown that, and no wonder'. Churchill then retorted that the Irish were lucky to have a Celt in the British Cabinet to put their case. See Jones, *Whitehall Diary*, 206.

[55] It is not clear why Collins had a problem with the common law. It is also referred to in Kennedy's letter (see above) but there are no further references to this either by Collins or by any of the Irish team.

[56] CAB43/7, 93–8.

wishes of both sides. Griffith pointed out that there were two parties to the Treaty and that Britain could not expect to dictate its own interpretation when lawyers on each side differed. There were arguments over the Canadian position also, with Lloyd George arguing that safeguards as to practice could not be embodied in a Constitution. In the end, Griffith promised to answer the letter and the six questions the next day.[57]

In the meantime, the Irish delegates travelled home to inform their colleagues of the situation. On the 2 June, Collins reported to the Irish Cabinet that the British government had definitely rejected 'our Draft Constitution' but that they did not quarrel with the proposed arrangements as to internal matters.[58] This was true in that, for the most part,[59] the British were concerned about the absence of the British symbols such as the King as head of Parliament and the oath and did not express much interest in the provisions relating to internal governance.

Collins informed his Cabinet of the letter from Lloyd George containing the six questions and the fact that a reply had to be sent that night. He also noted that, when the British brought up the question of the Appeal to the Judicial Committee of the Privy Council, he had told them that 'they could go to hell on that'.[60] Griffith also attended the Irish Cabinet meeting the next day, after he had sent the reply to Lloyd George. He reported that the situation was very serious and that the British would not hesitate to go back to war if they were not 'satisfied on the Constitution'. He noted that the British had objected to putting down constitutional practice in writing. They had informed him that this had been objected to at the last Imperial Conference. This was something he hoped to change.[61]

Griffith's reply

Griffith's reply to Lloyd George's letter began by introducing the Irish position, giving a brief introduction on the drafting of the Constitution and then the six questions were answered, all to the satisfaction of the British Cabinet, although the answers in relation to the treaty-making power and the Privy Council remained vague.[62]

In relation to the first question on the position of the Irish Free State within the Empire, Griffith answered: '[I]t is intended that the Irish Free State shall be, not merely associated with, but a member of and within the Community of Nations known as the British Empire and on the basis of common citizenship as explicitly

[57] *Ibid.*
[58] Notes on Cabinet Meeting, 2 June 1922, in Papers of George Gavan Duffy, P152, University College Dublin Archives.
[59] The external ministers provision was an exception.
[60] Notes on Cabinet Meeting, 2 June 1922, in Papers of George Gavan Duffy, P152, University College Dublin Archives.
[61] *Ibid.*
[62] Griffith noted that this particular question 'raises a matter of no small delicacy in Ireland'. CAB24/137, 73.

provided by the Treaty.'[63] He was a little more obscure in relation to the second question on Dominion status, stating that he believed there was a difference of interpretation as between the Irish and British. However, he affirmed that 'in all matters in which the Crown is constitutionally effective ... the position of the Crown is beyond question to be the same in Ireland as it is in Canada, Australia, New Zealand and South Africa'.[64] As to whether the treaty-making power of the Irish Free State was to be the same as that of Canada in question three, he simply answered in the affirmative.

The fifth and sixth questions were also answered succinctly in that Griffith wrote that if the British government was still not satisfied that the oath had been sufficiently incorporated, it would be expressly set forth in the Constitution and he agreed that all members of the Irish Provisional Government (including external ministers) would be required to sign the declaration under Article 17 of the Treaty.

It was the answer to the fourth question on the Privy Council to which Griffith gave most consideration. First, he pointed out that contemporary opinion[65] predicted the future abolition of the Appeal. He indicated that there were further reasons why the Appeal should not apply to Ireland, including the fact that the Judicial Committee comprised persons who had used their positions for 'party political purposes hostile to the Irish people'.[66] This, he noted, had 'aroused keen indignation and antipathy to the Tribunal of which they are members'. In addition, he observed that the great volume of Irish litigation was concerned with 'very small money interests' and thus the Appeal would be 'a rich man's appeal which may be used to the destruction of a man not well off'.[67] He stated that he did not think the insertion of the Appeal to the Privy Council in the Constitution was a necessary incident of the Treaty position. Finally, he noted that he had not gathered from Lloyd George's letter whether the British felt the point was vital or in what form they felt it should be insisted upon.[68]

In response, the British Cabinet agreed that, although certain parts of the answers were not clear, it afforded no ground for a break.[69] Lloyd George was then to inform Griffith that they were prepared to consent to the resumption of negotiations and to inform him 'personally and privately that while there were one or two important outstanding difficulties, the Irish reply had, on the whole,

---

[63] CAB24/137, 71.

[64] CAB24/137, 72.

[65] He mentioned Sir Robert Borden, Mr Hughes, General Smuts, Professor Berriedale Keith and Duncan Hall.

[66] CAB24/137, 74. Presumably, he means Carson and Atkinson, who were also criticised by Jones for being involved in politics as judges. See Jones, *Whitehall Diary*, 204.

[67] CAB24/137, 74.

[68] CAB24/137, 67–75.

[69] CAB43/7, 104.

created a favourable impression on the Cabinet'.[70] Since this episode had come to some sort of conclusion, the next stage of revision could begin and Kennedy and Hewart were set to work again.

Redraft

On 10 June, the British and Irish signatories all convened for a meeting during which the remaining issues of contention were discussed and many of the issues were finally agreed upon. It was also agreed to leave the (as yet undecided) transitional provisions on the courts out of the published Constitution. The original draft had not provided for the administration of justice during the period prior to the establishment of the courts of the Irish Free State. In order to prevent a hiatus, the British, who were keen to prevent any possible strengthening of the republican Dáil courts, drafted a provision whereby the existing British courts were to be used. The Irish objected to the provision and Kennedy was appointed to redraft a suitable alternative. By this date, 10 June, Kennedy had not yet completed his redraft and he suggested that it might be necessary to leave the subject out of the published draft and to say that temporary provisions were under consideration. It is unclear what exactly the Provisional Government objected to because the provision eventually produced by Kennedy was along the same lines as that originally suggested by the British.

Kennedy was evidently apprehensive in relation to the possible reaction in Ireland to a decision to use the 'enemy courts' during the transitional period. The republicans appeared to be under the impression that the Dáil courts were to continue but, as E.J. Duggan, Minister for Home Affairs, pointed out, these courts were not suitable as they had no licensing jurisdiction nor any lunacy or probate jurisdiction. However, Casey suggests that it may have been under British pressure that the decision was made to suspend operation of the courts.[71]

Given the anger which was expressed following the suspension of the courts, it was wise of Kennedy not to include the transitional provisions in the published draft of the Constitution. However, as Mary Kotsonouris has commented, 'Some of the fears might have been eased if the public had been told that the hated Resident Magistrates were not being brought back, but those gentlemen themselves had not yet been told!'[72]

Towards the end of the meeting, Griffith wondered whether 'the other side' would hold him to the publication of the Constitution before the election. In any case, he felt that the Constitution need only be published a day or two before the election. Possibly, he felt that they had conceded too much in relation to Irish

---

[70] CAB23/30, 183.
[71] See James Casey, 'Republican Courts in Ireland 1919–1922' (1970) 5 *Irish Jurist* 321, 337–8.
[72] Mary Kotsonouris, *Retreat from Revolution: The Dail Courts, 1920–24* (Dublin, 1994), 86.

independence and perhaps he felt that the pro-Treaty side might be punished by the electorate because of it. Lloyd George observed that Griffith would be charged with a breach of faith if the Constitution was not published. While Lloyd George may have had his own reasons for this piece of advice,[73] it was to prove crucial in relation to the validity of the Constitution afterwards.[74] Finally, the meeting was terminated with the agreement that Kennedy and Hewart would meet again on 12 June for a final redraft.

On 12 June, another meeting took place during which the Irish signatories (excepting Collins) met with the Southern Unionists and Churchill, who chaired the meeting. Griffith explained all of the safeguards which had been agreed upon for the protection of minorities but Lord Midleton complained that some of the Seanad provisions were only transitory, the Seanad itself was too small and the delay of legislation was too short. Talks resumed the next day with the addition of Collins. Eventually, it was agreed to have a Seanad of 60 with two representatives from the National University of Ireland and two from Dublin University, 56 elected (by all the citizens of the Free State who had reached the age of 30) from a panel where two-thirds would be nominated by the Dáil and one-third by the Seanad. The delay was extended to 270 days and it was provided that three-fifths of the Seanad could demand a referendum.[75] Joint debate was also provided for but not joint voting. The decision on whether a bill was a money bill was to be certified by the Speaker, subject to appeal to a committee of privileges selected from both Houses and presided over by a Supreme Court judge. For the first Seanad, half the senators were to be nominated and half elected by the Dáil.

A great effort was made to accommodate the Unionists, possibly in the hope that co-operation would prove to them that they would not be lost or overlooked in a united Ireland. However, the Unionists were evidently not impressed. During a Cabinet meeting on 15 June, Lloyd George read the alterations made since the meeting with the Southern Unionists, and Churchill compared Lord Midleton's attitude and the Southern Unionists' 'graceless answer' to the good spirit of

---

[73] For one thing, when the Draft was published, the Irish could no longer go back on any of it. However, failure to publish before the election could also reflect badly on the British; and Lloyd George, who was always conscious of British and Dominion public opinion, would have been anxious to avoid this. Furthermore, if the Draft was not published and the anti-Treaty side gained popularity because of it, the resulting instability would not bode well for Britain either.

[74] Even though they were criticised for failure to publish the Constitution until the morning of the election, at least the Provisional Government could claim that the Constitution had the support of the people, who had seen it that morning and still voted in favour of the pro-Treaty side. Had the Constitution not been published, it could have been disastrous for Collins and Griffith. In any case, it would not have been possible to publish the Constitution before the morning of the election as the terms were not agreed upon until the day before.

[75] This was amended in the final draft so that a simple majority was needed to demand a referendum.

Griffith and Collins. He proposed to ask them whether they could not say anything better and Chamberlain advised him to remonstrate with them.[76]

Amended Draft completed

Kennedy finished the Draft with Liddell and Greer, working until midnight on 14 June. Finally, a Draft appeared which pleased the British. In comparison with the original Draft which had been brought to London, the first major change was the inclusion of a 'preliminary' in place of the Preamble,[77] which had been already omitted by the Irish for fear of aggravating matters.[78] This preliminary declared that the Constitution was to be construed with reference to the Treaty, which was given force of law in the Free State.[79] The significance of the wording of this preliminary was crucial in that, ultimately, it gave the Treaty pre-eminence in Irish law. The Constitution was to be interpreted in accordance with the Treaty and together with Article 47;[80] this meant that any amendments which were considered to offend the Treaty would be unconstitutional.

In Article 47, the Irish had resisted the British desire to add a proviso that a law altering the Constitution must be confirmed by an Act of the Imperial Parliament. Hewart instead pressed for 'within the terms of the Treaty', which was eventually accepted.

Henri Bourassa, a Quebec nationalist leader, met with Douglas in order to discuss the Constitution and he warned Douglas about the use of this preliminary; 'he felt sure that it would be used against us in the future ...'.[81] Indeed, it was to have major implications later on in the political development of the Irish Free State, and many members of the Constituent Assembly, including government supporters, were extremely unhappy about this provision.[82]

---

[76] CAB43/7, 181.

[77] 'Whereas in the good providence of God an end has been made of foreign rule in Ireland and the sufferings and sacrifices of its people have been rewarded with freedom by Divine Mercy, we the people of Ireland, acknowledging that all lawful authority comes from God, and in the exercise of our National right, do hereby proclaim this to be the Constitution of Saorstát Éireann.'

[78] Before the Draft was taken to London it was decided to sacrifice this provision in the hope that the British would be prepared to accept some of the more important provisions.

[79] 'These presents shall be construed with reference to the Articles of Agreement for a Treaty between Great Britain and Ireland ... which are hereby given the force of law and if any provision of this Constitution or of any amendment thereof ... is in any respect repugnant to ... the Scheduled Treaty, it shall, to the extent only of such repugnancy be absolutely void and inoperative.'

[80] This was the amendment provision, which became Article 50 in the final document.

[81] J. Alfred Gaughan (ed.), *Memoirs of Senator James G. Douglas (1887–1954): Concerned Citizen*, (Dublin, 1998), 89.

[82] Gavan Duffy was particularly outspoken in relation to this issue. In a letter to Collins dated 14 June, he expressed the following opinion: 'Apart from the provision as to the oath which is abominable, the Preamble is the worst thing in the draft. It makes

The other major amendments included the fact that Article 1, which had contained nationalistic language stating that Ireland was a free and sovereign nation, was deleted and replaced with a less nationalistic provision which provided that Ireland was a co-equal member of the British Community of Nations. Surprisingly, Kennedy was the one who suggested this change. In a letter to Collins, Kennedy noted that he was going to propose omitting parts of Articles 1 and 2 which were suggested to be of a 'communistic tendency'.[83] In a further letter he seemed to be delighted (if a little surprised) that the British accepted his 'new Article 1 so easily'. He confessed that he had to drop Pearse's declaration as it would have been spoiled by the proposed amendments.[84]

So the declaration that the sovereignty of the nation would extend to all possessions and resources of the country was now omitted but the Irish were adamant that the provision on the sovereignty of the people should remain. This provision stated that 'All powers of Government in Ireland are derived from the people of Ireland'. This was one area where the Irish dug their heels in because this provision was central to the whole document and was vital in order to convince the people to accept the document. The British wanted to state that, although all powers would be derived from the people, they would be vested in the King. However, Kennedy found this to be objectionable and eventually the British were forced to concede on this point. It was one of the rare Irish victories however, as, for the most part, everything else required by the British was eventually achieved.

Inevitably, the oath was made mandatory for all members of Parliament and external ministers. However, the Irish had objected to taking the oath before the representative of the Crown so it was agreed to substitute the Chairman of the House. Article 39a[85] was added. This Article dealt with the power of the King's representative to withhold assent or reserve a bill for the signification of the King's pleasure. In addition, the King's representative was to be styled Governor-General and not High Commissioner, as the Irish had wanted. In Article 44, the referendum had originally applied to Acts but this was changed to bills so as to avoid the involvement of the representative of the Crown until after the referendum had been held.

Other changes included the structure of the legislature, which was now to be

the Treaty a part of the Constitution and it seems to make the Constitution derive its force from the Treaty. I am quite sure we could hold out on this, as the Treaty does not provide for these stipulations going into the constitution. The second part of the Preamble is almost worse for after giving the Treaty the force of law it goes on, quite unnecessarily and quite offensively, to declare that any law which breaks the Treaty shall be void. I think the preamble is thoroughly rotten and I trust you won't in any final way agree to it.' Papers of George Gavan Duffy, P152, University College Dublin Archives.

83 Hugh Kennedy Papers, P4/362 and 363, University College Dublin Archives. Churchill had described the Articles as 'Bolshevik'.

84 *Ibid.*

85 This later became Article 41.

made up of the King and both Houses; Parliament was to be summoned and dissolved in the name of the King; the Executive Council was given the exclusive right to decide on dissolution;[86] Executive authority was to be vested in the King; and judges were to be appointed by the Governor-General on the advice of the Executive Council. Eventually, the Irish conceded to allow the Crown to confer honours on Free State citizens, although the consent of the Executive Council was to be required.[87] Significantly, the Appeal to the Privy Council was also included in Article 66. Given the trenchant opposition expressed earlier by Griffith and Collins, it is surprising that the provision was eventually agreed to and it is unclear what led to its inclusion. It seems most likely that the Irish were forced to agree since the British refused to back down on what they felt was a crucial provision.[88] Irish fears may also have been calmed by promises of the South African position[89] and hopes that the Appeal might soon be abolished.

Another noteworthy amendment was that all originally Irish terminology was removed as the British found it to be crude and uncivilised.[90] However, certain words such as Dáil, Seanad and Oireachtas survived the culling process.

One provision which had worried the British was the provision on external ministers. They were unfamiliar with and unimpressed by the idea of such a scheme. They highlighted the fact that the idea whereby these ministers would not have to take the oath was a subterfuge and insisted that these ministers should also be obliged to take the oath. Unfortunately, this action ended the dreams of those

---

[86] This was something which the British had argued for all along but the Irish had managed to resist until the last minute.

[87] Article 5. This was a hard-fought battle for the Irish delegates, who bitterly contested the right of the King to bestow titles on Irish citizens and cited the example of the corruption of the early 1800s. The original drafts had specifically prohibited the possibility of British titles being conferred upon Irish citizens. However, the British were adamant that the King would retain this power. Eventually this compromise was reached whereby titles could be granted only with the consent of the Irish government. This compromise survived in the 1937 Constitution in Article 40.2.2.

[88] The British had made it clear that war was the alternative to agreement.

[89] O'Briain has given the following explanation of the South African position in relation to the Privy Council Appeal: 'The general rule is that no leave is given where the question is one that can best be determined in South Africa, or if it is essentially a South African question, no matter how important it may be.' See Barra O'Briain, *The Irish Constitution* (Dublin, 1929), 120. It has also been described in a South African legal text book as follows: 'The privy council will not readily grant leave to appeal. It will not do so in cases raising questions of a local nature; it may do so in cases raising serious constitutional questions. Very few appeals indeed are heard from the appellate division of the supreme court by the privy council.' See W.P.M. Kennedy & H.J. Schlosberg, *The Law and Custom of the South African Constitution* (London, 1935), 376.

[90] There was an attempt made to include the names of institutions etc. in both languages but this apparently gave the appearance of a very cluttered-looking document. In the *Morning Post* on 17 June 1922, the Draft Constitution was criticised for the inclusion of 'certain interpolated bastard Irishisms'. Even Hewart raised the question of the 'Erse' terminology. See CAB43/7, 177.

who had hoped that this provision would allow de Valera and his supporters to re-enter government and further alienated the anti-Treaty side. Additionally, the British decided they did not like the fact that these ministers could remain while the Dáil had been dissolved and a new Dáil constituted; they felt it would create a 'permanent oligarchy' in the Free State. The British did not insist on amendment of this provision, though. However, eventually a number of members of the Dáil also became suspicious in relation to this provision and, as Mohr has noted, 'by the time the Constitution came into force the proposal had been diluted out of all recognition.'[91]

The published Draft

The Draft Constitution (minus the transitional provisions)[92] was published on 16 June, the morning of the Irish election.[93] A complete version was published in Britain as a White Paper on 19 June and was also circulated to the British Cabinet. The five reserved articles were also published in the morning papers that day. The Constitution was greeted with mixed reactions on both sides of the Irish Sea but both governments claimed to have succeeded in what they had set out to do.

The British views on the election Pact had certainly affected the direction of the negotiations but a further reason for disagreement was that the British and Irish had completely different views as to the interpretation of Treaty provisions: 'The British demanded rigid adherence to the letter of the Dominion framework, the Irish its qualification by the living law of a new order.'[94] When broken down to its most basic elements, the difference between the Irish and the British positions was that the Irish looked at the Treaty and noted that that it was not specified in that document that any of the British symbols had to be included in the Constitution and it did not mention the appeal to the Judicial Committee of the Privy Council. In fact, there is no direction at all on the Constitution; the only mention of that word in the Treaty is in the form of the oath whereby members have to swear 'true faith and allegiance to the Constitution of the Irish Free State'. This is a fair point.

---

91 Mohr, 'British Involvement', 172. Because of the many changes made during the debates in the Constituent Assembly, the scheme which emerged bore little resemblance to the one originally proposed by Douglas. For more on this see Chapter 8.

92 The provisions which were not published were draft Articles 73, 74, 75, 76 and 79 which became Articles 75–83 of the final document. These Articles dealt with the administration of justice for the transitional period before the Irish court system was established, as well as the formation of the first Seanad, the transfer of the administration of public service and British officers.

93 On the morning of the election, Collins advised the electorate to vote 'without regard to the panel of candidates agreed by the Pact'. See B.P. Murphy, 'Nationalism: The Framing of the Constitution of the Irish Free State, 1922 – The Defining Battle for the Irish Republic' in Joost Augusteijn (ed.), *The Irish Revolution 1913–1923* (New York, 2002).

94 Kohn, *Constitution of the Irish Free State*, 79.

On the other hand, the British claimed that Dominion status required these forms to be adopted. One can understand the British argument in that the Constitution, as it had been presented to them, was essentially that of a republican state and this would never have been acceptable to the British. However, while it was reasonable for the British to insist on the inclusion of certain references in relation to the power of the King's representative etc., there was no real need to force the inclusion of the oath, since it was already incorporated in the Treaty, and, since the Treaty made no mention of the appeal to the Judicial Committee of the Privy Council, there should have been no reason to include that particular provision in the Constitution either.

Thus, it is submitted that, although the reasons for the British approach were valid, it seems that the Irish argument against the addition of British symbolism carried more weight. This is because the symbolism meant little to the British in reality whereas its inclusion in the Constitution meant that many anti-Treaty radicals would never accept the document. The Draft Constitution which was brought to London was one which might have gained the acceptance of the anti-Treaty side but the Draft which was published after the London negotiations contained British symbols and other provisions which were insisted upon by the British and which consequently damaged the possibility of universal acceptance of the document in Ireland. While these additions may not have been significant in practice and were mostly theoretical, they had essentially tainted the document in the eyes of the anti-Treaty side. The Irish were forced to accept these controversial provisions, and the inclusion of these elements was a feature in the spiral to civil war.

However, what the document did manage to avoid was a return to hostilities between Ireland and Britain, and it is interesting how both sides believed they had achieved what they wanted. The Irish believed they had effective sovereignty while the British believed they had retained some element of control and importantly, they had not been seen to submit to republican sentiments. So, it is to the credit of Kennedy and Hewart that they managed to devise a compromise, which walked such a fine line between the interpretations of both sides.

Conclusion

Although the British managed to force the Irish to compromise on many issues, the Irish had still managed to retain quite a sovereign and democratic document. Although it might appear that the Crown was given power, this was in fact only illusory. For example, judges were to be appointed by the representative of the Crown, but he was given no discretion because the appointment had to be on the advice of the Cabinet. So, in fact, the decision would be made by the Irish Cabinet. The situation was the same in relation to the President of the Executive Council, who had to be nominated by the Dáil before being appointed by the Crown's representative. Also, the Oireachtas was summoned and dissolved by the representative but, again, only on the advice of the Executive Council. Furthermore, the oath of allegiance, which all members of Parliament had to swear, was different from that taken by members in the Dominions as instead of swearing loyalty to the Crown the Irish members swore allegiance to the Irish Constitution first and only afterwards was faithfulness to His Majesty mentioned. Essentially, all of the Articles dealing with the Crown were devoid of substance.[95]

The Provisional Government had lost much of the tone of its draft, and, with it, they had also lost any hope of gaining the support of the anti-Treaty side. However, Griffith, Collins and their team should have been proud of the democratic document which they had managed to produce against the odds. Furthermore, despite the changes made at this stage, the central themes of popular sovereignty, democracy and an anti-party system still permeated the Draft Constitution. Kohn has described it as 'not a new Bill "for the better government of Ireland", but a most comprehensive and, in spirit, essentially republican constitution on most advanced Continental lines ... Its archaic symbols had to be introduced, but their meaninglessness for Ireland was writ large on every page.'[96] All that was required now was to pass the document through the Constituent Assembly.

---

[95] As early as 1927, it had been emphatically affirmed that the Crown was nothing but a fiction in the Irish Free State. In *Re Reade*, Chief Justice Kennedy stated: 'The Crown is in each Dominion the permanent symbol of executive government, but the actual government is in fact and in constitutional reality in the hands of the national ministers responsible to, and changeable at the will of, the national parliament.' [1927] IR 31, 50. This statement was not revolutionary because it was obvious in Ireland at the time. Kevin Costello has shown how during the discussions on the 1922 Constitution with the British 'the Crown was degraded to a purely symbolic position'. And he has correctly noted how 'The Crown was removed from the sphere of administration, and from the exercise of those common law executive powers known in those jurisdictions which adopt the English constitutional model as prerogatives'. See Kevin Costello, 'The Expulsion of Prerogative Doctrine from Irish Law: Quantifying and Remedying the Loss of the Royal Prerogative' (1997) 32 *Irish Jurist* 145, 172–9.

[96] Kohn, *Constitution of the Irish Free State*, 80.

5

Debates in the Constituent Assembly

Introduction

The passage of the Constitution through the Dáil, sitting as a Constituent Assembly, was a crucial stage in the drafting process as it was at this stage that the Constitution was solidified. The idealism of the early drafting period was replaced here with realism and the need to provide the new state with a working constitution; many of the originally strong Articles dealing with issues such as public ownership of land and natural resources were watered down due to the needs of political reality.[1] However, that is not to say that the themes which the Committee had ingrained in the Drafts had disappeared. On the contrary, by the end of this process, the ideas of popular sovereignty, democracy and anti-party politics, which are easily identifiable as key concepts in the three Drafts, had now been embedded in the Constitution.

By modern standards this stage was completed with considerable speed, with the Assembly finishing its consideration after only 19 days. However, this is an indication of the prevailing political circumstances and the need to stabilise the position of the embryonic Irish state. The Provisional Government had a difficult task before it in that it hoped to gain the support of the Constituent Assembly for a document which now contained many British flourishes, and, while these may have been mostly meaningless, they were enough to alienate many of the more radical republicans. There would be much debate, argument and, inevitably, many amendments before the Constitution would eventually receive the approval of the Assembly.

---

[1] These Articles were significantly diminished so as not to frighten the property-owning class whose funds were needed to maintain the economy.

The aftermath of the election

When the Draft was finally agreed upon in London, it was published in the morning papers of 16 June, which was the day of the Irish general election. The Provisional Government was criticised for its failure to publish the Draft at an earlier stage but, as Mohr points out:

> The reality was that publication was impossible until the deliberations of the London conference on the draft Irish Constitution had been completed. These negotiations continued right up to the last moment. Final agreement was only reached between the delegations on 15 June, the day before the Irish election. Lloyd George actually authorized the publication of the draft before the British cabinet had formally approved it in order to accommodate the Irish in this matter.[2]

In addition, it is quite probable that supporters of the Treaty were going to approve the Constitution just as the anti-Treaty side would oppose it.

The pro-Treaty Sinn Féin party won the election with 239,195 votes to 132,163 for anti-Treaty Sinn Féin,[3] and so, in essence, the Draft Constitution had been approved by the Irish people. The new government now had the task of putting the Constitution through the Constituent Assembly. It had been planned to do this as soon as possible but with the official outbreak of the Civil War on 28 June,[4] this had to be postponed until September. By September 1922, the Free State forces had taken all of the major towns and the anti-Treaty side was reduced to guerrilla fighting and acts of sabotage. At this stage, although it had now lost its two leaders,[5] the government felt it could move to consider the Constitution.

Because members of the anti-Treaty side had declined to take their seats in the Dáil, it was made up of pro-Treaty Sinn Féin representatives and also Labour, Independent and Farmers' Party representatives. The backgrounds of members were quite diverse, comprising professions such as a shopkeeper, engineer, vet and trade union official, and it is estimated that at least ten members were also members of the legal profession.[6]

---

[2] Thomas Mohr, 'British Involvement in the Creation of the Constitution of the Irish Free State' (2008) 30 (1) *Dublin University Law Journal* 166, 176.

[3] Michael Gallagher (ed.), *Irish Elections 1922–44: Results and Analysis* (Limerick, 1993), 13.

[4] This is the date generally given as the official beginning of the Civil War as it was on this day that the bombing of the Four Courts by the Irish Free State forces began.

[5] Arthur Griffith died of heart failure on 12 August 1922. Collins was assassinated 10 days later.

[6] According to the Oireachtas website www.oireachtas.ie, out of the 92 (of course Collins's and Griffith's deaths would bring this figure to 90) members who took their seats in the third Dáil, there are 19 members whose professions are not listed. Other professions include: 10 farmers, seven trade union officials, seven professors, six writers or journalists, five merchants, five doctors, three company directors, one editor, one newspaper proprietor, one assistant commissioner of An Garda Síochána,

Introduction of the Bill

On 18 September 1922, the Dáil, sitting as a Constituent Assembly,[7] began its detailed consideration of the Constitution, which lasted until 25 October.[8] During this time, the bill went through each of the conventional stages of legislative consideration.[9] The Minister for Home Affairs, Kevin O'Higgins, introduced the bill. He spent some time explaining to deputies that, despite British elements being included in the document, these really meant nothing and that now they had substantially what they wanted in a constitution. He explained:

> On the face of it this Constitution is not a republican Constitution; perhaps I would not be wrong in saying that it is as little a republican Constitution as a British Constitution. It contains the trappings, the insignia, the fiction and the symbols of monarchical institutions, but the real power is in the hands of the people ... In Ireland under this Constitution, the real power is in the hands of the people acting through their Parliament, no matter what fictitious or theoretical powers are stated to reside elsewhere.[10]

O'Higgins was referring to the apparent power of the Crown in his last sentence. He went on to point out each instance in which the Crown seemed to have power but in fact it was only *de jure* power; 'all through this Constitution you have that clash as it were of the law and the facts ... where you have the written word of the Constitution stating one thing, and the actual practice and constitutional usage of the country quite another thing'.[11] He also commented on the oath that 'this particular oath prescribed in the Treaty, and in the Constitution for the Free State, is a much more innocuous matter than the full-blooded Oath of Allegiance

---

one shopkeeper, one draper, one brick and stone layer, one accountant, one engineer, one businessman, one vet, one surgeon, one station master, one flour miller, one insurance broker, one book dealer, one army officer, one Harbour Commissioner secretary, one teacher, one manager and one auctioneer.

[7] The third Dáil was elected as a Constituent Assembly with the passing through of the Constitution its sole purpose. Chief Justice Kennedy explained this in *State (Ryan) v. Lennon* [1935] 1 IR 170, 203: '[T]he Constitution was enacted by the Third Dáil, sitting as a Constituent Assembly, and not by the Oireachtas, which, in fact, it created.'

[8] The Constitution was discussed on 16 out of the 19 days during which the Dáil sat.

[9] The second reading of the bill was carried on 21 September, after a two-day debate by a vote of 47 to 16. Donal O'Sullivan has noted that the minority consisted of members of the Labour Party and that their action seemed to have been conducted on the principle that it is the duty of the opposition to oppose. The Committee stage lasted eight days and the Report stage two days. The bill finally passed without division on 25 October 1922. See Donal O'Sullivan, *The Irish Free State and Its Senate: A Study in Contemporary Politics* (London, 1940), 84.

[10] *Dáil Debates*, vol 1, cols 477–8, 20 September 1922.

[11] *Ibid.*, col 479.

taken in these three Dominions'.[12] Many deputies remarked that this was not the Constitution the Irish people would have given themselves had conditions been different, and Figgis agreed. He mentioned that Collins had believed that

> if the first draft of the Constitution had been taken over two or three months before it was taken over, ... it would have passed and would not have come back in the form in which it did come back. The change having been wrought because of the action of certain men in this country who had created disturbance from one end of the nation to the other.[13]

Gavan Duffy stated that perhaps it would be better to wait until the next Imperial Conference before 'moulding in cast iron' anything regarding Ireland's relationship with Britain or the other Dominions. He felt that the status of the Dominions was going to change at this next conference[14] and it would be wise for Ireland to go in the same direction.[15] However, President Cosgrave brushed aside these comments with the observation that Ireland clearly needed the stability of a Constitution and they would not wait around in limbo for foreign bodies to decide Ireland's fate.[16]

O'Higgins wound up the debate following what he termed 'a certain amount of vague generalities, a certain amount of poetry, a certain amount of emphasis on the desire, which many here share, for better things, if such were attainable, but very little practical, useful, constructive criticism of the Constitution'.[17] He concluded by providing, in response to requests from deputies, the Articles which the government felt should not be changed:

> Article 12 is one. Articles 1 and 2 are agreed as stating the position, and we would consider it inadvisable to alter them. Article 12 is the first serious one; Article 17, Article 24 or certain portions of it, Article 36, Article 40, Article 41, Article 50, Article 55, Article 58, Article 65, Article 67, Article 77, Article 79.[18]

---

[12] *Ibid.*, col 480, 20 September 1922. The three Dominions he refers to are Canada, Australia and the Union of South Africa.

[13] *Ibid.*, cols 498–9, 20 September 1922. Churchill said something similar but in relation to the election Pact: 'Had the proposed Election been a bona fide one they could have put pressure on us to stretch the Constitution to suit them. As no election of value is contemplated we are in a position to be much more searching in our examination of the Constitution.' British Record of Negotiations CAB43/7, 12.

[14] This conference happened in the autumn of 1923 but the big changes Gavan Duffy had anticipated never came to pass.

[15] *Dáil Debates*, vol 1, cols 542ff, 21 September 1922.

[16] *Ibid.*, cols 545–7.

[17] *Ibid.*, col 571.

[18] *Ibid.*, col 578. Articles 1 and 2 described the constitutional position of the Irish Free State, Article 12 stated that the legislature would consist of the King and two Houses, Article 17 contained the oath, Article 24 stated the Parliament would be summoned and dissolved in the name of the King, Article 36 was on the appropriation of money, Articles 40 and 41 dealt with the role of the King in legislation, Article 50 stated that executive power was vested in the King, Article 55 concerned external ministers, Article 58 dealt with the Governor-General, Article 65 gave the Supreme Court final

The Committee stage and major controversies

During the Committee stage, many of the 'agreed' articles were questioned by deputies but the government consistently insisted that these provisions would remain as agreed in London. However, there were many other changes made,[19] the most obvious being to the executive proposals, and there were many heated discussions over certain provisions contained in the Draft. One issue which was brought up and continued to be debated for some time was the fact that the Draft had been brought to London before the Dáil had seen it. Gavan Duffy requested full disclosure and he insisted that the Dáil should be provided with the Draft which had been sent over to London. He speculated on why the government would want to hide the original Draft from the Dáil and claimed that it would be better to admit that they tried to obtain more than was given:

> It would have been very easy for the Government to come to this Dáil, anxious as we all are to support it, in implementing the Treaty properly, come and say: 'Here is the Draft we took to London last June. There were certain things in that Draft that did not commend themselves to Downing Street in relation to Clause A, B, or C, which we specify to the Dáil. Mr. Lloyd George informed us that if we insisted on our interpretation of the Treaty and what we were advised was the legitimate interpretation of the Treaty, he would tear up the Treaty in shreds and in the face of that insistence we felt it our duty to come away and to yield to the English interpretation.' The Government could have said that and have gone on to say 'we recognise we were rather precipitate in our yielding, but whether we were right or wrong then, we tell the Dáil, that at the moment, when civil war is raging in this country, it is impossible for the Government to do otherwise than to accept these interpretations which are thrust upon it at the pistol point.'[20]

He also spoke of the Australians passing their Constitution in 1900. When the English insisted they include an appeal to the Privy Council the Australians replied to the English: 'very well, there is our draft, take it to your Parliament. If you alter a comma in it you will alter it in the light of day and everyone will know if we accept your Privy Council that we do so, because you forced us to it.'[21] Gavan Duffy felt this to be a dignified position. There was much more discussion on this point before O'Higgins addressed the Dáil. He conceded that they went to London

jurisdiction but also allowed for appeal to the Privy Council, Article 67 stated that judges would be appointed by the representative of the King, Articles 77 and 79 were transitory provisions.

[19] The main changes included; the alteration of the external ministers scheme, transfer of university representation to the Dáil, removal of the proposed equality guarantee, changing of the provision on constitutional amendment; and there were many other minor amendments.

[20] *Dáil Debates.*, vol 1, cols 999–1000, 29 September 1922.

[21] *Ibid.*, col 1001.

with the spirit of a man who knows well that he is not going to get all that he is asking for and therefore aims high. We aimed high and we got what I have already described here, and what in my judgment is a strict but fair interpretation of the Treaty. I take it, it was strict because of the circumstances of the time. I am sure if circumstances were otherwise, that we would have got a more pleasantly worded Constitution, but I do not believe that we would have got a Constitution differing, in any material respect, from the Draft Constitution that is now before the Dáil.[22]

He then went on to reiterate that the Draft was sent over to London at that stage to test the waters and measure the reaction so they would know whether the British Parliament would eventually approve the document or not.

One of the other major points of controversy during the Committee stage was the oath of allegiance. Many of the deputies were very much against the whole principle of an oath; some called for exemptions to be provided for, while others felt it was a matter which could be left to the standing orders of the Dáil and was not necessary to be included in the Constitution. Moreover, Collins had originally believed that the inclusion of the oath in the Treaty was enough and it would not have to be expressly provided for in the Constitution but the discussions in London ended this idea. The British had insisted on the inclusion of the oath in the document itself and now the government was forced to persuade deputies that this should be adopted. Daniel Morrissey, a Labour Party TD, spoke before the issue was put to a vote and his sensible words seem to have won over the House eventually as the Government's position was upheld:

> I think when the General Election came the people understood the oath, and they knew what they were casting their votes for when they were voting for the Treaty. At any rate, so far as I am concerned, I intend to support it, not because it is palatable, but simply because I believe, as we are told, it is essential to the carrying out of the Treaty, and that means it is essential for the return of prosperity and peace to this country. I believe that the majority of the people in this country do not want this oath, but I believe that the people know that in the circumstances that prevailed at the time of the Treaty, and in the circumstances that prevail at the present time, they have accepted it, and are prepared to make the most of it. We hear a lot about Republicans. We are all Republicans and we must see what is the best means to attain it. I hold as one, and that is the reason I support this oath, that as this is the quickest road to a Republic we should support it.[23]

The question of university representation in the legislature also proved a decisive issue. The Draft Constitution had provided for university representation in the Seanad and this had also been guaranteed by Griffith to the Southern Unionists during negotiations. Following much debate and many speeches on the importance of university representation, it was decided to change the Constitution so as to provide for representation in the Dáil, instead of the Seanad. Professor Magennis, a university representative, moved the proposal and O'Higgins indi-

---

[22] *Ibid.*, cols 1008–9.
[23] *Ibid.*, vol 1, col 1074, 3 October 1922.

cated that there was no official attitude on the question and no unanimity within the government itself. Notably, Figgis opposed the motion in that it interfered with the 'one man one vote' principle. But university representatives themselves were very vocal during this discussion and were quite anxious not to be exiled to a House which, they evidently felt, would be insignificant. This change was inserted into the final version of the Constitution as Article 27.[24]

Another significant change which was effected at this stage was the amendment to the eventual Article 50 of the Constitution, whereby the Constitution could be amended by ordinary legislation for an initial period so as to facilitate any teething problems. This idea had not been proposed until the debates in the Constituent Assembly and it is interesting that it seems to have had the support of the whole Assembly. Even Gavan Duffy congratulated the Minister 'very heartily' on his proposal. Obviously nobody present anticipated the use which would subsequently be made of this particular provision or the fact that it would eventually lead to the dismantling of the Constitution.[25]

There was some discussion when the Dáil Committee came to discuss Article 65[26] and the Appeal to the Judicial Committee of the Privy Council. There were objections to the Appeal itself which, as was explained by the government, was, in effect, part of the Treaty and so was non-negotiable at this stage. Nevertheless, O'Higgins attempted to assuage the Assembly: 'I have shown on the strict interpretation of the Treaty, we would have been bound to the Canadian position. We have in effect secured a position very much more favourable than that of Canada.'[27] He also elaborated on this favourable position:

> Now, what is secured in this Article 65 is the most favourable position, i.e., the South African position. I do not know just how many appeals there have been taken from South Africa since the Union was set up, but I believe the number will be found to be very small. An appeal would not lie in the case of ordinary routine domestic legislation, but only in cases where international issues were raised was permission for such special appeal granted, as provided in this Article.[28]

Thus it was presumed that internal or local issues could not be made the subject of an Appeal but only cases which involved 'some great principle'.[29] This seemed

[24] Article 27 stated that 'Each University in the Irish Free State ... shall be entitled to elect three representatives to Dáil Éireann upon a franchise and in a manner to be prescribed by law'. The Electoral Act 1923 provided the detail whereby the National University of Ireland and Dublin University would each elect three members to the Dáil. The Constitution (Amendment No. 23) Act 1936 (No. 17/1936) repealed this.

[25] See Chapter 9.

[26] This became Article 66 in the final document.

[27] *Dáil Debates*, vol 1, col 1403, 10 October 1922.

[28] *Ibid.*, col 1402.

[29] These are the words of Viscount Haldane giving judgment in the joined cases of *Hull v. McKenna, The Freeman's Journal Ltd v. Fernstrom* and *The Freeman's Journal Ltd v. Follum Traesliberi* [1926] IR 4025. Haldane confirmed the view put forward above that the Privy Council would not concern itself with internal matters: 'We are

to ease the pain sufficiently for Dáil members so as to enable the provision to obtain the (reluctant) assent of the House. Thus, at this stage, it was expected that this aspect of the Constitution would remain purely theoretical. O'Higgins read an extract from the work of Professor A.B. Keith which stated that: 'for practical purposes the appeal from the Union [of South Africa] is a matter of mere theoretic interest'. Most of the TDs who spoke in the debate believed that nobody in Ireland would bring an appeal to the Privy Council. Even the great British authority on constitutional matters, Professor Dicey, stated that 'the Imperial Government is now ready at the wish of a Dominion to exclude from its constitution, either partially or wholly, the right of appeal from the decision of the Supreme Court of such Dominion to the Privy Council'.[30] Professor Dicey must have been misled, however, as it seems this was never the British position.

There were other objections to the wording of the Article[31] which seemed to provide a contradiction in that it specified that all decisions of the Supreme Court would be final and conclusive and not reviewable by any other court or body but then the Appeal to the Privy Council was provided for. However, O'Higgins countered that this contradiction was apparent rather than real. There was also some concern as to the composition of the Privy Council itself, with some deputies fearing the possibility of Irish cases being heard by a 'Downing Street' Council. However, surprisingly enough it did not take long for the government to persuade the doubters. O'Higgins admitted: 'We do not like this Appeal. We tried not to have this Appeal, but we attempt to show here its exact proportion to the whole matter, and it is not worth the time spent discussing it here in view of the existing conditions.'[32] In the end, the Article was agreed upon with minimal protestation.

Gavan Duffy raised an astute point in relation to the judiciary. According to draft Article 67,[33] all judges were to be appointed by the representative of the Crown on the advice of the Executive Council. He pointed out the inconvenience of having 'every little justice in the country'[34] appointed in this manner. He accepted that it was necessary, under the Treaty, for superior judges to be appointed by the representative of the Crown so as to follow Dominion precedent.

> not at all disposed to advise the Sovereign unless there is some exceptional question, such as the magnitude of the question of law involved, or it is a question of public interest in the Dominion to give leave to appeal.' He stated that importance was to be attached to the wishes of the Irish Free State in the matter and that 'she must in a large measure dispose of her own justice' (406). However, this interpretation was ignored in subsequent cases which came before the Privy Council. See Thomas Mohr, 'Law without Loyalty – The Abolition of the Irish Appeal to the Privy Council' (2002) 37 *Irish Jurist* 187, 190.

30 See A.V. Dicey, *The Law of the Constitution* (8th edn, London, 1927), xxxi.
31 See *Dáil Debates*, vol 1, col 1404 (Thomas Johnson), 1405 (Liam de Roiste) and 1406 (Professor William Magennis), 10 October 1922.
32 *Dáil Debates*, vol 1, col 1415, 10 October 1922.
33 Article 68 in the final document.
34 *Dáil Debates*, vol 1, col 1418, 10 October 1922.

However, he noted that there was no precedent in relation to appointment of lower judges in this manner.[35] O'Higgins agreed to consider this and stated: 'we will probably alter it'.[36] The matter was postponed until the next reading but it never came up again and the Article stood as it did in the Draft.

In fact, Gavan Duffy, who had at this stage become one of the most vocal critics of the Draft, having resigned his post as Minister for Foreign Affairs the previous July, made many interesting suggestions. As Mohr has outlined, 'Some of his legal arguments seemed to split hairs. Others could be described as ingenious. None would have cut any ice with the British.'[37] Indeed Mohr points out that if any of his proposed changes had been accepted 'the British would certainly have condemned them as breaches of the Treaty with predictably catastrophic results'.

The major debate which arose during the Committee stage was the debate on the external ministers scheme. Under the Draft, the Executive Council was to consist of not more than 12 ministers. Four of these would be members of Dáil Éireann and up to eight would be 'external ministers' who would not be members of the Oireachtas. O'Higgins explained the process:

> Dáil Éireann selects the President, the President selects the Vice-President and the other Ministers who will be members of the Dáil. As for the Ministers who, it is proposed, will not be members of Dáil Eireann, they are selected by a method to be determined by the Dáil so as to be impartially representative of the Assembly as a whole.[38]

He also explained that a committee of the Dáil would 'nominate each Minister of the eight for a Ministry with special regard to his suitability for that particular office'[39] and later that 'they will be judged by the Dáil only by the efficiency with which their department is run, and the soundness or otherwise of the measures'.[40]

While the Assembly approved of the plan to eliminate what was referred to as 'British-style party politics' and many deputies spoke out against the evils of such a system, there seemed to be a lot of confusion surrounding the executive scheme, with repeated questions on the details of the scheme, and many deputies seemed suspicious of it. The majority of the objections can be brought down to two main aspects of the scheme. First, there was to be a distinction in relation to ministerial responsibility, in that the four 'internal ministers' would be subject to collective responsibility but the eight would only be individually responsible for their departments and a vote of no confidence in the government would not

---

[35] O'Rahilly had come up with an alternative scheme in his Draft but it seems this was not considered at this stage.

[36] *Dáil Debates*, vol 1, col 1418, 10 October 1922.

[37] Thomas Mohr, *The Irish Free State and the Legal Implications of Dominion Status, 1922–1937*, (Unpublished PhD Thesis, University College Dublin, 2007), 99.

[38] *Dáil Debates*, vol 1, col 1242, 5 October 1922.

[39] *Ibid.*, col 1244.

[40] *Ibid.*, col 1248.

affect them. The other aspect was the question of whether these external ministers would form part of the actual Executive Council and participate in the full range of government matters or whether they were simply appointed to look after their own department without any actual place in the Executive Council. The fact that they could not be members of the Oireachtas was also a point of controversy.

Following much discussion on these points, Deputy Professor Liam Thrift[41] proposed that the details of this scheme should be referred to a Committee of the House for consideration. The Committee subsequently produced a report which recommended a simplified version of the original scheme. However, there was still too much confusion for the Assembly to be persuaded and, despite the support of the Government, the report of the special committee was eventually rejected by a vote of 30 to 31. Eventually, the Ceann Comhairle decided that they would vote on and amend each executive Article individually. The recommendations of the report were moved as amendments to the articles so that the Dáil could approve those they agreed with and dispense of those which were not agreeable.

The voting on the executive proposals demonstrates just how suspicious the Irish deputies were of this experimental system, and it was eventually decided that there would be no requirement to appoint external ministers, but that they could be appointed and, even if appointed, they would not be members of the Executive Council. All of this, effectively, weakened the scheme and reduced its significance.[42]

The subsequent readings of the bill were uncomplicated, with amendments mainly dealing with matters of detail and language. Before the bill was put to the Assembly, O'Higgins gave a final speech in which he emphasised that the Treaty and the Constitution should be regarded as Ireland's greatest success. Many more deputies spoke and all spoke favourably of the Constitution. Padraig Mac Ualghairc[43] summed up the opinion of the majority:

> This Constitution, to my mind, is, as the Minister for Home Affairs carefully said, a strict but fair interpretation of the Treaty. It may not be everything that everyone would desire in this country, but what it lacks are not things that are of really material essential value. They are the trimmings that might be sentimentally valuable but substantially they are of very little consequence. The thing that really matters is we have in this instrument here now the framework and machinery without which a country cannot proceed in its own way to do its work by its own methods.[44]

Following more speeches and a few more minor amendments, the Constitution was passed by the Constituent Assembly.

---

[41] Independent university representative.
[42] For further explanation of the scheme and the various changes made, see Chapter 8.
[43] Patrick McGoldrick, pro-Treaty Sinn Féin representative.
[44] *Dáil Debates*, vol 1, col 1923, 25 October 1922.

A congenial debate?

Members who contributed most to the debate were: O'Higgins, Blythe, de Róiste, Milroy and Duggan from the pro-Treaty side; Gavan Duffy, Figgis, Fitzgibbon, Thrift and Magennis, who were Independents; Johnson, O'Brien, O'Shannon and O'Connell from Labour. In general, it was quite a free debate with deputies voting according to their own principles rather than according to the party line. During the debates, O'Higgins had stressed that this was the way he would like things to run in the future: '[I]t is very desirable there should be as much freedom as possible for individual members of the Dáil – that it should not be always a matter of Party Whips and people voting contrary, perhaps, to their own particular ideas and particular feelings on certain matters.'[45] It seems that, for the most part, this is what happened. Professor Magennis conceded that, in relation to one debate at least, '[t]he Whips were not put on, and it was left open'.[46]

Mohr has commented that '[The] Provisional Government had to rely on rigid party discipline to push the unpopular aspects of the draft Constitution through the Dáil'.[47] It is true that the government stated that it would stand over the provisions already agreed in London but, in general, the voting was not rigid or party-based. On the contrary, mostly it was quite free. The fact that there was little party pressure can be seen from the voting statistics, where often even the government's own supporters voted against it and, on the other hand, sometimes members of the opposition happily supported the government.[48]

Thus, for the most part, the debates were constructive, not restricted to party lines, and, despite the short time, mostly quite thorough. While certain amendments effected at this stage, such as the changes to the external ministers scheme and to constitutional amendment, would have a profound effect on the future of the Irish Free State Constitution, the final document had still retained much of the spirit and inspiration of the original Drafts and the work of the Committee still shone through.

---

[45] *Ibid.*, vol 1, col 488, 20 September 1922.
[46] *Ibid.*, vol 1, col 1917, 25 October 1922. Although the situation might have been different had members on the anti-Treaty side decided to take their seats.
[47] Mohr, 'British Involvement', 178.
[48] During various different debates, pro-Treaty members such as Liam de Róiste and Eoin MacNeill can be seen voting with the opposition, and, in more, opposition members such as Thomas Johnson voted with the government, even when the rest of the Labour Party voted against the particular measure. Furthermore, even when the Labour Party voted against the government, sometimes it appears this was simply for the sake of acting as opposition. See O'Sullivan, *The Irish Free State and Its Senate*, 84.

Conclusion: the finished document

The Constitution, as it emerged from the Constituent Assembly, did not deviate too far from the document which had returned from London. Looking at the document as a whole and knowing the context behind all of the provisions, it is possible to extrapolate the key themes of the Constitution. As in the original Drafts, the most significant element in the Constitution is the idea of sovereignty of the people. It is around this principle that all of the other provisions are built. Having navigated through the various stages of drafting, from the original documents to the final published Constitution, we can now see how the document was originally intended to function and what was originally envisaged for the infant Irish state. The main differences were the executive changes, university representation and other minor amendments. Despite the addition of the British symbolism and the dilution of the external ministers scheme, the Constitution retained much of the original drafts. As Figgis explained, 'it is the essential plan that matters – not the feudal trumperies with which it is adorned ... marring its simple truth but not otherwise injuring its effectiveness for its purpose'.[49] Figgis also usefully elucidated that fundamental purpose, which was 'to make the mechanism of Government malleable at every stage to the will of the people of Ireland'.[50] In concluding the debate, O'Higgins, in a similar sentiment, drew on the words of Collins in addressing the people of Ireland: 'The country is yours for the making, make it.' [51]

---

[49] Darrell Figgis, *The Irish Constitution Explained by Darrell Figgis* (Dublin, 1922), 6.
[50] *Ibid.*, 5.
[51] *Dáil Debates*, vol 1, col 1909, 25 October 1922.

6

Themes and influences

No nation can pursue the path to self-government free from all external considerations and untrammelled by the intellectual influences descending from the past.[1]

Introduction

In order to understand the thinking behind the 1922 Constitution, it is necessary
to consider the document in the light of its intellectual and political context. The
1920s were years of momentous significance for Ireland because, after centuries
of oppression and revolutionary struggle, the Irish people had finally gained
the freedom to construct a new State for themselves. However, the turmoil of
the Land Wars and past risings were still fresh in the minds of the people and the
Gaelic revival was now at its zenith. The drafting Committee was very aware of
all of these events and experiences and the impact which they had on the Irish
psyche, and it took cognisance of them during the drafting process. As Kohn has
aptly put it:

> The aspirations which had been the moving force of the Gaelic Revival and the
> Insurrection of 1916 had long ceased to be a mere sectarian current. They had grown
> into a national stream which, when the offer of liberty came, overflowed and in the
> result transformed the constitutional framework which was to have shaped it.[2]

Before moving on to examine in detail the central aspects of popular sovereignty,
democracy and anti-party politics, which together form a leitmotif which runs
through the Constitution, it will be useful to consider first some influences and
themes which are identifiable throughout the original drafts and the final document. While there is no evidence to suggest that members of the Constitution

---

[1] Nicholas Mansergh, *The Irish Free State: Its Government and Politics* (London,
   1934), 15.
[2] Leo Kohn, *The Constitution of the Irish Free State* (London, 1932), 23.

Committee were predisposed to any particular philosophy or ideology, something often seen with other constitutions,[3] there are certain very clear influences which will be discussed below. While various movements could be mentioned here, such as the influence of the Home Rule movement, the original Sinn Féin, the Irish Republican Brotherhood, the Gaelic League etc., all of which influenced the Constitution in different ways, we will confine our discussion to the intellectual influences from the ancient Gaelic state as well as the influence of foreign constitutions, before considering how these manifest themselves in the Constitution.

Intellectual influences

Ideas from the Gaelic state

Pádraic Pearse, like many other nationalists, was obsessed with history. He wrote: 'Now the truth as to what a nation's nationality is, what a nation's freedom is, is not to be found in the statute-book of the nation's enemy. It is to be found in the books of the nation's fathers.'[4] Many of the nationalists looked back to a time when Ireland was Gaelic only and believed this was the state to aspire to. Darrell Figgis, in particular, had a great interest in ancient Irish customs. Tom Garvin has described this phenomenon, explaining that 'Irish people were commonly described as being obsessed by history; they were not possessed by a love for it, nor often of a well-informed view of it, but a habit of mind that referred all things present to things past for explanation or, at least, cultural mapping'. Garvin also points out that 'Irish political radicals often had a fascination with the past, but this could often be analysed rather easily into a hatred for the "long present" ...'[5]

One element in common in all strands of Irish separatists was their nostalgia for the ancient Irish past. The Gaelic state represented a utopia which had existed before the British ever arrived. It was idealised as a place in which everyone lived in harmony, and land, power and wealth were shared among the whole community. The people were interested in history, philosophy, poetry, music and storytelling. The ideal of a return to the ancient ways of the Gaelic state was seen as a sort of purification which would wipe out the pollution which was English rule.

One of the essential attributes of the Gaelic state which made it so attractive to separatist thinking was that 'The people were the state(ship), and the state(ship) was the people, for with them the power finally lay'.[6] Popular sovereignty was

---

[3] The United States Constitution is said to have been influenced by Rousseau, Montesquieu, Locke and others, the Weimar Constitution by Kant, various French constitutions by Voltaire, Montesquieu and Rousseau.

[4] Pádraic Pearse, *Collected Works of Pádraic H. Pearse: Political Writings and Speeches* (Dublin, 1916), 263.

[5] Tom Garvin, *Nationalist Revolutionaries in Ireland: 1858–1928* (New York, 1987), 108.

[6] Darrell Figgis, *The Gaelic State in the Past and Future* (Dublin, 1917), 17.

a motif which ran through Irish separatist thought, from Theobald Wolfe Tone through to the Irish state-builders. The fact that they could locate it in the Gaelic state was an added advantage.

Another facet of life in Gaelic Ireland which appealed to the separatists was the public ownership of land. But there were many more elements which convinced the separatists that this civilisation was one to aspire to. One example is the attitude towards law. Figgis described the ancient Brehon legal system as follows:

> Law in the old Irish State was not a mere technical contrivance to be argued from black-letter, as now happens, by a few men whom the people universally distrust; it was founded on a whole nation's sense of justice. Nor was it lawyers who put it into execution; but a stateship of freemen, acting in community who enforced its obedience or expelled the offender by withdrawing all dealings with him.[7]

It also appears that, unusually for the time, women were accorded an equal status in the Gaelic state. Figgis praised this aspect of the state for the equal dignity it gave to women: 'Whether women exercised political rights or not it is impossible to say; but in the social and economic spheres they took their place as the equal of men ... Never once do we find the law of the Irish State recognising any inequality between the sexes; and that again was remarkable in the Europe of the time.'[8] Perhaps it was for this reason, among others, that all women over the age of 21 were accorded the vote in the Irish Free State, six years before it was given in Britain.[9]

Figgis, in particular, was highly impressed by the ancient state, arguing that it would be 'hard to find a statecraft so complete, so wise and so soundly based on a people's will, while compact in itself'. He emphasised the equality which existed between members of the society, pointing out that, when the Normans arrived, 'they commented on the familiarity that existed between the members of a stateship and its king'. It was a society that valued the arts, which

> did not exist at the whim of a lordly patron, but were maintained at the people's charges. Each stateship conceived it an honour that Poetry, Music and History should be accorded the highest rank in its economy. Their professors were furnished land for their maintenance, and sat as equals at the king's table. The same was true of the Doctors of Medicine. These were all public servants, serving the public and maintained at the public charge.[10]

Collins also advocated a return to the ancient ways. He described the Gaelic system as follows:

---

[7] *Ibid.*, 23.

[8] *Ibid.*, 26.

[9] Article 14, Irish Free State Constitution.

[10] Figgis, *Gaelic State*, 34–5. Figgis's views were highly idealised, however, and ignored the fact that it was a hierarchical society.

The Irish social and economic system was democratic. It was simple and harmonious. The people had security in their rights, and just law. And suited to them, their economic life progressed smoothly. Our people had leisure for the things in which they took delight. They had leisure for the cultivation of the mind, by the study of art, literature and the traditions. They developed character and bodily strength by acquiring skill in military exercise and in the national games. The pertinacity of Irish civilization was due to the democratic basis of its economic system, and the aristocracy of its culture.[11]

Collins felt that the democratic social polity was the essence of the Gaelic civilisation and must provide the keynote for the future.

James Connolly[12] also discovered links between the Gaelic state and socialist thinking. This link fitted nicely with Connolly's brand of nationalist socialism. He pointed to the practices of public ownership of land and wealth in ancient Ireland to strengthen the argument for a return to the Gaelic ways. Aodh de Blacam, writing in 1919, described the Ireland which would emerge under a Gaelic nationalist socialism:

> But if Ireland, securing Self-Determination, has won her independence, these democratic stateships will become the vital framework of the most distinctive civilisations. The National Government, when raising revenue, will draw from the communal wealth of these stateships, and so the harsh and unequal incidence of taxation will no longer fall upon the individual ... The decentralisation effected by the stateships will, as of old, keep the professions and the industries healthily in touch with the land, and, in turn, will keep the farmer agreeably in touch with other phases of life than the agricultural. ... The diffusion of small private property, which will follow a widespread stake in the land, will increase stability, personal independence and good citizenship. In short, the greater the degree of adhesion to traditional Gaelic social principles, the greater will be the beauty, security and nobility of the restored Gaelic State.[13]

De Blacam, like Connolly, believed in an independent, democratic, Catholic, socialist state. Unlike the Bolsheviks, Connolly and his supporters believed it was possible to reconcile religion and socialism.

There are echoes of socialism in the writings of others at this time also. Collins wrote that 'The growing wealth of Ireland, will we hope, be diffused through all our people, all sharing in the growing prosperity, each receiving according to what each contributes in the making of that prosperity, so that the weal of all is assured'.[14] He also talked about the 'national wealth' and about the distribution of land. However, Collins's theories were based on the old traditions in the Gaelic

---

[11] Michael Collins, *The Path to Freedom* (Dublin, 1922), 98–9.

[12] Co-founder of the Labour Party in 1912 and organiser for the Irish Transport and General Workers' Union in Belfast. He was the leader of the Irish Citizen Army and one of the leaders of the Easter Rising.

[13] Aodh De Blacam, *Towards a Republic: A Study of New Ireland's Social and Political Aims* (Dublin, 1919), 28–9.

[14] Collins, *Path to Freedom*, 112.

state, rather than socialism, as he also commented: 'At the same time I think we shall safely avoid State Socialism, which has nothing to commend it in a country like Ireland, and, in any case, is a monopoly of another kind.'[15] Collins's economic aspirations were based on self-sufficiency.

The Gaelic state and its system of Brehon law was useful to the Committee because it represented a state to aspire to; Brehon law was much more than a legal system – it was a way of life. The state was seen as one which placed people, life and nature above things like property, and laws were an expression of the moral power of the people. It was this sort of scenario that the Committee wished to recreate. The influence of the Gaelic state can be seen in many provisions in the Constitution but was particularly strong in the original drafts in relation to the provisions on public ownership of land and resources, Irish language, equality, popular sovereignty, functional councils and all of the experiments which attempted to bring politics closer to the people.

Of course, this portrayal of the ancient Gaelic state was significantly romanticised; the aspects which were concentrated upon were those which would allow Ireland to assert its own unique identity and to provide inspiration for the new state. Other elements, such as the fact that it was a structured society involving layered classes from royalty to 'servitors', were conveniently ignored.

Lack of any realistic thinking on state-building and institutions

In general, much Irish thought at this time was quite idealistic and sometimes quite divorced from any sort of reality. Garvin has noted that, because the Irish politicians had been excluded from political power, they were 'never required to test their political ideas in the practical, everyday world, and a rather pathological divorce between political dreams and a low-grade unambitious empiricism developed in the political sub-culture of separatism'.[16] Garvin has pointed out that even 'pragmatic minds like those of Griffith and Collins tended to be infected by the impulse to retreat to political dream-worlds'.[17] These dream-worlds tended to be places where Ireland would be Irish through and through, run by Irish people by means of Irish institutions and all of the people (who would all be speaking fluent Irish) would be happy. The view of many people at the time was that, once the British and their institutions were gone, Ireland would suddenly be a better place. Bill Kissane has noted that 'the ideas that British institutions had brought the country to a demoralized impasse and that the revival needed new constitutional structures were widespread among Irish radicals'.[18]

However, it is clear that the Irish separatists did not put too much thought

---

[15] *Ibid.,* 115.

[16] Garvin, *Nationalist Revolutionaries in Ireland,* 118.

[17] *Ibid.,* 118.

[18] Bill Kissane, 'The Constitutional Revolution that Never Was' (2009) 104 *Radical History Review* 77, 92.

into what would replace these maligned institutions. As Garvin put it simply: 'Republicans believed that with the coming of independence, political problems would be easily solved'.[19] Elsewhere he notes:

> The Irish rebels were good at agitational politics and conspiracy, but knew nothing about real government. They fondly imagined that the independent Irish state that was to be born would solve problems of culture, and even problems of human nature; economic problems would be easy. Unfortunately, they had a subconscious assumption that an independent Irish state would have the kinds of capabilities which they witnessed in the British imperial state: the full implications of Irish independence did not impinge upon them, and they did not understand that the weaknesses of Irish society and economy would be reflected in the structure and performance of any state that emerged in Ireland.[20]

There is nothing particularly Irish about this: in other former colonies, the idea that the expulsion of the governing state would lead to happiness and prosperity was also widespread.

However, there was not a complete absence of thought on this subject in Ireland. John J. Horgan, a well-known writer and Parnellite from Cork, contributed articles which discussed suitable political institutions for the country. He put forward ideas such as proportional representation and a second Chamber with the function of protecting minority rights; ideas which, as Garvin has noted, came to fruition in 1922.[21]

In relation to Irish public opinion, Wilfrid Ewart, an English journalist, made a journey around Ireland in 1921, during which he interviewed people as to their opinions on the political circumstances of the time. Among those he spoke to were Castle officials,[22] including the Dublin Castle spin-doctor Basil Clarke, Old Irish Party nationalists and former Home Rule MPs such as William O'Brien, George Russell (Æ), Sinn Féin members including Liam de Róiste and activists in Cork and Limerick and Northern Unionists as well as a number of ordinary people with whom he came into contact along his journey. The general feeling of the time seemed to be that, despite a general hostility towards Britain, most Irish people would be willing to accept a 'generous offer of Dominion Home Rule' provided that this was in good faith. Most felt that the North could and should come into a Parliament in Dublin. However, Unionist feeling was completely opposed to this. Significantly, the ordinary people did not express any preference for forms of government as long as it was self-government but certain members of Sinn Féin and others mentioned a possible federal-type system along Swiss lines.[23]

Garvin has described the people of the time as 'pre-political'. Many of them had no real political theories and believed that the advent of Irish independence

---

[19] Tom Garvin, *1922: The Birth of Irish Democracy* (Dublin, 2005), 12.
[20] Garvin, *Nationalist Revolutionaries in Ireland*, 131.
[21] *Ibid.*, 120.
[22] Members of the British administration in Ireland who worked in Dublin Castle.
[23] Wilfred Ewart, *A Journey in Ireland* (Dublin, 2008) (first published in 1922).

would mean 'being left alone'.[24] The Irish people were also somewhat anti-political, something which stemmed from hostility to the British state. They had associated politics with corruption and subjugation for so long that trust in any political system, Irish or not, simply would not be guaranteed. That the politicians and architects of the 1922 Constitution were aware of this is obvious in the language used to convince the people that this new Constitution would be their Constitution; sovereignty would be vested in the people and the people would hold the ultimate political power by the devices of referendum, initiative, judicial review etc. which were all included in the Constitution. This would constitute a break from the old system in that, because of the devices mentioned, the people would truly be the masters. The people would hold the power and could object to laws, propose their own laws and have recourse to the courts to rectify unconstitutional legislation and vindicate their rights. In the 1922 Constitution, there is an obvious effort to prove to the Irish people that finally, there exists an Irish State which will work for the people.

Foreign constitutions

Another major influence which must be mentioned is the impact of foreign constitutions on the drafting process. As preparation for the drafting of the Constitution, the members of the Committee wrote to various personages in different countries around the world requesting copies of their Constitutions and explanatory or historical introductions, and they made studies of these.[25] The collection included many constitutions[26] which proved useful to the drafting Committee, including those of the Dominions (Canada, South Africa, Australia), the older constitutions such as the Swiss, French and American constitutions, the postwar constitutions of Poland, the Baltic states, Germany, Austria, Czechoslovakia and Estonia as well as a mix of other countries such as Mexico, Norway, Sweden and Denmark. The Committee was impressed with the enthusiasm for democratic ideals and popular sovereignty which permeated the postwar constitutions. In particular, the German (Weimar) Constitution of 1919 was frequently referred to during

---

[24] Interview with Tom Garvin, University College Dublin, 13 July 2010.

[25] These documents were subsequently published and presented to the Constituent Assembly in order to aid its deliberations on the Draft Constitution. See *Select Constitutions of the World* (Dublin, 1922).

[26] Countries included in the book which was later published (see above) are as follows: The Kingdom of the Serbs, Croats and Slovenes, The Polish Republic, The Republic of Austria, The Estonian Republic, The Czechoslovak Republic, The German Reich, The Russian Socialist Federal Soviet Republic, The United States of Mexico, The Kingdom of Denmark, The Union of South Africa, The Commonwealth of Australia, The French Republic, The Swiss Confederation, the Dominion of Canada, The Kingdom of Belgium, The Kingdom of Norway, The Kingdom of Sweden and The United States of America. In the files of the Constitution Committee, there are also documents on Bohemia, Italy and Holland.

Committee discussions. That the postwar constitutions had an influence on the drafters is obvious from a quick overview of the main themes contained in those documents and, while constitutions from other countries, such as the Dominions, may have been useful, it is from the postwar constitutions that the Committee took much of its inspiration.[27]

Postwar constitutions

A useful flavour of the postwar constitutions is given in a book by Agnes Headlam-Morley, written in 1928. The author concentrates on the contemporary constitutions of Germany, Poland, Czechoslovakia, Yugoslavia, Finland, Sweden and the Baltic states. (She does not deal with the Irish Free State.) She writes that the interest in these documents

> lies in the fact that an attempt has been made to give to the democratic principle its most complete and logical expression. Sovereignty rests with the people; the people are not only to control the Government, they are to be the direct holders of political power. Parliament is elected by the widest possible system of universal suffrage and by proportional representation. Nevertheless, the people do not surrender their authority to Parliament. The Representative Assembly is controlled by direct legislation or by a President who has considerable constitutional powers and is himself the direct representative of the sovereign people.[28]

Her subject is democracy and she deals with the material not by individual countries but under various headings including: Political Theory, Federalism and Local Government, Popular Sovereignty, Universal Suffrage and Proportional Representation, the Electoral System and Political Parties, Referendum and Initiative, Second Chambers, Legislative Functions of the President, Dissolution, Formation of Cabinet, Social and Economic Duties of Government, An Economic Constitution. As can be seen, many of these themes and devices also appear in the Irish Constitution of 1922. Much of the commentary in the book concentrates

---

[27] Throughout the book it will be seen that the postwar constitutions were a significant influence on the Constitution of the Irish Free State. In particular, the Weimar Constitution of 1919 was an extremely influential model. Recent scholarship has argued that the Weimar Constitution was also an influence on the 1937 Constitution, and similarities between the documents have been noted. See the Binchy Memorial Lecture, Burren Law School, 'Some Thoughts on the Origins of the Constitution', 5 May 2012, delivered by Mr Justice Gerard Hogan (unpublished). However, many of the similarities between these documents may be explained by the fact that Weimar influenced many of the 1922 provisions, and many provisions from the 1937 document were taken word for word from 1922. Thus, rather than being a direct influence on the 1937 Constitution, it is more likely that many of the Weimar provisions came through from the 1922 Constitution.

[28] Agnes Headlam-Morley, *The New Democratic Constitutions of Europe: A Comparative Study of Post-War European Constitutions with Special Reference to Germany, Czechoslovakia, Poland, Finland, The Kingdom of the Serbs, Croats & Slovenes and the Baltic States* (Oxford, 1928), 2.

on the misapplication of these democratic devices, leading almost to the failure of democracy. In hindsight, the same commentary could be applied to the Irish Free State.

The conception of popular sovereignty which underlay the postwar constitutions was based on Rousseau's claim[29] that sovereignty cannot be delegated; rather, it remains with the whole body of citizens, and, for that reason, Parliament cannot be sovereign – it is only one of the organs which can be established. This idea was perfect for what the drafters wanted for the Irish Free State Constitution and it fitted in nicely with the perpetual claim that the Irish people had always remained sovereign just as Ireland had always remained a nation. As mentioned above, most of the devices associated with popular sovereignty which appear in the postwar constitutions are also found in the Irish Free State Constitution: popular sovereignty, universal suffrage, proportional representation, referendum and initiative and a second Chamber.

However, one facet of the postwar constitutions which was not followed (besides the feature of a president, which would not have been permitted under the Treaty) was that of state intervention. Headlam-Morley wrote that

> The most characteristic feature of the new constitutions is the recognition of the fact that one of the chief functions of the State must be to secure the social well-being of the citizens and the industrial prosperity of the nation. Industry must be organised as a collective whole for the good of the community and not of the individual.[30]

While this sentiment might have suited some of the earlier Irish drafts, it was not something which appeared in the final document because of its radical nature and the fear that it might alienate a certain section of the electorate.[31]

Older established constitutions

The constitutions of Switzerland and the United States, while considerably older than the postwar documents,[32] were also hugely influential on the Irish Free State Constitution because of the fact that the sentiments contained in those documents reflected those that attracted the Constitution Committee to the postwar documents. The features of popular sovereignty, democracy and equality contained in those Constitutions were to prove worthy models for the Constitution of the Irish Free State. As we shall see later, the Swiss Constitution proved an important

---

[29] *Ibid.*, 32.

[30] *Ibid.*, 264.

[31] Like some of the more radical ideas of Connolly and the Gaelic state, this ideology was also a victim of circumstances in that, as much as the architects would have liked to include these ideas in the final Draft, the government was aware that it would need the support of the wealthy conservative class in order to secure the economy, and many of these ideas would have been too radical for them.

[32] The United States Constitution was adopted in 1787 and the Swiss Constitution which the Constitution Committee would have studied was that of 1874.

example as it was from this document that inspiration for the external ministers scheme came. It also provided inspiration for the provisions on the legislative referendum and the initiative. Furthermore, it is quite probable that the inspiration for the inclusion of judicial review and the provisions in relation to individual liberty in the Irish Constitution came from the American example.

Dominion constitutions

The Committee also made a study of the Dominion constitutions, and in particular, those of South Africa and Canada (which was proposed by the British as a model for the Irish Free State) were frequently referred to. Popular sentiment in the Dominions was noted by the Irish and the occasional objections of the Dominions to the rigidity of Cabinet government[33] may have strengthened the case for external ministers in the Irish Free State Constitution. However, it is clear that the Irish were not interested in borrowing from the Dominion constitutions and referred to them only for matters which were expressly required by the Treaty, such as the Governor-General, for which the Canadian provisions were useful, and the Appeal to the Judicial Committee of the Privy Council, where the South African position was adopted.

Kennedy noted in a speech to the American Bar Association in 1928 that, in framing the Irish Free State Constitution, the Committee 'did not simply turn to any of the existing Dominion Constitutions to find a ready model ... The framers of our Constitution were conscious of the much more important fact that special conditions in Ireland required special treatment.'[34]

One possible reason for the lack of influence from the Dominion constitutions is that, in drafting style, they read very much like British statutes rather than constitutions. This is compounded in the lack of an eloquent preamble and their passionless introductory lines: 'An Act for the Union of Canada ...' or 'An Act to constitute the Union of South Africa'. And as regards content, Kohn has noted that the Dominion constitutions were 'in origin no more than measures of technical devolution necessitated by the exigencies of geography'.[35] In contrast to the emphatic declaration of statehood in the Irish Constitution, the Dominions were clearly not states. The constitutions of South Africa (1909) and Canada (1867) each contain frequent mentions of the King or Queen, a feature which was anathema to the drafters. Another reason for the unsuitability of the Dominions as models is that their constitutions were concerned with the union and federation of their respective states and provinces and so were framed with this in mind.

---

[33] See A.B. Keith, 'Notes on Imperial Constitutional Law' (1922) 4 (4) *Journal of Comparative Legislation and International Law*, Third Series 233, 236.

[34] Hugh Kennedy, 'Character and Sources of the Constitution of the Irish Free State', An Address delivered at the meeting of the American Bar Association at Seattle, Washington, 25 July 1928, 1928 14 (8) *American Bar Association Journal* 17–18.

[35] Kohn, *Constitution of the Irish Free State*, 103.

The impact of these influences on the 1922 Constitution

These influences manifested themselves in diverse forms and to varying degrees in the Drafts of the Constitution and in the document itself. Not all would survive the Conference in London or the debates in the Constituent Assembly but some became very influential, such as the idea of popular sovereignty, which became the cornerstone of the document.

Popular sovereignty

The idea which, without any doubt, constituted the greatest influence on the drafting and eventual document of 1922 was the idea of popular sovereignty. There are various different reasons for this. To begin with, the British system was based on Parliamentary sovereignty and the Irish were particularly anxious to move away from that system.[36] In addition, popular sovereignty could also be associated with the Gaelic state. The ideal was espoused in the 1916 Proclamation and the documents drawn up in 1919 for the sitting of the first Dáil. It was also a principal feature of the postwar constitutions: 'Each of the new constitutions begins with a preamble stating that the people of the country concerned have given themselves a constitution ... the constitution in each case goes on to state that the people are sovereign; that all powers of government emanate from them.'[37] Hence, it is not surprising that popular sovereignty was made a central feature of the Irish Constitution.

In line with this, Article 2 of the Irish Free State Constitution contains a declaration that 'All powers of government and all authority, legislative, executive and judicial, in Ireland, are derived from the people of Ireland'. While the British were not enamoured with this aspect of the Irish Constitution, the Irish were adamant that popular sovereignty would remain. In fact, popular sovereignty was made the foundation of the whole document and, as we shall see, many of the provisions were deduced from this concept: the referendum and initiative,[38] to ensure that the people ultimately held the power; functional councils,[39] to give an extra voice to the people in choosing the government; wide franchise and proportional representation (single transferable vote) (PR-STV),[40] to provide for

---

[36] This was due to Irish hatred of British-style politics, particularly the corruption and bribery which had led to the Act of Union in 1800 and disestablishment of the Irish Parliament. For more see Chapter 8.

[37] Headlam-Morley, *New Democratic Constitutions*, 89–90.

[38] Articles 47 and 48.

[39] Article 45.

[40] Article 14 declared that 'all citizens who have reached the age of 21 years ... shall have the right to vote'. As mentioned earlier, STV was not actually specified in the Constitution but it was this system which was intended and which was implemented.

a fair system of voting; judicial review and the independence of the judiciary,[41] to ensure the people had recourse to the courts if Parliament overstepped its role; entrenchment,[42] to ensure that the document would be difficult to amend in order to protect the people from arbitrary actions.[43]

For the sake of clarity, it is important to distinguish here between popular sovereignty and state sovereignty as the two are often confused and combined. Popular sovereignty is the idea that the people are the source of all political authority within a state. It is popular sovereignty which runs through Irish political thought and history as the dominant theme. State sovereignty, which is the idea that a state has full autonomy in its relations with other states and is not subordinate to any other authority, did not become as big an issue until some time after the 1916 Rising. This is because many separatists, before this, were quite prepared to accept various forms of internal independence. The issue of state sovereignty came to the fore during the Treaty negotiations, when the Irish declared that what they were entitled to was complete and total separation from Britain (and any other country).[44] It was following the Treaty signing that arguments began as to whether the Irish Free State was truly sovereign. It was argued at the time that the Irish Free State was not sovereign vis-à-vis Britain because of the Treaty ports and the oath, among other things. It could also be argued that the Treaty itself was a limitation on the sovereignty of the state, in that any amendments to the Constitution had to be within the terms of the Treaty and, if not, were to be declared void.

Public ownership of land and natural resources, private property

In the original Drafts of the 1922 Constitution, Articles 11, 12, 41 and 42[45] provided for unfettered public ownership of land and natural resources. This particular principle was very popular with the Committee. The memorandum which was used to draft the Articles was written by C.J. France, and his socialistic ideas certainly had a strong influence on these provisions.[46] However, it is submitted that the principal reasons for the inclusion of these provisions in the Drafts were the influence of the Gaelic state, where all land was held communally and for

---

[41] Articles 65 and 69.

[42] Originally, the Draft Constitution did not contain any period of grace in relation to constitutional amendments. All amendments were to be submitted to the people.

[43] This theme is discussed in further detail in the next chapter.

[44] Tone had preached separatism but was prepared to negotiate with the French, and Pearse would have been quite happy to install a Hohenzollern monarch on the throne of independent Ireland, as an alternative to the British King. See F.S.L. Lyons, *Ireland Since the Famine* (London, 1973), 370.

[45] Drafts B and A, although Draft C contained similar provisions. See Chapter 3.

[46] France submitted a memorandum to the Committee entitled 'The Natural Endowments of the State' contained in Document 24. He also penned the draft 'Economic Provisions' in Documents 35 and 37. His primary focus was on an economic foundation for independence. See Box III, Papers of E.M. Stephens, MSS 4236, Trinity College Dublin Archives.

the good of the community, and possibly also the influence of the famous land agitators such as John Mitchel,[47] Thomas Davis[48] and James Fintan Lalor[49] who associated popular sovereignty with public ownership of land.

Furthermore, the influence of the Land War was still very strong at the time; indeed, some of the most passionate debates which took place in the Dáil in relation to the Treaty were on the subject of land. Therefore, it would have been very important to the public that the land was transferred to the Irish state so that it could then be redistributed to the people.

However, the economic circumstances of the time intervened; the fact that the state had a large budget deficit must have always been at the back of the minds of the politicians, and the fact was that they could not risk alienating the property-owning class, as they were needed to bankroll the economy. As a result, the provisions were significantly watered down and the version which appears in the Constitution is but a shadow of the original radical drafts.[50] However, the absence of an express right to private property is still notable.

While many of the constitutions of the postwar states contain private property guarantees, many of these are also subject to significant exceptions; the Constitution of the Kingdom of the Serbs, Croats and Slovenes (1921) guarantees a right to private property in Article 37 but only if it is not injurious to the interests of the community and the scope, extent and limits to that right are regulated by law. Article 24 of the Estonian Constitution (1920) guarantees private property but then specifies that this may be expropriated without the consent of the owner if public interest so requires. In the German (Weimar) Constitution (1919),

---

[47] James Quinn, *John Mitchel* (Dublin, 2008).

[48] See Helen Mulvey, *Thomas Davis and Ireland: A Biographical Study* (Washington, 2003).

[49] Natural law and the Social Contract provided the underlying basis for his ideas, which centred on intense agrarianism which, in turn, could be used to promote the cause of political liberty. He believed that Irish internal sovereignty was based on the will of the people. See L. Fogarty, *James Fintan Lalor Patriot and Political Essayist (1807–1849)* (Dublin, 1918), and David Buckley, *James Fintan Lalor: Radical* (Cork, 1990).

[50] When the Draft was submitted to George O'Brien (see Chapter 3) for criticism he suggested combining Articles 11 and 12 into one milder and toned-down article: 'The rights of the State in and to natural resources, the use of which is of national importance, shall not be alienated. Their exploitation by private individuals or associations shall be permitted only under State supervision and in accordance with conditions and regulations approved by legislation.' This provision survived the British negotiations but was watered down again during the debates in the Constituent Assembly. When Article 11 came up for consideration during the Committee stage, Figgis, Johnson and William O'Brien all submitted amendments intended to bring the Article back to the original spirit. O'Higgins commented that these might 'frighten timid people' because they looked 'very much like a Communist doctrine'. *Dáil Debates*, vol 1, col 707, 25 September 1922. The amendments failed and Article 11 remained as it was until the fourth stage when O'Higgins put forward the final form of Article 11 as an amendment, apparently with a view to satisfying Figgis, Johnson and others who objected to the Article. The new amendment was accepted despite protests by Figgis. See *Dáil Debates*, vol 1, 18 October 1922.

Article 158 states that, while property is guaranteed, this also imposes obligations and its use must at the same time serve the common good. The majority of the postwar constitutions also contain provisions which claim all resources, forests, mineral wealth, water etc. for the state.[51]

Like the Constitution of the Irish Free State, the constitutions of the Dominions do not contain any right to private property. However, this is due more to the absence of any sort of bill of rights in these documents than to a conscious decision not to include the right to private property.

The Irish language

The guarantee contained in Article 4 which declares Irish as the national language is an obvious result of the work of the Gaelic League and of the fact that many of the 'Irish political elite'[52] wished for a return to a version of the Gaelic state. Thus, the ideal of promoting the Irish language was initially of extreme importance, although other issues soon came to take precedence. The Irish language was still in a weak position in 1922, despite the efforts of the revivalists. There was little effort by the State to prevent the decline of the language in Gaeltacht areas but enormous resources were used in order to provide English-speaking children with a rudimentary knowledge of Irish.[53] Furthermore, many of the politicians, Eoin MacNeill in particular, did not believe in excessive state intervention and felt that the language revival would happen naturally. This fact, combined with a lack of suitably qualified Irish teachers, undoubtedly led to the failure of the 'Gaelicisation' of the state. While the aspirations may not have come to fruition, the fact that a language which was spoken by such a small minority of the population was declared to be the national language is significant in itself and, of course, the symbolism was hugely important. As Kohn has put it, the enunciation of Irish as the national language 'marked the consummation of the process of national emancipation'.[54]

Equality

Oran Doyle has commented that '[T]he drafters of the 1922 Constitution had ... been aware of [the] constitutional trend in continental Europe and had chosen not to include an equality guarantee'.[55] However, this statement does not accurately reflect the early work on the Constitution. The original Drafts of the Irish Free

---

[51] See generally *Select Constitutions of the World* (Dublin, 1922).
[52] Tom Garvin, 'Cogadh na nCarad: The Creation of the Irish Political Elite' in Tom Garvin, Maurice Manning & Richard Sinnott (eds), *Dissecting Irish Politics: Essays in Honour of Brian Farrell* (Dublin, 2004), 11.
[53] See John Coakley & Michael Gallagher (eds), *Politics in the Republic of Ireland* (Dublin, 1993), 30.
[54] Kohn, *Constitution of the Irish Free State*, 23.
[55] Oran Doyle, *Constitutional Equality Law* (Dublin, 2004), 52. By 'trend' he means including guarantees of equality in constitutions.

State Constitution contained strong guarantees of equality; an early draft Article proclaimed the following:

All Irishmen and women have as citizens of Saorstát Éireann fundamentally the same civil rights and duties. All Irishmen and women are members of one common society. For the better ordering of their common affairs, to adjustment of their mutual interests, for the care and nurture of their physical and moral well-being and development, and for the binding together of them in life and liberty, certain powers of Government are devised by them.[56]

In the same draft, another Article appeared which provided: 'All Irishmen and women are equal before the law, and no law can be of effect that in any way impairs that equality.'[57]

There may be many reasons for the original enthusiasm of the drafters to enshrine the right to equality. One influence was certainly the Gaelic state. As mentioned above, there was a belief that equality, and in particular equality between the sexes, was very important in this society:

In ancient Ireland, under Brehon Law, the lowest clansman stood on an equal footing with his chieftain. For example, it is recorded that when several Irish Kings visited Richard II in Dublin, the Irish kings sat down to dinner with their minstrels and entire retinue as was their custom. The English were appalled by such a display of egalitarianism and soon rearranged things so that the Irish royalty ate separately from the rest of their attendants. The Irish gave in to this demand of the English in order to be courteous guests even though it went very much against their inclination and custom.

It should not be surprising that it was in this race of Gaels, where the equality of man was so well understood and practiced, that woman stood emancipated from the remotest time. Indeed, women in ancient Ireland were often eligible for the professions, and for rank and fame. They were druidesses, poets, physicians, sages, and lawgivers ... Under Brehon Law women were equal to men with regard to education and property. After marriage, the woman was a partner with, and not the property of, her husband. She remained the sole owner of property that had been hers prior to marriage. Property jointly owned by her and her husband could not be sold without her approval and consent.[58]

Another motivation would have been the fact that equal suffrage had been promised by the 1916 Proclamation.[59] Equality was also a major theme in the postwar

---

[56] Document 3, Hugh Kennedy Papers, P4/320, University College Dublin Archives. This was before the Committee decided to submit separate drafts.

[57] *Ibid.*

[58] Loreta Wilson, 'The Brehon Laws', *Hedgemaster – Periodical of the Irish Cultural Society of the City Garden Area* (New York, 1989), 1.

[59] 'Until our arms have brought the opportune moment for the establishment of a permanent National Government, representative of the whole people of Ireland and elected by the suffrages of all her men and women, the Provision Government, hereby constituted, will administer the civil and military affairs of the Republic in trust for the people.'

constitutions, which all contained explicit guarantees of equality and abolished all titles, classes and distinctions.[60] Even the older Swiss Constitution, which was a particular source of inspiration for the Committee, contained an equality guarantee.[61]

However, the original enthusiasm for equality in the Drafts did not transfer to the eventual document; alterations to the equality provision were made throughout the course of the drafting process, and the Draft which emerged following consideration by the Provisional Government contained the simple guarantee: 'All men and women have equal rights as citizens.' This sentence would at least have retained some of the original sentiment but, by the time the Constitution had been passed through the Constituent Assembly, even this sentence had disappeared. One of the principal reasons for this omission appears to stem from a meeting between Kevin O'Higgins and a group of women, at which it seems an interpretation of the proposed Article was noted, which would render unconstitutional any legislation which discriminated between the sexes in any way.[62] William Cosgrave's comment that such a situation would create 'endless bother' seems to be a sentiment which was shared by a number of politicians. Ernest Blythe also commented at the time that many women would prefer that the intention to pursue egalitarian values to be taken for granted rather than spelling it out in a constitutional provision![63] The result of this was that the intended provision was simply left out and thus the Committee's hopes of an equality provision were ruined.

One reason for this may have been the fact that women were not organised enough to campaign for these rights at the time. Another reason may have been that the issue of class equality was more pressing at the time than equality between the sexes and a huge emphasis was put on the attempt to abolish class and privileges from the Irish Free State in Article 5, which originally abolished all titles of nobility. However, the British were opposed to this in that this was considered a prerogative of the monarch and so the provision was altered to provide that 'No title of honour in respect of any services rendered in or in relation to the Irish Free State may be conferred on any citizen of the Irish Free State except with the approval or upon the advice of the Executive Council of the State'. This was still a victory as it effectively prevented the conferring of any new titles and helped to eliminate the idea of an 'upper class'. The provision was retained and now appears in Article 40.2 of the 1937 Constitution.

In light of the strength of the equality theme in all of the influences mentioned

---

[60] Article 96 of the Constitution of the Polish Republic, Article 4 in the Constitution of the Kingdom of the Serbs, Croats and Slovenes, Article 6 in the Constitution of Estonia, Articles 106 and 128 in the Constitution of Czechoslovakia, Article 109 in the Constitution of the German Reich, Article 7 in the Constitution of the Republic of Austria.

[61] Article 4.

[62] See Thomas Mohr, 'The Rights of Women under the Constitution of the Irish Free State' (2006) 41 *Irish Jurist* 20, 24.

[63] *Ibid.*, 35.

above, it is surprising and disappointing that the general equality guarantee failed to survive the final document.

Religion and the Church

One notable absence from the list of influences is the Roman Catholic Church. This is simply because the Catholic Church does not seem to have influenced the drafting of the Irish Free State Constitution. While the liberal nature of Article 8 (which guarantees free practice of religion and does not recognise any specific religion) of the Irish Free State Constitution has been downplayed by some,[64] who point to the fact that religious neutrality was required by the Treaty,[65] the truth is that there was absolutely no reluctance by the Irish in relation to this position. In fact, it seems to have been welcomed. There was virtually no debate in the Dáil on the matter and no criticism following promulgation.[66] Besides, the Church does not seem to have shown any interest in lobbying at the drafting stage of the 1922 Constitution, and certain members of the Church even refused to become members of criticising committees.[67] The reason for the nonchalance of the Catholic Church at this time may have been that the demographics of the 1911 census pointed to more than 90 per cent Roman Catholic majority[68] and the Church felt it had nothing to fear from the new government; it expected to be respected as even the British government had respected it.

---

[64] See Gerard Hogan's foreword in Dermot Keogh & Andrew McCarthy, *The Making of the Irish Constitution 1937* (Cork, 2007), 20.

[65] Article 16 of the Treaty provided the following: 'Neither the Parliament of the Irish Free State nor the Parliament of Northern Ireland shall make any law so as either directly or indirectly to endow any religion or prohibit or restrict the free exercise thereof or give any preference or impose any disability on account of religious belief or religious status or affect prejudicially the right of any child to attend a school receiving public money without attending the religious instruction at the school or make any discrimination as respects State aid between schools under the management of different religious denominations or divert from any religious denomination or any educational institution any of its property except for public utility purposes and on payment of compensation.' There was no prohibition in the Treaty on the creation of an established church, such as existed in Britain. However, this may have been implied. Either way, the Irish government had no intention of creating an established church.

[66] See J.H. Whyte, *Church and State in Modern Ireland 1923–1979* (Dublin, 1980), 14.

[67] See NAI, S8952: series of letters between Figgis and Collins in March 1922, discussing a possible 'criticising committee'. However, the Catholic bishops were kept up to date with the draft provisions on religious matters and they discussed the draft Article 8 at a conference in Maynooth in September 1922. They were not happy with the unfettered nature of the provision as they felt it could be interpreted as allowing polygamy or ritual murder in the name of religion. The Constituent Assembly subsequently followed their recommendations and specified that the right be subject to public order and morality. See Thomas Mohr, *The Irish Free State and the Legal Implications of Dominion Status* (Unpublished Thesis, University College Dublin, 2007), 117.

[68] Gerard Hogan, 'Law and Religion: Church–State Relations in Ireland from Independence to the Present Day' (1987) 35 *AJCL* 47.

However, despite the absence of any special place for the Catholic Church in the new Constitution, there was no attempt made to secularise the state either. On the contrary, during the Civil War the Catholic Church was to excommunicate the republicans[69] and, in return for this support, Cumann na nGaedheal was quite happy to leave matters such as education and health in the hands of the Church, which already had a good deal of control over these matters anyway.[70] As Michael Gallagher has noted in relation to Cumann na nGaedheal:

> Its character was shaped by other strong political figures of a broadly conservative disposition, a conservatism that was reflected in a new close relationship with the Catholic Church. Although the 1922 Constitution was an entirely secular document, the new Government quickly moved to show its deference to Catholic moral values. Thus divorce was prohibited, restrictions were placed on the sale of alcohol and censorship of films and publications was greatly intensified.[71]

In addition, certain ministers were quite happy to defend the hold which the Church had over education.[72]

The contrast between 1922, when the Catholic Church had little to no influence on the drafting of the Constitution, and 1937, when the Church played a major part, is interesting. It is intriguing even when one notes that circumstances had not substantially changed; the Catholic Church still had a huge majority in 1937 and the Irish government obviously held pro-Catholic values so the Church had less reason to feel threatened than in 1922. However, the reason for a more interventionist policy by the Church in 1937 is more obscure. It is possible that the Church had no reason to interfere in 1922 as it was given control of education and health and it knew it had the support of the government, whereas in 1937 there were many more liberal ideas coming to the fore and the Church had to ensure that its values, rather than any modern secular ideas, would be enshrined in the new Constitution.[73] It has also been suggested that Ireland was seen by the Vatican as a

---

69 A joint pastoral letter of 10 October 1922 declared the Irish Free State to be legitimate and that to resist it by force of arms would be grievously wrong. For more see Conor Cruise O'Brien, *States of Ireland* (London, 1972), 108, and Whyte, *Church and State*, 10. See also Emmet Larkin, 'Church, State, and Nation in Modern Ireland' (1975) 80 (5) *American Historical Review* 1244, 1274.

70 Since The Stanley Letter of 1831, there was *de facto* denominational control of primary education.

71 Coakley & Gallagher, *Politics in the Republic of Ireland*, 15.

72 Whyte quotes Professor John Marcus O'Sullivan, Minister for Education from 1925 to 1932, his successor, Thomas Derrig, another Fianna Fáil Minister for Education, Sean Moylan, and General Mulcahy who was Minister for Education in the inter-party governments of the 1950s, who all accepted and endorsed the Catholic viewpoint on education and the managerial system. See Whyte, *Church and State*, 19–20.

73 In relation to this point, it appears that Archbishop Byrne was good friends with Cosgrave. See T.J. Morrissey *Edward J. Byrne 1872–1941: The Forgotten Archbishop of Dublin* (Dublin, 2010). See also Dermot Keogh, *The Vatican, the Bishops and Irish Politics: 1919–1939* (Cambridge, 1986), 89–90 (n. 43), where Keogh states: '[Archbishop] Byrne of Dublin did not feel overly concerned; there

potential model Catholic state in 1937 and the Church sought to bring this about.[74] Furthermore, because the 1937 Constitution required popular approval by referendum, the Church would have had a strong position of influence.[75] As J.M. Kelly has noted, de Valera would have been aware that 'outright opposition from the Church might have sunk his whole constitutional project'.[76] Thus it made political sense to involve the Church in 1937.

State intervention

The theme of ministerial deference towards the Church, mentioned above, is indicative of a reluctance towards excessive state involvement in the lives of the general public. In fact, there was a marked lack of enthusiasm for any kind of state intervention during this period,[77] possibly due to the inexperience of those running the country and the fact they had a lack of resources and had to rely upon those who had already been running things under the British, who had more conservative notions.[78] There was no interest in following Britain's lead in the creation of the 'welfare state'; as early as 1911, Erskine Childers denounced the economic paternalism of those British measures.[79] The only signs of any sort of state intervention seem to have been the Shannon hydroelectricity scheme in

---

was no need for the Church to supervise the drafting of the constitution. There was no real conflict of interest or ideology.'

[74] See for example Dermot Keogh, 'The Constitutional Revolution: An Analysis of the Making of the Constitution' in Frank Litton (ed.), *The Constitution of Ireland 1937–1987* (Dublin, 1988), 50, where he details the Pope's wishes for the Irish Constitution: 'Ireland was *the* Catholic country of the world, and he thought we should have made a very special effort to give to the world a completely Catholic constitution.' See also Dermot Keogh, *Ireland and the Vatican: The Politics and Diplomacy of Church–State Relations, 1922–1960* (Cork, 1995), xxi, where he details a conversation between de Valera and Pope Pius XIII in which the latter stated that de Valera's Constitution 'was meant to be an instrument of "prudence, justice and charity" at the service of a "community which has never, through its long Christian history, had any doubt about the eternal as well as the temporal implications of that common good, which it professes to seek through conjoined prayer, toil and often times heroic sacrifice of its children"'.

[75] This was something which de Valera would have been all too well aware of since during the Civil War many of the anti-Treatyites were excommunicated by the Church and this had a grave effect on their campaign.

[76] J.M. Kelly, 'The Constitution: Law and Manifesto' in Frank Litton (ed.), *The Constitution of Ireland 1937–1987* (Dublin, 1988), 209.

[77] Of course the original plan in Draft Articles 11 and 12 might have led to a different pattern. See above.

[78] The government relied heavily on experienced civil servants, such as Joseph Brennan and James J. McElligott, who were quite conservative in attitude. See Leon O'Broin, *No Man's Man: A Biographical Memoir of Joseph Brennan, Civil Servant and First Governor of The Central Bank* (Dublin, 1982).

[79] Erskine Childers, *The Framework of Home Rule* (London, 1911).

1925 and the government's early vigorous promotion of the Irish language.[80] The provision for the referendum and the initiative in the Constitution may also have been an attempt to reduce the possibility of excessive state intervention.

Curiously, as noted earlier, the postwar constitutions contain many features requiring state intervention; for example Article 26 of the Yugoslav Constitution provided that 'The Government has, in the interest of the whole and based upon the spirit of the law, the right and duty to intervene in the economic affairs of its citizens in the spirit of justice and for the prevention of social adversity'.[81] It is strange that the Irish Constitution does not follow the trend. Of course, as the years passed, the government became more interventionist and the amendments to the Constitution reflect this trend.

Conclusion

The ideas and influences mentioned in this chapter undoubtedly shaped the tone and foundation of the entire 1922 document. It is clear that the Irish Free State Constitution was a product of many diverse inspirations and ideologies, as well as being a product of its period in history. However, there are vast differences between some of the earlier drafts, the document which actually emerged and the manner in which that document was treated. In practice, many other factors, such as the unrest which led to the Civil War, the unrest in the North, pressure from the British and from the anti-Treaty side and more, all affected the drafting and outcome of the 1922 Constitution. As time progressed, many of the original devices that had so inspired the drafters had disappeared and, with them, much of the enthusiasm and original spirit of the Constitution. This is due partly to the political reality of the time, with the Civil War legacy and economic and political difficulties, but also to the conservative nature of many of the politicians. Those in government may have believed in the original spirit of the Constitution but during the early years in government they were more concerned with stabilising the country and trying to achieve public safety rather than furthering popular sovereignty or democracy. While some of the ideas were ruled out and some were phased out, others remained and can even be seen in Bunreacht na hÉireann today.

Having touched on the various themes involved in the 1922 Constitution we can now proceed to examine in further detail the leitmotif of the document – the idea of a constitution for the people.

---

[80] As mentioned above, there was a huge effort in the beginning to provide English-speaking children with a rudimentary knowledge of Irish. See Coakley & Gallagher, *Politics in the Republic of Ireland*, 30.

[81] Headlam-Morley, *New Democratic Constitutions*, 267.

7

The people's Constitution

This Constitution should be prized by the people. It was won in toil, in danger, and in stress. It was negotiated on the cliff's edge, and it gives to Ireland the care of her own household. It puts into the hands of the Irish people the making and moulding, and the amending or repealing of their own laws. It gives them full fiscal control; it gives them power to develop in peace and reconstruction towards the fullness of National life.[1]

Introduction

While it may not be known for it, one of the principal aims of the 1922 Constitution was to ensure that it was the people, rather than any organ of government, who held the ultimate power in the state. The Constitution was intended to function as a protector of people's rights, in a country where the people would ultimately hold the power. In the first place, it was attempted to embody the purest form of democracy in the Constitution, something which, it was hoped, would inspire trust in the new system. Secondly, in the collective memory of the Irish people, it was corrupt government which had led to suppression and poverty and it was believed that an Irish state run by the Irish people would solve many problems. For this and many other reasons, the 1922 document was an attempt to create a sovereign, democratic Constitution for the people.

Sovereignty

Popular sovereignty

In the UK, it is the 'Crown in Parliament' which is sovereign. This is a fundamental doctrine of UK constitutional law and it means that Parliament is 'the

---

[1] *Dáil Debates*, vol 1, col 1908, 25 October 1922 (Kevin O'Higgins).

supreme legal authority in the UK, which can create or end any law. Generally, the courts cannot overrule its legislation and no Parliament can pass laws that future Parliaments cannot change.'[2] In complete contrast to the British idea, the Irish Constitution Committee decided on the idea of popular sovereignty for the Irish Free State Constitution.[3] Popular sovereignty is the idea that the people are the source of all political authority within the state.[4] It is the idea that the people can create their own state, write their own laws, build their own institutions, set down their own rules, elect their own representatives and have the power to remove those representatives. Irish writers, such as Pearse, saw popular sovereignty as the solution to the unjust imposition of British law in Ireland. Popular sovereignty would thus give the new state legitimacy in the eyes of the Irish people.

The declaration of sovereignty contained in Article 2 of the Free State Constitution is certainly one of the most significant aspects of that document.[5] It provides that 'all powers of government and all authority, legislative, executive and judicial in Ireland are derived from the people of Ireland'. A.G. Donaldson has noted that this declaration of the origin of popular power 'is wider than that contained in the United States Constitution, and was therefore even further away from the constitutions of the older Dominions'.[6] In fact, none of the Dominion constitutions contained anything close to a declaration of popular sovereignty. O'Higgins highlighted this point during Dáil discussions on the Constitution: 'It is the first time, I think, that in any Constitution which the British had to do with, that that fundamental, democratic principle of power deriving from the people of a country was explicitly recognised.'[7] Kohn has also reasoned that a pronouncement 'of such theoretical character and revolutionary antecedents' could clearly have found no place in the Constituent Acts of the British Dominions, 'under which all legal authority in the latter is derived from the sovereign fount of the Parliament of Westminster'.[8]

There is a further significance relating not to the details of the provision but to the fact that it was one of the 'agreed clauses'.[9] The fact that the British explic-

---

[2] Website of the UK Parliament, www.parliament.uk/about/how/laws/sovereignty. cfm. See also Bradley, who notes that '[I]t is regarded as a fundamental constitutional rule that there are no legal limits upon Westminster's legislative powers'. A.W. Bradley, 'The Sovereignty of Parliament: Form or Substance?' in Jeffrey Jowell & Dawn Oliver (eds), *The Changing Constitution* (5th edn, Oxford, 2004), 29.

[3] This was not a spontaneous decision: as will be seen below, the idea had existed in Ireland for some time.

[4] Donald Lutz wrote: 'To speak of popular sovereignty is to place ultimate authority in the people.' See D.S. Lutz, *Popular Consent and Popular Control: Whig Political Theory in the Early State Constitutions* (Baton Rouge, 1980), 38.

[5] The constitutions of the other Dominions do not contain any such provision.

[6] A.G. Donaldson, *Some Comparative Aspects of Irish Law* (London, 1957), 138.

[7] *Dáil Debates*, vol 1, col 655, 21 September 1922.

[8] Leo Kohn, *The Constitution of the Irish Free State* (London, 1932), 114.

[9] *Dáil Debates*, vol 1, col 578, 21 September 1922.

itly approved of the Article is surprising, especially when the British preoccupation with the sovereignty of the 'King in Parliament' is considered.[10]

So popular sovereignty was a novel departure where the British were concerned. The same doctrine had been asserted in Ireland in the not so distant past during the period of the first Dáil and before that in the 1916 Proclamation.[11] But the roots of the doctrine can be traced back further still. Emmet Larkin has written that by the end of the 1860s:

> [T]he crucial constitutional concepts about sovereignty, consent and rights had settled in the Irish mind in a way that was basically inimical to the English Victorian Constitution. The Irish had not only evolved a doctrine of popular sovereignty as opposed to parliamentary sovereignty, but they had opted for a radical rather than a liberal view of the nature of consent as being delegatory rather than representative.[12]

However, while the idea of popular sovereignty in Ireland had existed for some time, Kohn has observed that the difference now was that the claim to popular sovereignty was no longer *ex parte*.[13]

The inclusion of the doctrine of popular sovereignty was essential in order to gain the trust of the people for the new system, particularly one which had not yet freed itself completely from the shackles of the Crown. Crown, Parliament and politics were traditionally regarded with suspicion in Ireland. However, if the people were to hold the power in their own hands then perhaps the evils of the previous system could be avoided. It was one way of ensuring an autochthonous constitution. The declaration of popular sovereignty was seen by the people also as a republican aspect of the Constitution; a sign that the Irish Free State was not going to be controlled by the Crown. No doubt many felt comforted by that fact that their rights would be protected in a system in which it was the people who were declared to be sovereign. As proof that the declaration was not just rhetoric, many other devices were included in the Constitution in order to invest the idea with 'concrete reality'.[14]

---

[10] The word 'preoccupation' is used not in a strictly negative sense but rather because of the devices which have been thought up to preserve some semblance of authority in the idea of the 'King in Parliament', such as the process whereby the Privy Council gives judgment in the form of advice to the King.

[11] 'We declare the right of the people of Ireland to the ownership of Ireland, and to the unfettered control of Irish destinies, to be sovereign and indefeasible.'

[12] Emmet Larkin, 'The Irish Political Tradition' in T.E. Hachey & L.J. McCaffrey (eds), *Perspectives on Irish Nationalism* (Lexington, 1989), 99. Larkin references a lecture given by Father P.E. Moriarty during about 1864 about English rule in Ireland, during which he delivered what Larkin states had become 'the pure milk of constitutional theory', that all authority and power of civil governments are derived from God and God had communicated that authority and power directly to the people.

[13] Kohn, *Constitution of Irish Free State*, 114.

[14] Kohn's phraseology. *Ibid.*, 116. These devices will be considered below.

Differing perspectives

The theory that the central theme underlying the Irish Free State Constitution was the idea of a Constitution for the people, based on popular sovereignty, may not be a view shared by all. The argument has been put forward that Westminster did retain some lawmaking power over Ireland even after the conclusion of the Irish Free State Constitution.[15] This was a view which the British actually held at the time,[16] even though the Irish vehemently disagreed.[17] Thomas Mohr has considered this question and, while he stops short of concluding that Westminster did in fact retain this power, he does note the argument that, according to Article 2 of the Treaty, the position of the Irish Free State in relation to the Imperial Parliament should be that of Canada and there was no doubt that Westminster could pass statutes that extended to Canada.[18] However, Mohr also points out the generally accepted legal view in the early twentieth century that 'a new Imperial statute could only be extended to a Dominion if the government of the Dominion had requested and consented to it'.[19]

If one accepts the argument that Westminster did in fact retain some lawmaking power over the Irish Free State, then it follows that true popular sovereignty would not have been possible in the state, if the people were not the true supreme authority. However, the essential point here is that those who drafted the Constitution did so with the belief that the Irish Free State was a truly sovereign state and that the people were the supreme authority within the state. This fact was later confirmed in cases such as *Re Article 26 and the Criminal Law (Jurisdiction) Bill 1975*,[20] where the Supreme Court drew attention to 'the all important distinction that the Constitution of Saorstát Éireann derived its authority, not from any Act of the Imperial parliament but from an Act of the Dáil, while the constitu-

---

[15] See Thomas Mohr, 'British Imperial Statutes and Irish Sovereignty: Statutes Passed After the Creation of the Irish Free State' (2011) 32 (1) *Journal of Legal History* 61; Thomas Mohr, 'The Colonial Laws Validity Act and the Irish Free State' (2008) 43 *Irish Jurist* 21; Thomas Mohr, 'The Foundations of Irish Extra-Territorial Legislation' (2005) 40 *Irish Jurist* 86.

[16] Successive British governments insisted that the Irish Free State, as a British Dominion, was subject to British Imperial statutes. See Mohr, 'The Colonial Laws Validity Act', 28. However, not everyone agreed; see the work of the great English Constitution writer A.V. Dicey, *Introduction to the Study of the Law of the Constitution* (10th edn, London, 1959), xxxiv.

[17] The Irish view was inserted into the final version of Article 12, which provided that 'The *sole and exclusive* power of making laws for the peace, order and good government of the Irish Free State (Saorstát Éireann) is vested in the Oireachtas' (emphasis added). As Mohr has noted, 'The Irish Government accepted that legislative uniformity with the United Kingdom and the Dominions might be desirable in certain key areas. However, it insisted that such uniformity be voluntary and based on a position of equality.' Mohr, 'The Colonial Laws Validity Act', 29.

[18] *Ibid.*, 22.

[19] *Ibid.*, 26.

[20] [1977] IR 129.

tions of the other Dominions derived their authority from Acts of the imperial parliament'.[21] Furthermore, as Mohr has noted: 'The decisions of the Supreme Court in *Byrne v. Ireland* and *Webb v. Ireland* were based on a perception of the Irish Free State as a sovereign state founded on principles of popular sovereignty from the time of its inception.'[22]

Thus, whether or not academics today choose to make the argument that full popular sovereignty was not possible under the Irish Free State Constitution, the crucial point is that the architects of that Constitution would have disagreed. The Constitution was written with the aim of providing full sovereignty for the Irish people; this was the intention of Constitution Committee and this is what the Constituent Assembly believed it had achieved. As Figgis made clear: '[The] Committee has just decided that the Constitution assumes sovereignty in a form stronger than any possible protestation of it. The entire Constitution is, to any reader, manifestly based on that assumption in every line.'[23]

Another point which has been disputed is the argument that the retention of Article 2 was a victory for the Irish during the negotiations in London.[24] Mohr has written that

In fact, it could be argued that Article 2 was not quite as revolutionary as it seemed at first glance. It had long been recognised by such authorities as A.V. Dicey that 'the prerogatives of the Crown have become the privileges of the people'. Once again, the Constitution of the Irish Free State had not created a new revolutionary precedent but had merely made explicit a principle that had long been recognised in practice in the United Kingdom and in the Dominions.[25]

What Mohr is saying is that British academic opinion was already beginning to argue that the Crown was really representative of the people. Thus, in Mohr's eyes, the vesting of sovereignty in the people was no more than a recognition of this principle. However, this is more representative of the emerging British view.

---

[21] *Ibid.*, 148. The British would disagree with this view. See also the decision of the Privy Council in *Moore v. Attorney-General of the Irish Free State* [1935] AC 484.

[22] Mohr, 'Irish Extra-Territorial Legislation', 109.

[23] Letter from Figgis to Professor Culverwell (mathematician and Professor of Education in Dublin University) in response to a comment by the latter that there should be an explicit declaration of sovereignty included in the Constitution. NAI, File 3/495/5, Box s–t.

[24] It is possible that the anti-Treaty side might have seen this as a pyrrhic victory. However, the objections of the anti-Treaty side were limited to aspects of the Treaty, such as the oath and the continuing connection with the British Empire. Because they claimed the Treaty signing was invalid, they simply ignored the Constitution. There is one mention of the Constitution in the anti-Treaty publication 'An Poblacht' on 2 July 1922. The short article states that the Constitution was 'dictated at the point of the bayonet by Lloyd George and Churchill' and that republicans could never accept the Crown. It was the conduct of the war, rather than the passage of the Constitution which occupied the minds of the anti-Treaty side and so there does not seem to have been any analysis of the Constitution from their perspective.

[25] Mohr, 'Irish Extra-Territorial Legislation', 136.

During the negotiations, Lloyd George remarked that 'the Crown was a mystic term which, as they well knew, in the British Commonwealth simply stood for the power of the people'.[26] Lloyd George was quite forward-thinking in this respect though and, while it is unclear whether his colleagues in government would have agreed wholeheartedly with him, what is certain is that the Irish would not have agreed.

The British had originally wanted to remove the popular sovereignty provision completely. When the Irish refused, the British proposed retaining the provision but clarifying that sovereignty was vested in the Crown. When the Irish refused to negotiate on this position, the British eventually relented once it was agreed that executive authority would be derived from the Crown in Article 51, and Mohr has commented that 'their concerns on this matter were diminished by the insertion of numerous references to the King in other provisions of the draft Irish Constitution'.[27] In his report back to the British government, Lord Chief Justice Hewart commented that 'if the Article [2] stood alone it might be open to remark, but when read in conjunction with other Articles in the Constitution it might be considered harmless'.[28] However, history has proved otherwise and Article 2 was, in fact, the cornerstone of the whole Constitution, with the Crown playing only a peripheral role.

The British view that vesting executive power in the Crown would trump popular sovereignty is questionable. The Irish people knew what sovereignty meant and the implications of popular sovereignty as opposed to sovereignty being vested in the Crown. However, executive power would hardly have been as significant in the eyes of the Irish people. In any event, while the Crown was theoretically to have a role in the executive, it was well recognised that the Crown was nothing but a fiction in the Irish Free State. In *Re Reade*,[29] Kennedy, who was at that stage Chief Justice, stated: 'The Crown is in each Dominion the permanent symbol of executive government, but the actual government is in fact and in constitutional reality in the hands of the national ministers responsible to, and changeable at the will of, the national parliament.'[30] This statement was not revolutionary because it was obvious in Ireland at the time. Kevin Costello has shown how, during the discussions on the 1922 Constitution with the British, 'the Crown was degraded to a purely symbolic position'. And he has correctly noted how 'The Crown was removed from the sphere of administration, and from the exercise of those common law executive powers known in those jurisdictions which adopt the English constitutional model as prerogatives'.[31]

Although the British may have seen the Crown as a symbol for the people,

---

26 British Record of Negotiations, CAB43/7, 94.
27 Mohr, 'Irish Extra-Territorial Legislation', 136.
28 CAB43/7, 134.
29 [1927] IR 31.
30 *Ibid.*, 50.
31 See Kevin Costello, 'The Expulsion of Prerogative Doctrine from Irish Law: Quantifying and Remedying the Loss of the Royal Prerogative' (1997) 32 *Irish Jurist* 145, 172–9.

this would never have been the case in Ireland, where it was seen as a symbol of oppression and a symbol of British sovereignty over Ireland. Those who drafted the Constitution wanted to make sure that the people knew that they were the sovereign power and that the Constitution was for them. This is one of the reasons why the popular sovereignty provision was so important and why so many other provisions flow from it.

Irish citizenship

The Irish citizenship provision, like Article 2, backed up the claims of the Treaty supporters that the Irish Free State was a distinct and sovereign nation. Kohn lists a distinctive Irish citizenship as the primary inference to be drawn from sovereignty of the people.[32] Article 3 declares:

> Every person, without distinction of sex, domiciled in the area of jurisdiction of the Irish Free State (Saorstát Éireann) at the time of the coming into operation of this Constitution, who was born in Ireland or either of whose parents was born in Ireland, or who has been ordinarily resident in the area of the jurisdiction of the Irish Free State (Saorstát Éireann) for not less than seven years, is a citizen of the Irish Free State.

The idea of a distinctive Irish citizenship was another novel departure, for, although certain types of Dominion nationality had been created, no other Dominion had conceived a truly national citizenship. Canada had created a Canadian nationality but only with regard to re-immigration into the jurisdiction and also in relation to the appointment of Canadian members to the Court of International Justice.[33] Kohn has also pointed out that 'in several of the Dominions disabilities and restrictions had been imposed upon natives of other parts of the Empire, but these had been directed exclusively against persons of coloured race and were not designed to affect the status of British citizenship as such'.[34] Mary Daly has described the form of 'local citizenship' which existed in the Dominions as purely domestic.[35] This notion was set out by Patrick McGilligan[36] during a speech to the Imperial Conference in 1930: 'At present when a Canadian, South African or New Zealand national goes to France or Germany or even to Great Britain he loses his national identity. He becomes one of the vast mass of British subjects without legal right or title to be proud of his particular nationhood.'[37]

---

[32] Kohn, *Constitution of the Irish Free State*, 116.
[33] See Clive Parry, *Nationality and Citizenship Laws of the Commonwealth and of the Republic of Ireland* (London, 1957), 450–1.
[34] Kohn, *Constitution of the Irish Free State*, 120.
[35] Mary Daly, 'Irish Nationality and Citizenship Since 1922' (May 2001) 32 (127) *Irish Historical Studies* 378.
[36] Minister for External Affairs at the time.
[37] 'Nationality and Citizenship, 1929–1930' (McGilligan Papers, P35b/103 (2), University College Dublin Archives), as cited in Daly, 'Irish Nationality'.

However, unlike the Irish, it seems the other Dominions were content with this position. As Daly has commented, 'while other dominions had been eager to assert their autonomy *vis-à-vis* Westminster, they appear to have been content with the existing position regarding citizenship. Ireland was the exception.'[38]

The Constitution Committee made the decision, quite early on, to include a citizenship provision in the Constitution. Obviously, it was a contentious point not only because of the difficulties of British and Commonwealth practice but also because of the Unionists and the Irish diaspora.[39] On 16 February, it was recorded in Stephens's notes that a formal decision had been taken to include a definition of citizenship in the Constitution rather than leave the matter for legislation. Stephens took a particular interest in this topic and he devoted many pages in his notes[40] to a consideration of various cases on citizenship. He also submitted a memorandum on the status of aliens.[41] The original citizenship provision in Drafts A and B was as follows:

> Every person domiciled in Ireland at the time of the adoption of this Constitution who was born in Ireland or either of whose parents was born in Ireland or who has been so domiciled for not less than seven years is a citizen of Saorstát Éireann provided that any such person being a citizen of another State may elect not to accept the citizenship hereby conferred; and the conditions governing the future acquisition and termination of citizenship in Saorstát Éireann shall be determined by law. All men and women have as citizens the same rights.

Draft C's alternative provided:

> All persons, irrespective of sex, born or naturalised in Ireland, who are subject to the jurisdiction of the Irish Free State and are not citizens or subjects of any other State, are Irish citizens. Details and conditions relative to the acquisition and extinction of citizenship or nationality, or to the acquirement or loss of political and civic rights by Irish citizens, shall, subject to this Constitution, be determined by law.

A more detailed version of the former provision was eventually accepted by the Provisional Government and then by the British. When the provision was put to the Constituent Assembly, the only changes made were the substitution of 'ordinarily resident' for 'domiciled' and the last sentence was changed to 'men and women have equal political rights'. This last sentence was then later taken out.[42] Otherwise the provision passed without comment.

The details of the provision caused some controversy in Britain. Under the

---

[38] Daly, 'Irish Nationality', 384.

[39] The questions of whether to include the diaspora and how the Unionists would react to inclusion in the citizenship provision provoked much discussion.

[40] Stephens's Notebook, Papers of E.M. Stephens, MSS 4235, Trinity College Dublin Archives.

[41] Document 17, Papers of E.M. Stephens, MSS 4236, Trinity College Dublin Archives.

[42] See Chapter 6, 92.

provision, citizenship was conferred upon those domiciled in the Free State at the time of the passing of the Constitution, who were either born in Ireland or to an Irish parent, or who had been ordinarily resident in the jurisdiction for seven or more years. Political membership of the Irish Free State was restricted therefore to those who satisfied these criteria only and, while non-Irish residents could become citizens, there was no distinction between British people and those of other foreign states; British subjects domiciled in Ireland but not satisfying the criteria were 'deprived of all privileges of active citizenship in the Free State'.[43] The British felt they were being discriminated against since Irish people living in Britain were in a more favourable position than British people living in Ireland.[44]

It was obviously envisaged by the Constitution Committee that legislation would be passed soon after the enactment of the Constitution in order to fill in the details and gaps regarding citizenship,[45] as the position under the Constitution was somewhat ambiguous. As Kohn has pointed out,

> Children born in the Free State [after the enactment of the Constitution] of Irish parents, since they were not 'domiciled in the area of the jurisdiction of the Irish Free State at the time of the coming into operation of the Constitution', are not Irish citizens ... Nor would the marriage of an Irishman to a woman not of Irish nationality confer on the latter the status of Irish citizenship.[46]

Clearly, supplementary legislation was needed, but this was not introduced until the Irish Nationality and Citizenship Act 1935.[47]

Article 3 and the creation of a distinct Irish citizenship were a triumph and a step forward for the Irish Free State, but as far as the British were concerned, and in relation to international law up until the 1935 Act, Irish citizens were still considered British subjects.[48] However, in practice, the change happened earlier,

---

[43] Kohn, *Constitution of the Irish Free State*, 121.

[44] Kohn describes how the Attorney General rejected calls in the House of Commons to take reciprocal measures against Irishmen residing in England, stating that all British citizens, whatever their origin, were equally entitled to the franchise. *Ibid.*, 121.

[45] Article 3 also stated: 'The conditions governing the future acquisition and termination of citizenship shall be determined by law.'

[46] Kohn, *Constitution of the Irish Free State*, 119.

[47] Daly has noted that the delay was caused by efforts to reach an accommodation within the Commonwealth. See Daly, 'Irish Nationality', 384. However, it was also caused because, according to an official in the Department of Justice in 1929, there was 'no real necessity ... to do anything in a hurry'. While the absence of legislation had given rise to anomalies such as the fact that those born after 6 December 1922 were not citizens under Article 3, Daly has commented that these problems do not seem to have caused much concern.

[48] The words 'common citizenship' appeared in the Treaty and also in Article 17 of the Constitution which contained the oath to be taken by parliamentarians. Even after the 1935 legislation, however, the matter was still not settled as Britain continued to insist that all persons born within the Irish Free State were British subjects. In fact, the situation was not finally resolved until the passing of the Ireland Act 1949, which

in April 1924, when the Irish government rejected the British demand that the description 'British subject' be printed on each Irish passport.[49]

Popular sovereignty was crucial in the establishment of Irish citizenship because, as Kohn has noted, 'if sovereign authority in Ireland was vested in the Irish people, it was clearly from this original source, and not from any secondary association with a wider political grouping, that citizenship of the Irish State must be derived'.[50] Furthermore, the establishment of Irish citizenship reinforced the idea of popular sovereignty as it proved that the doctrine was not simply rhetoric and that the Irish people could trust in the State because the State was prepared to fulfil the political, national and cultural aspirations of the people. So, in essence, Article 3, particularly when considered with the follow-up actions of the government, can be deemed an extension and substantiation of the declaration contained in Article 2.

The name of the State and the Irish language

One of the ways in which it was attempted to prove to the people that this was a fresh start with a new trustworthy Constitution was to entrench the idea of a Gaelic Ireland into the Constitution. The people needed to feel that this was their State and their Constitution, and the introduction of Irish terminology helped to reinforce this.[51] Furthermore, it was a signal to the rest of the world; our ancient language proved that we had always been a separate ancient nation.

The name *Saorstát Éireann*, which was translated as 'Irish Free State', is an assertion of the sovereignty of the State and a link to popular sovereignty. The appellation was the official title which was given to the State at the first session of Dáil Éireann in 1919 and then also in the Treaty. While literally translated it means 'free state of Ireland', its broader meaning is that of an Irish republic. There was no original direct translation into Irish of the word 'republic' besides the word Saorstát but the word 'Poblacht' was created as a gaelicisation of the word.

is the British response to the Republic of Ireland Act 1948. However, de Valera had always stated that the Irish position was supported by the Hague Convention of 1930, when it was stated that 'whether a person is or is not a national of a country is to be determined by the laws of that country'. For more on this see Daly, 'Irish Nationality', 377–407.

49 See J.P. O'Grady, 'The Irish Free State Passport and the Question of Citizenship, 1921–4' (November 1989) 104 (26) *Irish Historical Studies* 396, 398.

50 Kohn, *Constitution of the Irish Free State*, 116.

51 This was a policy of the government. A document in the papers of Desmond Fitzgerald recommends the renaming of towns back to their original Irish forms and he notes that general public opinion presumes that Gaelic terminology for the various offices and departments is being prepared. He comments: 'This would not only be useful for practical purposes but would have the important effect of keeping before the people the fact that the Saorstát is going to be Irish in names as well as in name and the rest will follow.' See Papers of Desmond Fitzgerald, P80/668, University College Dublin Archives.

Rather than base the name of the State on a foreign loan word, it was evidently decided in 1919 to use the true Irish term. The term 'Poblacht' is used in the 1916 proclamation but the Declaration of Independence and the other documents from 1919 all favour 'Saorstát'. The term 'Saorstát', the 'alternative neologism based on purer Gaelic roots',[52] was also used on official headed paper, including that which was used by de Valera in 1921 in order to provide credentials for the plenipotentiaries who negotiated the Treaty with the British.[53]

In his work *Peace by Ordeal*, Frank Pakenham refers to the 'current dispute among Gaelic purists whether the idea "republic" was better conveyed by the broader "Saorstát" or by the more abstract "Poblacht"'.[54] He also refers to a 'fragment of dialogue' between Arthur Griffith and Lord Birkenhead, where Griffith commented: 'You may prefer to translate "Saorstát Éireann" by "Free State" (instead of republic). We shall not quarrel with your translation.' Birkenhead answered: 'The title, Free State, can go into the Treaty.'[55] It is unclear whether the British truly understood the connotations of the Irish word.

The Irish language was declared to be the national language of the state in Article 4, although the English language was to be equally recognised as an official language. Kohn has described this as 'novel inspiration'. He describes how bilingual developments in the Dominions differed, in that, in both Canada and South Africa, English was always the official language and while 'the use in official discourse of French and Dutch ... was admitted ... such admission implied no derogation from the preponderant status of the English language'.[56] Furthermore, in the Dominions just mentioned, the languages of French and Dutch were in use by a considerable section of the population. On the other hand, in Ireland, the native language was spoken by very few and yet it was designated the national language.[57]

Professor Keith criticised the choice of a language which has 'the worst of all systems of spelling' as a national language. He lamented the fact that the Irish youth would waste time on the language which could better be spent 'in acquiring the familiarity with one or other of the great European speeches, not to mention English'.[58] It is likely that the Committee did not give much thought to such considerations when it was recommended to designate Irish as the national

---

[52] John Coakley, '"Irish Republic", "Eire" or "Ireland"? The Contested Name of John Bull's Other Island' (2009) 80 (1) *The Political Quarterly* 49, 50.

[53] Tom Garvin, *1922: The Birth of Irish Democracy* (Dublin, 2005), 55.

[54] Frank Pakenham, *Peace by Ordeal: An Account from First-Hand Sources of the Negotiation and Signature of the Anglo-Irish Treaty 1921* (3rd edn, London, 1962), 83.

[55] *Ibid.*, 244.

[56] Kohn, *Constitution of the Irish Free State*, 123.

[57] Of course French and Dutch were not native to Canada or South Africa.

[58] A.B. Keith, *The Constitutional Law of the British Dominions* (London, 1933), 127–8.

language.[59] Rather it was a question of sovereignty and 'Irishness'. If the Irish Free State was to be recognised as a free and sovereign nation, indeed even by its own citizens, then its cultural identity as a separate nation was crucial. The ancient Irish language was an essential part of this identity. Figgis, in particular, had very strong views about the importance of the Irish language:

> The state of the future might be built on the foundations of the past, but the Nation inhabiting it would not be the same Nation if it spoke by the tongue of a foreigner ... The recovery of the language in daily use is not a sentimentalism but a national necessity if the Nation is to act with the full certainty of its hereditary mind ... Ireland will utter her State aright when she utters her own speech aright, and when she does both, other nations will look at her, think separately of her and deal directly with her. Her dignity will be a national beauty and will aid her prosperity. For it is not when a Nation is crowned that its dignity is completed but when it speaks; and not when it lisps with a stranger's tongue but when it speaks with its own.[60]

The Irish language is further included in the Constitution by the renaming of institutions; for example, the Chamber of Deputies became the Dáil, the Senate became the Seanad and Parliament became Oireachtas. Originally, many other Irish terms had been included in the Constitution; however, the British had objected to the abundance of 'Erse'[61] terminology. Lord Chief Justice Hewart insisted upon the translation of the terms, which caused some difficulties.[62] An agreement was reached, whereby the English translations would be inserted in brackets following the Irish term but this was found to be too awkward and eventually many of the Irish terms were phased out. However, despite certain objections to the 'interpolated bastard Irishisms',[63] some of the Irish words remained and are, even now, part of everyday political speech.

The 1922 Constitution was also translated into Irish.[64] This process was effected after the English text had been agreed upon, unlike its successor which had both Irish and English drafts at the very beginning.[65] A committee was set up to translate the Constitution into the Irish language. It consisted of: the Minister for Education, the Irish scholar and historian Eoin MacNeill; the Leas-Cheann Comhairle, Pádraig Ó Máille; the Clerk of the Dáil, Colm Ó Murchadha; Piaras

---

59 Drafts A and B gave a special status to the Irish language. Draft C gave both languages equal status.

60 Darrell Figgis, *The Gaelic State* (Dublin, 1917), 83–4.

61 This word was considered a pejorative term in Ireland.

62 Kennedy noted the 'panicky minds' of the British ministers when it was explained that Uachtarán, the term which had been decided on as head of the Cabinet, meant President. The English term was later changed to President of the Executive Council. NAI, Dept of Taoiseach, S8955.

63 *The Morning Post*, 17 June 1922.

64 File 2, Papers of E.M. Stephens, MSS 4235, Trinity College Dublin Archives.

65 See Micheál Ó Cearúil, *Bunreacht na hÉireann: A Study of the Irish Text* (Dublin, 1999), 10. He notes that parts of the English text of the 1937 Constitution were actually based on the Irish Draft.

Béaslaí; Liam Ó Rinn and Professors Osborn Bergin and T.F. O'Rahilly. Again, unlike the 1937 Constitution which, in case of conflict with the English text, gives supremacy to the Irish version, the Irish translation of the 1922 Constitution was recognised as just that. However, this must not take away from the precedent which was set in translating the document. It was a momentous work, particularly because many of the technical terms required new Irish words to be created.[66] Undoubtedly, the Irish version added an element of prestige to the already uniquely Irish document.

Like the citizenship provision, the name of the state and the status of the Irish language were fundamental in strengthening the idea that the Constitution, and the state, belonged to the people. There may have been some British symbolism included in the Constitution but the symbolism of a free Irish state where Irish would be the national language of the people was much more important. Cultural identity had become increasingly significant in Ireland since the end of the nineteenth century, and Irish institutions were seen as a key part of building a new Irish state. In order to prove to the people that this was their state, it would truly have to be an Irish state and, in the eyes of the people, an Irish state meant one that would recognise and appreciate Irish history, customs and beliefs.[67] Thus, each of the above devices constituted, in itself, a further building-block on the edifice of popular sovereignty.

Democracy

The principle of popular sovereignty was also exemplified by the democratic devices included in the Constitution. Inclusion of such ideas as the referendum and initiative as well as the original type of constitutional amendment and suffrage chosen, all point to the precedence of the people in the political system. The establishment of a democratic system was essential to enhance the principle of popular sovereignty but also because, according to Figgis, a democratic system would be a link with and a return to the ancient Irish system, since democracy was the basis of the social and economic system of pre-Norman Ireland.[68]

The referendum

The referendum was an important feature of the Irish Free State Constitution, particularly so because it was not introduced solely as the means for effecting constitutional amendments. In addition to the constitutional amendment

---

[66] *Ibid.*, 10.

[67] See generally Wilfred Ewart, *A Journey in Ireland* (Dublin, 2008) (first published in 1922).

[68] Charles Townshend, 'The Meaning of Irish Freedom Constitutionalism in the Free State, 1922–1923' (1998) 6 (8) *Transactions of the Royal History Society* 45.

provision, Article 47 introduced the device of referendum for ordinary legisla-tion, which was in effect, a veto on legislation. So not only was there a require-ment that the people would decide on a change to the Constitution but also, if certain legislation which had passed through the Oireachtas was not agreeable to the people, then the people could, before the measure was signed into law, bring a petition demanding a referendum on the issue. Kohn has written that the model for this device

> is to be found less in the older American, Australian and Swiss precedents than in the post-War Constitutions of the new Continental Republics. In the latter democratic zeal, political doctrinarism and distrust of the mechanism of parties and parliaments had combined to produce a highly involved design of direct legislation interwoven with the fabric of representative institutions.[69]

No doubt these were also factors in the Irish situation and an examination of the referendum provisions in the postwar constitutions will reveal their influence on the Irish document. However, during a speech to the American Bar Association in 1928, Kennedy stated that an investigation had been carried out into the actual working of the systems in the United States and Switzerland and the Committee had been satisfied as to the utility and practicality of the device 'in our own condi-tions'.[70] Thus it seems that the postwar European constitutions as well as the older Swiss and American constitutions all provided sources of inspiration in relation to this provision.

By 1922 this form of direct legislation[71] had begun to grow in popularity, having been originally included in the old Constitution of the Swiss Cantons and the American states, and, as Kohn noted previously, it had also been incorporated in many postwar constitutions. The referendum is found in Article 89 of the Federal Constitution of the Swiss Confederation of 1874. The second paragraph of this Article states: 'Federal laws are submitted for acceptance or rejection by the people if a demand be made by 30,000 active citizens or by eight Cantons.' The device is also employed for amendment of the Constitution.[72]

The Reich (Weimar) Constitution of 1919 contained specific provisions pro-viding for the referendum. Article 73 of that Constitution stated:

> A law passed by the Reichstag shall, before its promulgation, be submitted to the decision of the people, if the President of the Reich so decides within one month.
>   A law the promulgation of which is deferred on the motion of at least one-third

---

[69] Kohn, *Constitution of the Irish Free State*, 238.

[70] Hugh Kennedy, 'Character and Sources of the Constitution of the Irish Free State', An Address delivered at the meeting of the American Bar Association at Seattle, Washington, 25 July 1928, 1928 14 (8) *American Bar Association Journal* 445.

[71] Referendum and initiative have been termed 'direct legislation' because of the fact that the people are directly involved in the legislative process, unlike representative democracy, whereby elected representatives make decisions on behalf of the people.

[72] Under Article 120, besides the normal referendum procedure, fifty thousad Swiss voters could demand a total revision of the Constitution.

of the Reichstag, shall be submitted to the decision of the people, if desired by one-twentieth of those entitled to the franchise.[73]

The similarities between this and the Irish provisions are evident. In addition, under Article 74 of the Reich Constitution, the President could call a plebiscite because of a disagreement on a law between the two houses of Parliament. Article 75 stated that a decision of the Reichstag could be annulled by the decision of the people if a majority of voters entitled to the franchise take part. Constitutional amendments, although permitted by ordinary legislation, could be made the subject of a referendum by Initiative of the people, according to Article 76.

Article 43 of the Austrian Constitution of 1920[74] stated:

> If the National Council so resolves or if the majority of members of the National Council so demands, every enactment of the National Council shall be submitted to a referendum upon conclusion of the procedure pursuant to Art. 42 above but before its authentication by the Federal President.

Article 44 stated that any total revision of the Constitution would also be submitted to referendum.

A referendum for ordinary legislation was also included in the Czechoslovak Constitution of 1920; Article 46 provided: 'Should the National Assembly reject a Government Bill the Cabinet may resort to a Referendum to decide whether the rejected Government Bill shall become law. Such a Cabinet resolution shall be unanimous.' However, here the right to resort to a referendum lay in the hands of the Cabinet only.

Nicholas Mansergh, writing in the 1930s, commented that 'In modern Europe direct legislation is regarded as the necessary postulate of democracy: it is almost universally accepted as a logical corollary to the theory of popular sovereignty. It is by the means of such machinery that the final expression of the people's will, of the *volonté générale*, can be ascertained.'[75] Undoubtedly, the idea of ensuring popular sovereignty was utmost in the minds of Committee members but, as Mansergh also notes, the device of the referendum had another function: that of acting as a safeguard for individual rights.[76] This would have been quite significant in a country which had seen little or no vindication of individual fundamental rights for centuries.

Although Barra O'Briain has noted that the device was included in the Australian Constitution,[77] in fact it is available only for amendment of that

---

[73] Article 73 of the Constitution of the German Reich, taken from *Select Constitutions of the World*. The third paragraph of this article also introduced the initiative.
[74] The Bundes-Verfassungsgesetz (B-VG) available at www.ris.bka.gv.at/Dokumente/ Erv/ERV_1930_1/ERV_1930_1.pdf.
[75] Nicholas Mansergh, *The Irish Free State: Its Government and Politics* (London, 1934), 137.
[76] *Ibid.*, 138.
[77] Barra O'Briain, *The Irish Constitution* (Dublin, 1929), 91.

Constitution and never included ordinary legislation. Moreover, as Donaldson has pointed out, the procedures for referendum and initiative, or what he terms 'the fifth main element' in the 1922 Constitution, 'had no counterpart in the constitutions of Canada, Australia, or South Africa'.[78] While the device of referendum is not included in the American Federal Constitution, it has been adopted by many state constitutions. During the Progressive Era[79] the referendum and initiative were adopted by many states as a response to corrupt state legislatures and as gesture of their commitment to pure democracy. In urging Americans to accept direct democracy, James William Sullivan wrote the following:

> There is a radical difference between a democracy and a representative government. In a democracy, the citizens themselves make the law and superintend its administration; in a representative government the citizens empower legislators and executive officers to make the law and carry it out. Under a democracy, sovereignty remains uninterruptedly with the citizens, or rather a changing majority of the citizens; under a representative government, sovereignty is surrendered by the citizens for stated terms to officials. In other words, democracy is direct rule by majority, while representative government is rule by a succession of quasi-oligarchies indirectly and remotely responsible to the majority.[80]

Since a study was made of the American practice, it is possible that American writings on the subject were also considered by the Irish Constitution Committee.[81] Much of the literature on the subject was written in the same type of language and tenor as this piece.[82] Undoubtedly, the Committee would have been impressed by such an argument as their central aim was to guarantee the sovereignty of the Irish people.

The Constitution Committee examined and was obviously influenced by both sets of constitutions and, whether the inspiration came from the older or newer documents, the referendum was a unanimous point of agreement. Together with the provision for the initiative, it was included in each of the three Drafts. O'Briain believed that this device was of such importance because of the 'desirability of impressing on the people that henceforth under the new Constitution the

---

[78] Donaldson, *Comparative Aspects*, 144.
[79] This began in 1877 and was initiated by groups of farmers attempting to break up the crop-lien system. The movement gradually grew into a massive democratic movement.
[80] J.W. Sullivan, *Direct Legislation by the Citizenship through the Initiative and Referendum* (New York, 1893), 6.
[81] There is no direct evidence to support this point but it is reasonable to speculate along these lines, given that American practice was studied.
[82] For example: Nathan Cree, *Direct Legislation by the People* (Chicago, 1892); P.S. Reinsch, 'The Initiative and Referendum' (1913) 3 (2) *Proceedings of the Academy of Political Science in the City of New York* 155; L.F.C. Garvin, 'The Constitutional Initiative' (1903) 177 (560) *The North American Review* 78; A.L. Lowell, 'The Referendum, and Initiative: Their Relation to the Interests of Labor in Switzerland and in America' (1895) 6 (1) *International Journal of Ethics* 51.

law would be their law'.[83] O'Higgins made the same point when introducing the provision in the Dáil:

> [P]ersonal, actual contact between the people and the laws by which they are governed is advisable in a country where the traditional attitude of the people is to be against the law and against the Government. The Referendum, we consider, will be a stimulus to the political thought and the political education of the people.[84]

Besides the need to reassure the people, the referendum had two more purposes; it was 'a device for enabling a substantial minority in the First Chamber to appeal to the electorate against a Bill passed by the majority and, on the other hand, as a solution of conflicts arising between the two Chambers'.[85]

Article 47 specifically provided the following:

> Any Bill passed or deemed to have been passed by both Houses may be suspended for a period of ninety days on the written demand of two-fifths of the members of Dáil Éireann or of a majority of the members of Seanad Éireann presented to the President of the Executive Council not later than seven days from the day on which such a Bill shall have been so passed or deemed to have been so passed. Such a Bill shall in accordance with regulations to be made by the Oireachtas be submitted by Referendum to the decision of the people if demanded before the expiration of the ninety days either by a resolution of Seanad Éireann, or by a petition signed by not less than one-twentieth of the voters then on the register of voters, and the decision of the people by a majority of the votes recorded on such Referendum shall be conclusive. These provisions shall not apply to Money Bills or to such Bills as shall be declared by both Houses to be necessary for the immediate preservation of the public peace, health or safety.

Basically, seven days had to elapse between the passing and signing into law of a Bill in order to allow for the possibility of a referendum. During those seven days, two-fifths of the Dáil or a majority of the Seanad could suspend the Bill for ninety days. Then, either by a resolution of the Seanad or by a petition of one-twentieth of registered voters, a referendum could be demanded. Essentially, it gave to the people the right to accept or refuse proposed laws (except money bills and those declared necessary for public peace and safety) and it rests on the idea of the people as the ultimate source of authority in the state.

Article 47 in practice

The first controversy involving Article 47 arose during the case of *R (O'Brien) v. The Military Governor of the Internment Camp, North Dublin Union*.[86] The case involved a *habeas corpus* application for Nora O'Brien, who was being held in

---

[83] O'Briain, *Irish Constitution*, 91.
[84] *Dáil Debates*, vol 1, col 1211, 5 October 1922.
[85] Kohn, *Constitution of the Irish Free State*, 238.
[86] [1924] I IR 32.

military custody. Mrs O'Brien relied on Article 6 and the liberty of the person in order to challenge her detention. Kennedy, in his capacity as Attorney General, also relied on that Article, the proviso of which states: 'Provided, however, that nothing in this Article contained shall be invoked to prohibit, control, or interfere with any act of the military forces of the Irish Free State (Saorstát Éireann) during the existence of a state of war or armed rebellion.' The case was first heard by O'Connor MR on 15 June 1923, when the motion was refused.

The prosecutor then appealed to the Court of Appeal[87] on 31 July. Chief Justice Molony and Lord Justice Ronan held that the 'state of war or armed rebellion' had ceased to exist and a writ of *habeas corpus* was made returnable the following morning. However, when the case was called the following morning in order for the prisoner to be released, the return to the writ stated that Mrs O'Brien was now being held by an order made by the Minister for Defence, Richard Mulcahy, under the Public Safety (Emergency Powers) Act, 1923, which had passed through the Oireachtas the previous day.

Counsel for the Prosecutor asked that the return be quashed as being in contravention of Article 47 of the Free State Constitution because the seven days required by Article 47 (so as to allow for the possibility of a referendum) had not yet elapsed and noted that the exception did not apply as there was no declaration that the Act was necessary for public peace and safety. He contended therefore that, although the Bill had passed through both Houses, it had not become operative or binding, because the provisions of Article 47 had not been observed. Kennedy argued that the seven-day period was now irrelevant as the Act had already received the assent of the Governor-General, and the Court was bound to assume that it had been properly converted from the bill stage to the Act stage.

Kennedy's argument may seem surprising, coming from one of the original advocates of the referendum; as Lord Justice Ronan commented, 'if we assented to the argument on behalf of the Crown, we would sweep the referendum out of the Constitution'.[88] Kennedy's claim, that because the royal assent had been given the Act was immune from Article 47, would effectively mean that the Crown, along with the President of the Executive Council, could veto the right of referendum. However, as Attorney General, Kennedy had no choice but to defend the constitutionality of the Act.

The Chief Justice took the case as an opportunity to interpret Article 47. He asked the question 'what does the Article mean?' and endeavoured to answer the question:

> A Bill has passed both Houses, but still the rights of the members of both Houses of the Legislature do not cease to exist. It may be that a number of members of the Legislature think, notwithstanding that a Bill has in fact passed a majority of both Houses, that the people should have the ultimate decision upon the question. How are they to express their views? The only way by which their views can be

---

[87] The old courts system was still in existence at this time.
[88] *Ibid.*, 51.

expressed under the Article is by a written demand. A written demand requires time. What time is to be given for that written demand? The Article says seven days. Consequently the scheme of the Article so far is this: A Bill passes both Houses, but notwithstanding that it passes both Houses two-fifths of the members of the Dáil or the majority of the Seanad may think that there should be a referendum and may express their thoughts in a constitutional manner under Article 47 by presenting a petition to the President of the Executive Council.[89]

He then addressed the proviso:

Now, it was seen by the framers of this Constitution that circumstances might arise in which that clog upon rapid legislation might work injustice and perhaps do very grave or serious harm in the country; consequently it was thought that in certain circumstances these provisions should not apply ... Of course, if a declaration was presented to us, we would have nothing further to do. There is no evidence that such a declaration was ever made.[90]

The Court held that Kennedy's argument was clearly contrary to the Constitution. The return was quashed and the prisoner was ordered to be released. However, the Act itself was not struck down for invalidity. Despite this, two days later a second Act was passed which incorporated the first, and, this time, it was declared necessary for public peace and safety and so the government did not have to abide by the time limit. The declaration was then frequently resorted to in order to circumvent the seven days' time limit.

This action was central to the eventual failure of the referendum. By choosing to evade the time limit, the government was effectively preventing the possibility of ever having a referendum. Granted, the intent of the government was not to undermine the right of the people to their democratic voice.[91] Civil war tensions were still running high and the government obviously felt it needed to take such extreme measures in order to implement unpopular safety measures. However, this is one of many examples of the political context of the time leading to failures in implementing the true spirit of the Constitution.

No attempt was made to invoke Article 47 until the passing of the Electoral (Amendment) (No. 2) Act 1927,[92] when an attempt was made to prevent the Bill from becoming law. However, the minimum of five per cent of the electorate was not obtained and the effort failed.[93]

---

[89] *Ibid.*, 48.

[90] *Ibid.*

[91] *Dáil Debates*, vol 3, cols 1984–6ff, 15 June 1923.

[92] This Act required candidates for election to make a declaration of intention to take their seats and to take the Treaty oath. It also set a time limit for the taking of the oath.

[93] The electorate in 1927 was 1,730,177 (according to Michael Gallagher (ed.), *Irish Elections 1922–44: Results and Analysis* (Limerick, 1993), 83). Therefore five per cent or one-twentieth would have been 86,509. Interestingly, Fianna Fáil managed to achieve nearly ten thousand more signatures than would have been required here a year later in its attempt to set up the initiative. See below.

Already, the Amendments to the Constitution Committee 1926 had recommended the abolition of the referendum, except for constitutional amendments, on the basis that it involved complicated machinery and heavy expense.[94] However, there was no action taken to abolish the referendum until Fianna Fáil's attempt to set up the initiative machinery in 1928.

The initiative

The initiative would have given power to the people to submit to the Oireachtas proposals for new laws or for constitutional amendments. The initiative was not actually established by the Constitution but Article 48 provided for the option of establishing initiation of legislation as follows:

> The Oireachtas may provide for the initiation by the people of proposals for laws or constitutional amendments. Should the Oireachtas fail to make such provision within two years, it shall on the petition of not less than seventy five thousand voters on the register, of whom not more than fifteen thousand shall be voters in any one constituency, either make such provision or submit the question to the people for decision in accordance with the ordinary regulations governing the Referendum. Any legislation passed by the Oireachtas providing for such Initiation by the people shall provide (1) that such proposals may be initiated on a petition of fifty thousand voters on the register; (2) that if the Oireachtas rejects a proposal so initiated it shall be submitted to the people for decision in accordance with the ordinary regulations governing the Referendum; and (3) that if the Oireachtas enacts a proposal so initiated such enactment shall be subject to the provisions respecting ordinary legislation or amendments of the Constitution as the case may be.

There obviously existed some reluctance to include this device in the Constitution, seeing as the Constitution did not simply establish the machinery itself and there was no compulsion on the Oireachtas to set it up. However, its adoption was still possible either by the Oireachtas or by the people themselves. This, in itself, was significant; as Kohn has pointed out, 'the provisions adopted went further than those of almost any of its Continental models in enabling an extra-parliamentary system of legislation to be set up'.[95] Donaldson has added to that remark by noting that 'not only were the Dominion precedents exceeded, but even the Continental provisions were surpassed in this endeavour to insure the predominance of popular opinion'.[96] It was another strengthening factor of the thread which ran through the Constitution and ensured the sovereignty of the people.

---

[94] See Patrick Fay, 'The Amendments to the Constitution Committee 1926' (1978) 26 (3) *Administration* 331.

[95] Kohn, *Constitution of the Irish Free State*, 241–2. Here we can presume he means the postwar constitutions as it can hardly be said that the Irish scheme went further than that of Switzerland.

[96] Donaldson, *Comparative Aspects*, 145.

However, there was some suspicion in relation to this provision. O'Briain wrote in 1929:

[S]peaking generally it may be said to be of very doubtful value. Experience of its working in various countries has shown that its advantages outweigh its disadvantages only when it is limited in its application to matters which concern the great bulk of the people, and of which they have a fair understanding and where it is exercised by an electorate, animated by a keen civic spirit, and endowed with more than average intelligence.[97]

Kohn has described the provision as one which shows great 'minoritarian bias', in that a very small minority of the electorate could have forced a vote on any particular issue.[98] However, this conjecture was never tested as, when the first attempt was made to activate the provision in Article 48, the government decided to remove it along with Article 47. The Fianna Fáil Party had decided to petition for the setting up of the initiative, as a means to remove the parliamentary oath from the Constitution. The petition was signed by 96,000 voters and was submitted to the Dáil on 3 May 1928. However, Article 48 did not set out the procedure to be followed when a petition was brought before the Dáil and this led to a debate as to the correct procedure to be adopted. Eventually, the Dáil decided to postpone the issue until proper procedure had been decided on. Apparently, it was intended to establish a Joint Committee to consider the procedure.[99] However, before this ever happened, the government introduced a Bill, which had been incubating for some time,[100] which provided for the abolition of the referendum and initiative.[101] An American writer has commented that 'In this manner, the constitution of 1922 was repeatedly punctured by the moves of party strategy'.[102]

This action caused immense controversy and fierce debate in the Oireachtas. The opposition claimed it was *ultra vires* to attempt to abolish the initiative when the people had already brought a petition before the Dáil. The government was accused of bad faith in postponing the procedure and effectively eradicating democracy. It was argued that 'The introduction of direct legislation alone could ensure an effective democracy and protect the liberties of the individual and the rights of the minority'.[103]

The government countered that the decision had been announced before

---

[97] O'Briain, *Irish Constitution*, 92.
[98] Kohn, *Constitution of the Irish Free State*, 242.
[99] *Dáil Debates*, vol 23, col 1907, 23 May 1928. The setting up of the Joint Committee was a suggestion made by Professor Thrift, an independent deputy.
[100] See Fay, 'Amendments to the Constitution Committee 1926'.
[101] Constitution (Amendment No. 10) Act (No. 8 of 1928).
[102] A.W. Bromage, 'Constitutional Developments in Saorstát Éireann and the Constitution of Éire II, Internal Affairs' (1937) 31 (6) *The American Political Science Review* 1050, 1054.
[103] This is Kohn's summation of the arguments against the removal of direct democracy from the Constitution. However, this was not something Kohn agreed with. See Kohn, *Constitution of the Irish Free State*, 243.

the preceding election, the result of which meant the government party was returned as the majority party. It was also contended by the government that the Constitution already contained sufficient safeguards for democracy in the fair distribution of constituencies, wide suffrage and PR-STV. It was argued that the initiative would destroy 'the coherence of representative government' and would be an 'easy tool for obstructionist tactics'.[104] In short, it was put forward that 'The presence of these Articles in the Constitution had engendered the belief that they could be used for nullifying an essential part of an international settlement: their abolition was thus imperative for the political pacification of the country'.[105] These were ironic arguments, coming from a government which had so vehemently supported the devices of referendum and initiative in 1922.

After three weeks and despite considerable opposition, the bill was passed by the Oireachtas together with a declaration designed to circumvent the seven-day period required by Article 47. Consequently, both the referendum and the initiative were removed from the Constitution without ever being used; thus the original spirit of the Constitution had started to dissipate.[106]

Like the circumvention of the seven days' time limit in order to prevent the operation of the referendum, the removal of both devices from the Constitution was not because it had been decided that the philosophy behind the introduction of the devices had been flawed. Rather it was because of political expediency due to the advent of Civil War politics. In theory, many members of the majority still believed in the ideals of direct democracy but the threat of initiative proposals from de Valera and his supporters proved too frightening.

It is quite possible that, even if adopted, this provision, along with that of the referendum, might have caused more problems than it was worth.[107] However, the adoption of these bold democratic devices in the Constitution was a brave step by those responsible and it was all done in the (perhaps naive) hope that the fledgling Irish State could prove to the world that it was truly a sovereign nation of its own right with democratic ideals above and beyond those of its former oppressor.

---

[104] *Ibid.*

[105] *Ibid.*, 244.

[106] These together with the external ministers scheme were vital components in the Constitution as originally drafted. The removal of these aspects greatly changed the tenor of the document. Donaldson has commented on this point that 'In this respect the Irish Free State veered away from Continental practice and moved back to the Commonwealth conception of representative government'. See Donaldson, *Comparative Aspects*, 147.

[107] Kohn has noted that the case against direct legislation had been growing at the time: 'Its crudeness in the face of the highly complex problems of modern legislation, its exclusion of the vital factor of authoritative deliberation, its anarchical interference with representative government, its inevitable production of incoherent legislation, its intolerance of religious and racial minorities – these and kindred defects of the system have often been stressed.' See Kohn, *Constitution of the Irish Free State*, 245.

Conclusion

Those who drafted the Constitution wished to prove to the Irish people that the new State would not involve simply painting red post-boxes green. They hoped that by showing the people that they were the sovereign power, the people would have faith in the new system and would work together for its prosperity. Moreover, they believed in the ideals of a democratic system. The creation of Irish citizenship as well as the promotion of the Irish language was important in terms of showing the people that the new system was truly Irish and that they were not afraid to proclaim this to the rest of the world; the dreams of Pearse and many other Irish patriots would be realised in the form of an Irish Ireland with democratic institutions and popular sovereignty.

However, while that was the ideal, the Constitution was manipulated in the opposite direction. The fact of civil unrest meant that the early governments were often more interested in public safety, keeping the peace and balancing the books than in promoting the spirit of the Constitution. The late addition to Article 50 which allowed the Oireachtas to amend the Constitution led to many amendments which were contrary to its original spirit. One can only speculate as to what would have happened if the original spirit of the Constitution had been allowed to develop.

8

Anti-party politics

It may be then that the political system has failed to serve the country as well in recent as in earlier years.[1]

Introduction: resistance to party politics

One of the central uniting features of the 1922 Constitution Committee was that each member wished to create a new political system which would not be associated with the corruption and mistrust of the previous regime and so there was a conscious move away from the British party style of government.[2] It is impossible to pinpoint why and when this anti-party feeling began in Ireland but it is clear that a number of factors contributed to this theme.

Andrew E. Malone[3] has pointed out that the members of the Constitution Committee had first-hand experience of the party machine in Ireland: 'They had all known its rigidity, its local bosses, its stern discipline, and its use of the spoils system of rewards for services rendered.'[4] Writing mainly about the 1880s, Conor Cruise O'Brien, in discussing the sacrifices which were made to produce the party machine of the Irish Nationalist Party, stated that the sacrifices often included 'the rejection of individuals of high integrity and ability in favour of pliant henchmen'.[5] Malone also noted that because of the abuse that some of the

---

[1] Joe Lee, *Ireland 1912–1985: Politics and Society* (Cambridge, 1989), 547.

[2] Collins also expressed a 'dislike' of the British party system. See J. Alfred Gaughan (ed.), *Memoirs of Senator James G. Douglas (1887–1954): Concerned Citizen* (Dublin, 1998), 81.

[3] Writing in 1929, Malone was a pseudonym of Laurence Patrick Byrne (1890–1939), a journalist who had run as a Labour candidate in the Seanad election of 1925 but failed to get elected.

[4] A.E. Malone, 'Party Government in the Irish Free State' (1929) 44 (3) *Political Science Quarterly* 363.

[5] That independent thought was not tolerated is also evident from O'Brien's statement

Committee members had suffered during the days when the Irish Nationalist Party dominated, 'they knew that a strong party organisation meant the inevitable suppression of independent political opinion, and they knew that in its earlier stages certainly the Irish Free State would require more than anything else freedom of political thought'.[6] He concluded that by the 1920s: 'The old party had been discredited in every way, and the new movement of political idealists endeavoured to avoid party domination.'[7]

Lee has explained that among members of Sinn Féin, and the drafting Committee itself, 'there was considerable suspicion of the idea of party either because party allegedly prostituted the national to the sectional, or because the techniques of compromise inherent in party politics proved repulsive to a particular type of temperament'.[8] It has also been suggested that the experience of the Home Rule Bills, which were 'tossed and torn in the tussle between two large British political parties', was also a factor in the anti-party feeling.[9] As Bill Kissane has commented: '[T]he inability of the Liberals to deliver Home Rule, and the Irish Parliamentary Party's dependence on them at Westminster, combined to heighten nationalist hatred of party government leading to an interest in alternatives.'[10]

However, at the time, there was also a general aversion to the British style of government in Ireland, which was seen as petty, corrupt and unjust.[11] This was laid at the door of the party system:

[B]y the end of the nineteenth century, the charge was being laid that party had replaced Parliament as the central institution in the political life of the country, and that the Prime Minister and Cabinet, combining the dual roles of leaders of the majority party and government ministers, had come to control the State.[12]

that a leader in *The Nation* had brutally stated: 'Ireland cannot afford to have representatives of the "independent" pattern' (July 1881). See Conor Cruise O'Brien, *Parnell and His Party 1880–1890* (Oxford, 1964), 148.

[6] Malone, 'Party Government', 364. Malone fails to refer to any specific incidents of the 'abuse' suffered by members of the Committee but he does make it clear that any sort of independent thought was not appreciated by the dominant party. He noted that epithets such as 'crank', 'sorehead', 'rainbow-chaser' and 'snake-in-the-grass' had been commonly applied to them by the bosses of the United Irish League.

[7] *Ibid.*, 364.

[8] Lee, *Ireland 1912–1985*, 87.

[9] Thomas Mohr, 'British Involvement in the Creation of the First Irish Constitution' (2008) 30 (1) *Dublin University Law Journal* 166, 171.

[10] Bill Kissane, 'The Constitutional Revolution that Never Was' (2009) 104 *Radical History Review* 77, 80.

[11] It was well known that bribery and corruption had brought an end to the Irish Parliament in 1800 and the blame for this was laid unequivocally at the door of the British government. Mohr describes the opposition to British-style party politics in Ireland as 'hostile'. See Mohr, 'British Involvement', 170.

[12] A.J. Ward, 'Challenging the British Constitution: The Irish Free State Constitution and the External Minister' (1990) 9 *Parliamentary History* 116, 117.

Party was associated with corruption. Warner Moss has written that the 'Sinn Féiners' had declared that the Irish Nationalist Party of Redmond had 'degenerated into a political machine' and that Sinn Féin claimed as its task 'the "purification" of Irish political life'.[13]

In the context of the time, there were no real political parties in existence in Ireland. The Irish Parliamentary Party had been discredited and reduced to rubble, Sinn Féin was simply an umbrella organisation with numerous different strands pulling in different directions[14] and even Labour was not a truly organised party but rather an offshoot of the Trade Union movement.[15] Furthermore, anti-Treaty Sinn Féin, particularly the more extreme members, did not believe in party politics at all. It is possible that this fact was also in the minds of the members of the Constitution Committee when drafting their proposals.

However, it must be noted that the Committee was not against political groupings *per se* but rather against the abuses which party politics can cause. It was abuse and corruption which the members of the Constitution Committee wished to avoid in the nascent Irish state. Indeed Moss has written, on the basis of a conversation he had with members of the Committee, that they simply 'sought to prevent the development of political abuses'.[16] Ward has stated their goals as follows: '[They] sought to weaken collective responsibility, enhance individual responsibility, and subdue party.'[17]

The Committee set about to achieve these goals by the inclusion in its proposals of a number of devices which it believed would help provide a better political system for the Irish Free State. Its members were 'consciously critical of many aspects of British political usage'; 'they (and their political masters in the early Irish cabinets) deplored the artificial character of parliamentary party conflicts, [and they] sought to create a more direct and active role for the people in public affairs and tried to erect some safeguards against executive dominance'.[18]

Each of these 'safeguards' was intended to lessen the possibility of a British party-style political system being created in the Irish Free State. These devices included:[19]

---

[13] Warner Moss, *Political Parties in the Irish Free State* (New York, 1933), 27–8.

[14] The disagreement on the Treaty was not the only source of discord within the Sinn Féin party; there were varying levels of republicanism and sometimes almost opposing beliefs among its members. When it came together as a successful party organisation in 1917 it was made up of a number of different nationalist organisations with the common aim of freedom for Ireland. They did not all necessarily agree on the means or the form of that freedom.

[15] Michael Gallagher, *Political Parties in the Republic of Ireland* (Dublin, 1985), 68–9.

[16] Moss, *Political Parties*, 48. Unfortunately, no detail is given on this conversation with Committee members.

[17] Ward, 'Challenging the British Constitution', 117.

[18] Brian Farrell, 'The First Dáil and After' in Brian Farrell (ed.), *The Irish Parliamentary Tradition* (Dublin, 1973), 214.

[19] The devices of referendum and initiative, discussed in the previous chapter, were also intended to complement this theme.

1. The use of PR-STV in elections which, it was believed, would have the effect of creating a number of smaller parties and so weaken the party system.
2. The external ministers scheme, which would include a number of outside experts in government in order to run specialised departments.
3. Functional representation, which would be achieved by the setting up of groups which represented the interests of the nation and by involving these groups in politics.
4. The Seanad as a House composed of 'senatorial persons', i.e. those who had greatly contributed to the life of the nation in some way, rather than an upper Chamber with the same type of representation as the Dáil.

Proportional representation

The system of voting by PR-STV was seen as an innovative alternative to the traditional block voting system. Malone described the system as follows:

> In itself the single transferable vote system of proportional representation holds safeguards against undue party encroachment, inasmuch as it encourages every variant of political and social opinion to nominate candidates representing its own peculiarities. Experiments can be tried with impunity because if the candidate nominated secures such small support that any chance of election is hopeless the votes cast for him are not lost, as they would be under the 'block-vote' system, but are transferred to the second, or later, preferences of the voters.[20]

The Constitution Committee was unanimous in agreement about the suitability of PR-STV for the Irish Free State from the beginning. On 13 February 1922, John Humphreys,[21] Secretary of the PR Society of Britain,[22] presented the case for PR-STV to the Committee.[23] Following this meeting, PR-STV is frequently mentioned in the Committee's notes and drafts with approval and it was adopted with relatively little debate.

At first glance, the quick and undisputed choice of PR-STV as the voting system for the Irish Free State may seem radical, when the 'first-past-the-post' method was still in use in Britain and possibly would have promoted stability in Ireland. However, when the number of reasons in favour of the newer system is

[20] Malone, 'Party Government', 365.
[21] A relentless campaigner, he travelled to South Africa to advise on the electoral system for the new Union of South Africa. During the war he also travelled to Australia and New Zealand, visiting Tasmania, which had been using STV since 1907.
[22] This is now known as the Electoral Reform Society. The Committee also received submissions from the PR Society of Ireland, of which Sir Horace Plunkett was president.
[23] Stephens recorded the meeting with Humphreys and a number of Committee discussions on the transfer of votes system. Letters were also received by the Committee from various persons interested in promoting the idea of PR-STV for the Irish Free State. See Stephens's Notebook, Papers of E.M. Stephens, MSS 4235, Trinity College Dublin Archives.

enumerated, the choice becomes clearer. The original motivation for the choice of PR-STV is multiple. Kohn speculates that the true purpose of the introduction of PR-STV was to fulfil the promise of Griffith[24] to the Unionists that the Constitution would contain safeguards in order to ensure fair representation of that section of society.[25] Lee also agrees with this conclusion.[26] But whether or not this was the original motivation, other motivating factors soon emerged. In short, the reasons for the choice were:

1. It would pacify the Unionists.[27]
2. It was seen as a more advanced and innovative method than the simple British method then in use.[28]
3. It was a move away from Britain.[29]
4. It was in use in the continental constitutions.[30]
5. The PR Societies of Britain and Ireland were very proactive in campaigning at the time.[31]
6. It had already been tested in Ireland.[32]
7. It would help to eliminate the party system.[33]

[24] Griffith was a supporter of the PR Society of Ireland and wrote in an article in his weekly publication *Sinn Féin* on 25 February 1911: 'PR secures that the majority of the electors shall rule and that minorities shall be represented in proportion to their strength. It is the one just system of election in democratic government.'

[25] Leo Kohn, *The Constitution of the Irish Free State* (London, 1932), 186. While we have evidence that the Southern Unionists specifically requested a second Chamber, it is not clear whether PR was among their political demands. However, on the afternoon of the Treaty signing, 6 December 1921, Griffith met with the Southern Unionists and promised them the adoption of PR-STV in elections and due representation in the Senate. See Donal O'Sullivan *The Irish Free State and Its Senate: A Study in Contemporary Politics* (London, 1940), 76.

[26] See below.

[27] Erskine Childers encapsulated this reasoning when he wrote that, if this system was seen by the minority to be safeguarding their interests, then it should be welcomed. See Erskine Childers, *The Framework of Home Rule* (London, 1911), 337.

[28] See Bill Kissane, 'De Valera, the 1937 Constitution, and Proportional Representation' in Eoin Carolan & Oran Doyle (eds), *The Irish Constitution: Governance and Values* (Dublin, 2008), 37.

[29] The Committee was anxious that the new Constitution would not be seen as a copy of the British or Dominion Constitutions so such experiments were welcome changes from the existing system.

[30] PR was being experimented with in many European jurisdictions. See generally *Select Constitutions of the World*.

[31] Kissane, 'De Valera', 36–7.

[32] Largely as a result of the work carried out by the PR Society of Ireland, PR-STV was included in the Home Rule Act of 1914 but was first used at a local election in Sligo in 1919 after the local Nationalist MP Thomas Scanlon piloted an enabling Act through the British Parliament. The Sligo experiment was seen as a success and so PR-STV was introduced for all local elections in Ireland under the Local Government (Ireland) Act 1919. See Proinsias Mac Aonghusa, 'Proportional Representation in Ireland' (1959) available at http://proinsias.net/publications/

This last point was possibly quite a strong one; it had been noted that the experience of PR in Europe had led to weaker parties, which in turn had prevented the possibility of a strong party government. William Shirer has described the German experience of PR, which led to a multitude of splinter parties, most of which represented the extreme ends of the political spectrum. This made it difficult for any party to establish and maintain a workable parliamentary majority.[34] This result was seen in Ireland as positive because it was hoped that the elimination of party politics would mean encouragement of independent thought and fairer government. Interestingly, despite the atmosphere of the time, there seems to have been little or no concern that such a situation in Ireland would lead to parties being at extreme ends of the political spectrum. Of course, another reason why PR-STV was adopted without contest was that there was no pressure group to advocate the first-past-the-post system and the Committee had not heard any evidence against PR-STV.[35]

PR-STV was inserted into the Irish Free State Constitution in Articles 26[36] and 32.[37] The general election of 1923 was then conducted under this system.[38] The results of that election meant that Cumann na nGaedheal won 63 seats, anti-Treaty Sinn Féin won 44, the Farmers' Party won 15, Labour won 14, the Businessmen's Party won three and there were 14 Independents.[39] Most parties made gains, mainly because the number of seats in the Dáil had been increased from 128 to 153,[40] but no party won an overall majority. This had been intended by the PR-STV system in order to ensure the representation of different interests and avoid domination by any one group.

There were three elections between 1923 and 1927 and the same type of results was seen each time.[41] While the new system did not lead to the development

---

pr_in_ireland/. PR was also specified in the Government of Ireland Act 1920. See Liam Weeks, 'Membership of the Houses' in Muiris MacCarthaigh & Maurice Manning, *Houses of the Oireachtas* (Dublin, 2010), 5. See also John Coakley & Michael Gallagher, *Politics in the Republic of Ireland* (4th edn, London, 2005), 107. For information on PR in Britain see Hugh Fraser, *The Representation of the People Act 1919 with Explanatory Notes* (London, 1918), 155–65.

[33] Malone argued that the PR-STV system would be a deterrent to party politics in that it would encourage the nomination of candidates representing all variants of opinion. See Malone, 'Party Government', 365.

[34] William Shirer, *The Rise and Fall of the Third Reich* (New York, 1960), 155.

[35] Cornelius O'Leary, *Irish Elections 1918–1977: Parties, Voters and Proportional Representation* (Dublin, 1979), 14.

[36] This provision provided that members of the Dáil would be elected on the principles of proportional representation. Although STV was not actually specified in the Constitution, this was the system which was intended and was implemented.

[37] This Article specified that Seanad elections would be held on the principles of proportional representation.

[38] The Electoral Act of the same year also provided for STV for future elections.

[39] See Gallagher (ed.), *Irish Elections 1922–44*, 47.

[40] *Ibid.*, 23.

[41] *Ibid.*, 23–4.

of many new parties,[42] it did prevent the dominance of the larger parties. Furthermore, as Proinsias Mac Aonghusa put it: 'What matters is that, because of P.R. minorities who had something more to think about than the niceties of a Republic, a Document Number-2 State or a Free State could and did elect representatives to voice their opinions in Parliament.'[43] However, this also led to a certain amount of dissatisfaction with the experiment among members of Cumann na nGaedheal, who felt that they would be in a much stronger position but for the PR-STV system.[44] In 1927, there were proposals to reform the system, and in 1933 the abolition of PR was a policy commitment on the Fine Gael election manifesto. However, in general the public was satisfied with the system and any change was fervently contested by the Southern Unionists. Thus the system was retained even in the 1937 Constitution.[45]

As we now know, the PR-STV system did not have the effect which was originally anticipated and it failed to eliminate the party system. Following the Civil War, the political system was left largely divided in two[46] and the atmosphere did not lend itself to the prosperity of small parties or groupings. However, PR-STV did have other effects; as Lee has pointed out:

> Devised originally to safeguard the minority unionists, the first major minority it protected was anti-Treaty Sinn Féin, presumably saved by PR from land-slide defeat in the early Free State elections. Without PR, it might have been more difficult for de Valera to persuade his followers to take the parliamentary road, for their prospects might have looked hopeless ... PR probably contributed, however inadvertently, to the stability of nationalist Ireland, though imposed with unionist sensitivities in mind![47]

Thus, as a result of the Civil War and other factors,[48] the PR-STV system did not achieve the goal of a multi-party Dáil. In fact, the system evolved into the

---

[42] Some smaller parties were established around this time but most did not last very long and many were unsuccessful. These included: the Business and Professional Group, which existed in 1922 and 1923; the Irish Worker League, which was founded by Jim Larkin in 1923; the National League, founded by William Redmond and Thomas O'Donnell in 1926; Clann Éireann, a splinter group of Cumann na nGaedheal founded in 1926; and later parties such as Cumann na Poblachta Éireann, Clann na Talmhan and Clann na Poblachta.

[43] Mac Aonghusa, 'Proportional Representation'.

[44] Kissane, 'De Valera', 42–3.

[45] Kissane has written that de Valera must have realised that abandoning the PR-STV system would only have increased his opposition. His own explanation was that he had retained his enthusiasm for the doctrine since 1919 and he felt that it needed constitutional protection. Kissane, 'De Valera', 43–4, 6.

[46] Of course, there were smaller parties in the Dáil and more small parties were established in later years. However, these parties always remained small and never posed a threat to the two major parties. Even Labour, as Gallagher has noted, was 'still merely the political wing of the trade union movement'. See Gallagher, *Political Parties*, 23.

[47] Lee, *Ireland 1912–1985*, 83.

[48] Had the anti-Treaty Sinn Féin members remained in the Dáil the situation might have turned out somewhat differently and the experiments might have had a fairer trial.

very situation which had been dismissed as unfair and unsuitable to the new state, namely the British dual-party system. This, in itself, is a contributing factor to the failure of the other experiments, which were designed with a plethora of parties in mind.[49] It seems that perhaps the forecasting was somewhat incorrect and that, rather than giving rise to large numbers of parties in the Dáil, PR-STV helped to guarantee minority representation, something which it had originally been intended to do. Thus, while the PR-STV experiment should not be considered a failure, in that it inadvertently ensured a level of representation for anti-Treaty Sinn Féin[50] and achieved a certain level of success in relation to anti-party politics in that it prevented the total ascendency of Cumann na nGaedheal, the ideal of a Dáil which represented numerous diverse and independent interests never came about. This was to be significant for the external ministers scheme.

External ministers[51]

In 1922, the external ministers scheme was intended to be the principal weapon in the fight against party politics. It was envisaged that a new form of executive could be created which would be above party and which would function simply for the good of the state. However, the end result was not quite what was anticipated in the very beginning.

Emergence of the scheme during the Committee stage

As outlined in Chapter 1, the genesis of this scheme has been attributed to Douglas, who suggested the creation of a two-tier executive during a meeting of the Constitution Committee on 2 February 1922.[52] The first group would be responsible for policy and would comprise the President[53] and ministers responsible for Defence, State, Finance and Foreign Affairs. The second group would be composed of a number of non-parliamentarians, appointed on the basis of their technical expertise. They would have responsibility for matters such as Agriculture, Education and Justice. The first group would be directly elected by the Dáil but the second group would be elected only following Cabinet nomination. Farrell has described how under Douglas's scheme the external ministers

---

[49] It was not simply PR-STV which led to this situation – it was also because of the particular split and mistrust which existed between the two dominant parties, which contributed directly to the failure of several experiments, which might have worked in a two-party system under different circumstances.

[50] Those who remained loyal to the republican ideal might have been wiped out under the previous electoral system.

[51] These are also referred to as extern or technical ministers.

[52] Brian Farrell, 'The Drafting of the Irish Free State Constitution I' (1970) *Irish Jurist* 115, 131.

[53] President of the Executive Council.

would serve for 10 years, the whole executive would 'resign *en bloc* if defeated in the house [but] a defeat of an "extern" minister (removable only on a vote of the whole house) would not involve the fall of the government'.[54] Plainly hanging over this was the anti-party theme.

This was the original scheme as it was first proposed. The idea was inspired by the Swiss system but, as Kohn notes, it was not a completely novel experiment for the Irish, as the idea was implemented in some form under the Dáil Constitution of 1919, when a 'Director of Trade', who was not a member of the Cabinet, was appointed.[55] However, it was on the Swiss model that Douglas based his proposals.[56]

France immediately encouraged Douglas's scheme. He felt that stability was needed for departments involving technical expertise and that changing ministers and fluctuating governments would not provide the stability which could be possible under the external ministers scheme.[57] Some of the others were not so sure. Notably, Kennedy expressed some early trepidation[58] although he later supported the scheme. Murnaghan also objected at this point, as did Figgis. Douglas pointed out that the PR-STV system, of which they had all approved, would not work under the traditional British parliamentary system because of the fact that it was expected to cause the emergence of many smaller parties. He felt that his scheme could better accommodate a system with many parties. Eventually Kennedy and France supported Douglas; O'Rahilly and Murnaghan proposed a similar plan; while Figgis, McNeill and O'Byrne submitted their own executive proposals.

Another consequence of Douglas's plan was that it would enable the anti-Treaty side to participate in government.[59] The main grievance of the anti-Treaty side was the idea of having to take an oath to the British King in order to sit in Parliament. But under this scheme, external ministers would not sit in Parliament. Therefore, there would be no requirement for them to take an oath. In addition, they would not have to signify their acceptance of the Treaty, as was required by Article 17 of the Treaty. Although Douglas and his allies used this as a selling point (in that in their memorandum to the Provisional Government they emphasised heavily the fact that de Valera could join the government), they also maintained that this was only a happy consequence of the plan and not the main motivation. Whether or not this was the main motivation, it is clear that Collins, who was very anxious to get his former colleagues back on board, was quite

---

[54] Farrell, 'Drafting I', 131.
[55] Kohn, *Constitution of the Irish Free State*, 38. However, Farrell has opined that the 'extra-Cabinet ministers' from 1919 were most likely modelled on British junior ministers and therefore he does not see the scheme as an early version of the 1922 scheme. See Brian Farrell, *The Founding of Dáil Éireann* (Dublin, 1971), 70–4.
[56] Letter to Provisional Government from signatories of Draft B, file 2, Papers of E.M. Stephens, MSS 4235, Trinity College Dublin Archives.
[57] Farrell, 'The First Dáil and After', 214.
[58] This would later be cited by Figgis in promoting his own executive proposals.
[59] Letter on Draft B, file 2, MSS 4235, Trinity College Dublin Archives.

taken with the idea, unlike Griffith, who wrote 'impossible' on the first draft of the scheme.[60] The plan, as included in Draft B, was eventually adopted by the Provisional Government.

British reaction to the scheme

When the draft Constitution[61] was taken to London, the British accused the Irish of trying to evade the Treaty and they insisted that all ministers would have to take the parliamentary oath. This reaction ended Collins's dream of inviting the anti-Treaty leaders into government. As outlined earlier in Chapter 4, the British disliked the external ministers scheme in general; they saw it as a way of attempting to create 'a permanent oligarchy in the Irish Free State'.[62] However, Mohr has noted that, because the British had already insisted on major amendments to the proposals, they 'seemed reluctant to press for even more amendments based on purely practical considerations'. It was concluded that 'as this was a matter of internal government, the British government were not concerned'.[63] Thus the scheme was retained following the London amendments, although much of the appeal had now been eliminated by the oath requirement.

Dáil reaction

A modified plan for external ministers was then introduced to the Dáil by O'Higgins on 5 October 1922. The plan, then contained in Draft Article 50, was set out as follows:

There shall be a Council to aid and advise the Government of the Irish Free State/ Saorstát Éireann to be styled the Executive Council/Aireacht. The Executive Council shall be responsible to the Chamber/Dáil Éireann, and shall consist of not more than twelve Ministers/Airí appointed by the Representative of the Crown, of whom four Ministers shall be Members of the Chamber/Dáil Éireann and a number not exceeding eight, chosen from all citizens eligible for election to the Chamber/Dáil Éireann, who shall not be members of Parliament/Oireachtas during their term of Office, and who, if at the time of their appointment they are members of Parliament/Oireachtas, shall by virtue of such appointment vacate their seats; Provided that the Chamber/Dáil Éireann may from time to time on the motion of the President of the Executive Council determine that a particular Minister or Ministers not exceeding three, may be members of Parliament/ Oireachtas in addition to the four members of the Chamber/Dáil Éireann above mentioned.

---

[60] NAI, Department of Taoiseach, S8953.
[61] Draft B with some modifications, which was eventually accepted by the Provisional Government having considered Drafts A, B and C and heard evidence from outside experts on each. See Chapter 3.
[62] Mohr, 'British Involvement', 171.
[63] *Ibid.*

In addition, it was provided that the external ministers could speak, but not vote, in either House and they would be individually responsible to the Dáil and so not subject to the collective responsibility of the 'inner' ministers. During his explanatory speech, O'Higgins underlined that the intention of the scheme was 'to forestall the party system of government'.[64] He outlined the fact that PR-STV had been agreed upon as the proper election system and, while this would safe-guard the Unionist minority,[65] it would also weaken the powerful British-style party system. He asserted that PR-STV was incompatible with the British parlia-mentary system:

> Under Proportional Representation you will have not so many great solid parties like in England, which make the party system a fairly good working arrangement, but you will have rather a lot of groups in this Dáil not bound together particularly, but voting independently on the different issues that may arise.[66]

For this reason, he explained, it was necessary to implement a different style of executive which might be better suited to the new system.

Under the proposed system, it was asserted that external ministers could run their departments free from political pressures; rejection by the Dáil of a particu-lar policy of an external minister would not mean resignation of the minister or the government and a defeat of the government would not mean that the external ministers would have to resign. External ministers would be under no obligation to align themselves with every government policy. As O'Higgins put it: 'Why lose your best servant because he does not agree with you on matters outside the scope of his work?'[67] In addition, Dáil deputies 'would be free to vote without Party divisions and Party distinctions'.[68]

Ward has termed the scheme 'a clear attack on the role of party in the British system'.[69] This much is evident from the words of the deputies: 'As far as I am concerned, I would not like to see the Party system in England working in this country';[70] 'Are you going to adopt the British party system here, where you have two parties who continually keep fighting with each other, and where you have no Minister at all who will be independent of these parties?';[71] 'There is every reason to expect that the evils of the party system in England would be very much exaggerated over here.'[72]

Although it was something which did not provoke much discussion in the Dáil, another function of the external ministers scheme was that it would operate

[64] *Dáil Debates*, vol 1, col 1246, 5 October 1922.
[65] See above. Also see *Dáil Debates*, vol 1, col 355, 18 September 1922.
[66] *Dáil Debates*, vol 1, cols 1242–3, 5 October 1922.
[67] *Dáil Debates*, vol 1, col 487, 20 September 1922.
[68] *Ibid.*, col 488.
[69] Ward, 'Challenging the British Constitution', 120.
[70] *Dáil Debates*, vol 1, col 1322, 6 October 1922 (Deputy Davin, Labour Party).
[71] *Ibid.*, col 1565 (Deputy Mac Ualghairg, pro-Treaty Sinn Féin).
[72] *Ibid.*, col 1266 (Deputy Thrift, Independent).

in conjunction with the functional or vocational councils which were to be established under Article 45. The idea was that, once these councils were up and running, the external ministers could then be chosen by these groups.

However, the scheme proved to be a contentious point among Dáil deputies and it was the one which caused the most discussion during the debate on the Draft Constitution. As outlined earlier in Chapter 5, deputies had various fears and suspicions about the scheme and many seemed quite confused by it as there were repeated requests for explanations. Although there were various minor objections,[73] deputies seemed to have had two major problems with the scheme. The first was the lack of collective responsibility,[74] as it was only the inner ministers who were subject to this, the external ministers being only individually responsible for their own departments. The second objection came from the fact that these external ministers would be part of the actual Cabinet but would not have any responsibility for policy.[75] However, it was also argued that if the external ministers were responsible for policy matters then the situation could arise whereby policy decisions could be made by ministers who had not been elected by the people. It was questioned whether it was wise to include the external ministers in the actual executive at all.

Deputies were concerned about attempting such an experiment which they believed had not been tested outside of Switzerland, where it worked differently due to the federal system in place in that jurisdiction. However, as Kohn has noted:

> [The idea was] not, in fact, so unprecedented an innovation as was considered by members of the Constituent Assembly steeped in the British conventions of parliamentary government. Continental constitutions frequently permit of the appointment of Ministers from outside the ranks of the legislature, provided they enjoy the support of the majority in the latter.[76]

But, precedented or unprecedented, many of the Dáil deputies simply could not get their heads around the scheme. There were many more claims such as the contention that the scheme would create an executive within an executive, or that all the power would be concentrated in a very small group as the external ministers would not hold much power. Eventually, following much confusion, discussion and argument, it was decided to refer the matter to a committee. President Cosgrave nominated Deputies Fitzgibbon, Thrift, Johnson, Davin, Gavan Duffy, O'Connell, Gorey, McGoldrick, Sears and McCarthy to consider the matter. It was decided that they should examine Articles 50 to 59 of the Draft Constitution,

---

[73] An example of a minor objection is Deputy Gavan Duffy's objection to specifying foreign affairs as an internal ministry at col 1273. There were many more minor objections in relation to the wording of the provision. See *Dáil Debates*, vol 1, cols 1249–60, 5 October 1922.

[74] *Ibid.*, col 1275.

[75] *Ibid.*, col 1276.

[76] Kohn, *Constitution of the Irish Free State*, 279. Kohn fails to give any examples.

dealing with the executive proposals, examine witnesses if necessary and report back to the Dáil four days later.[77]

The report was completed by 10 October and considered by the Dáil on 12 October. Deputy Fitzgibbon explained that the committee had 'recast Articles 50B to 59 inclusive, of the Draft Constitution, in accordance with our instructions'.[78] The committee had come up with the idea of separating the ministers completely, so that the external ministers would not actually form part of the Cabinet and so that they would be a minority. He attempted to convince the Dáil that the committee had solved the problems with the scheme:

> We have met the two main objections urged in this Dáil – the objection that the policy of the country will be dictated by people not elected by constituents – by providing in our draft that no member of the Executive Council can be taken from Ministers who have not been elected to this Chamber. We have endeavoured to meet another objection by providing that, whatever number of Ministers may be chosen from people outside the Chamber, they shall not be a majority – that is, the entire Executive Council and the majority of Ministers, whether Executive Council or not, must be men elected to this Dáil by their own constituents and who are Members of this Dáil.[79]

Unfortunately, agreement could not be reached and the debate raged on. O'Higgins attempted to bring the debate back to basics and explained again that the whole idea was to avoid the British system:

> We pointed out that it would be desirable to cut away as far as possible from the party system and the obvious evils of the party system; that it was particularly desirable, in view of the system of franchise now in existence in this country, in view of Proportional Representation and the kind of Assembly that Proportional Representation will give here – an Assembly composed ... of a number of small groups ... And so the suggestion is that collective responsibility be limited to a number which may be five, or six, or seven – at most seven, and at least five – and that those five or seven men would take collective responsibility for broad matters of policy, and that they would stand or fall together upon these matters of policy; but that outside that you would have Ministers individually responsible for the conduct of their own Departments.[80]

Despite O'Higgins's appeals for support, when the report of the committee was eventually put to the Assembly, it was rejected by a vote of 31 to 30. The recommendations were then voted upon separately as amendments. When this process was completed, the scheme which Douglas had originally envisaged had been markedly changed.

---

[77] *Dáil Debates*, vol 1, col 1350, 6 October 1922.
[78] *Ibid.*, vol 1, col 1535, 12 October 1922.
[79] *Ibid.*, col 1537.
[80] *Ibid.*, cols 1556–7.

The final scheme

The external ministers scheme, as it was finally to appear in the 1922 Constitution, was to function as follows. There would be a two-tier ministry. The first tier was the Executive Council, which would comprise between five and seven members, including the Prime Minister. These ministers would be responsible for policy and would be 'collectively responsible for all matters concerning the Departments of State administered by Members of the Executive Council'.[81] They would resign *en bloc* if defeated in the Dáil on a vote of confidence. The second tier could also consist of five to seven members, who would be nominated by a committee of the Dáil. This committee would be 'impartially representative of Dáil Éireann'.[82] Members of the second tier would not be members of the Executive Council and were not subject to collective responsibility but rather were individually responsible for the conduct of their departments and removable only by a vote of the Dáil. Their term of office was the term of the Dáil, not the term of the government. Kohn has observed that 'The framework of government as it emerged from the Constituent Assembly was in the nature of a compromise. It retained the complexity of the scheme of the Draft Constitution, but it lacked its inspiration.'[83]

Changes in the proposal as between Draft B and the 1922 Constitution

In the original plan by Douglas, contained in Draft B, the Executive Council was to consist of four ministers, who were to be members of Dáil Éireann, and up to eight external ministers, who would not be parliamentarians. The four 'internal' ministers would consist of the President, Tánaiste, Minister for External Affairs and Minister for Finance.[84] When the provision came before the Dáil, the idea was almost the same in that the Executive Council would consist of not more than 12 ministers, four to be members of the Dáil and another eight to be chosen from among all citizens eligible for election to the Dáil (but not members of either House) but, on the motion of the President, up to three of the eight could be members of the Oireachtas.

Under the provisions which were finally adopted, the situation differed significantly: Article 51 provided that the Executive Council would consist of between five and seven ministers, who would all be members of the Dáil. A second tier of ministers could be appointed,[85] provided the total number did not exceed 12, but these ministers were not to be members of the Executive Council.

---

[81] Article 54.
[82] Article 55.
[83] Kohn, *Constitution of the Irish Free State*, 279.
[84] It was anticipated that both the President and Tánaiste would hold portfolios, one of which would be Defence. The Department of State was also suggested as an internal ministry.
[85] Article 55 stated that 'Ministers who shall not be members of the Executive Council *may* be appointed' (emphasis added).

So, the appointment of external ministers was now to be permissive rather than mandatory and they would be external in a different sense in that they would not form part of the actual Cabinet. Furthermore, because the appointment of external ministers was now permissive, all ministers could be members of the Dáil provided no external ministers were appointed.[86] Thus, an essential facet of the scheme was lost.

The scheme in practice

The reality is that, as sometimes happens with political theories, the practice did not quite follow the theory. The Constitution came into effect on 6 December 1922 and an election immediately followed. Under the new Constitution, a ministry was formed under the leadership of William Cosgrave, which included three external ministers, who were all pro-Treaty Sinn Féin deputies: Deputy P.J. Hogan[87] was elected as Minister for Agriculture, Deputy J.J. Walsh[88] as Postmaster-General and Deputy Fionán Lynch[89] as Minister of Fisheries. The external ministers were unanimously elected without much controversy.[90] Another election was held in August 1923 but the same ministers were re-elected except for one addition: this time there were four external ministries, Local Government being added to the list. It was at this stage that the cracks in the edifice that was the external ministers scheme began to show.

One of the major flaws of the scheme, and something which precipitated its downfall, was the lack of clarity in the divide between political and non-political ministries. The premise of the scheme had been that there were certain ministries which were non-political and therefore could be run expediently by experts in the field rather than politicians. However, apart from off-the-cuff examples given by Douglas and O'Higgins,[91] these departments most suited to external ministries were never specified. This led to some controversy. In 1923, Deputy T.J. O'Connell[92] objected to the fact that Education had again been chosen as an internal ministry. He proposed that Education should be 'kept as far as possible from politics or political concerns'.[93] He pointed out that

---

[86] If it was decided not to appoint any external ministers, the number of ministers would be restricted to seven.

[87] He was a solicitor and farmer.

[88] As a young man, he passed the Civil Service exams for the postal service and later worked in Cork as a clerk in the Post Office. He spent three years in London at King's College, studying for the Secretary's Office but did not succeed and returned to Cork to work on the Entertainments Committee of the Cork International Exhibition.

[89] He was a qualified teacher and later a barrister and judge.

[90] *Dáil Debates*, vol 2, 14 December 1922.

[91] Finance and External Affairs had always been put forward as internal ministries. There were various recommendations on the types of suitable external ministries depending on the number of external ministers at each stage of amendment.

[92] Labour Party TD.

[93] *Dáil Debates*, vol 5, col 45, 20 September 1923.

The Minister for Education should be in the position that he could take the Dáil fully and wholly into his confidence, and every Party in the Dáil, in framing his proposals. He cannot do that if he is a member of the Executive Council, because it would mean if the proposal that he brings forward happens to be defeated, and happens not to meet with the wishes of the Dáil, it is immediately a question of policy, and as the Minister is a member of the Executive Council, the Council stands or falls, the Government stands or falls, on this educational proposal.[94]

However, Eoin MacNeill was the obvious choice as Minister for Education and, because of his personal standing, Cosgrave evidently felt he could not be left out of the Cabinet.

The argument went the other way also. It was contended by Deputy R. Wilson[95] that agriculture was so important to the country that its minister should be a member of the Cabinet. The reply given by Cosgrave shattered, in an instant, the credibility of the entire scheme: 'With the exception possibly of two or three Ministries the selection of the Executive Council is not a matter of particular Ministries, but the inclusion of certain persons.'[96] This statement could not have been more disastrous for proponents of the scheme, for as Ward has noted:

[It] destroyed an essential premise of the two-tier ministry, that there were two kinds of ministry, those inherently suited to be either in or out of the Executive Council. Now Cosgrave was arguing that if a particularly important politician had to be in the Executive Council but was best suited to administer a 'technical' department, that department would find itself in the inner council of government.[97]

Furthermore, there were allegations of bias on the part of the government in choosing the external ministers. It turned out that the predictions of the PR-STV system were incorrect and, instead of consisting of many large groups, the Dáil comprised only one major party; the second biggest party chose not to sit in the Dáil. Because of Cumann na nGaedheal's[98] huge majority, the candidates for external ministries were all 'Government nominees'.[99]

One of the biggest problems, which had never been anticipated, was that of finance. Kohn explained the situation well:

---

94 *Ibid.*
95 Farmers' Party.
96 *Dáil Debates*, vol 5, col 48, 20 September 1923.
97 Ward, 'Challenging the British Constitution', 125.
98 The party is referred to as Cumann na nGaedheal here for ease of reference, even though the party was not formally launched until April 1923.
99 *Dáil Debates*, vol 5, col 193, 10 October 1923 (Deputy Redmond). The government party did not make much of an attempt to deny this. Deputy O'Mahony commented as follows: 'Surely all this is a pretence of piety. I wonder what would the Labour members do if they were in a majority? I wonder what would the Farmers do if they were in a majority? I wonder what would the Independents do if they were in a majority? They would do exactly what they accused the Government members of having done last week.' See col 197.

The work of every department, however technical its scope, involves expenditure which necessarily must fall on the central fund of the State. Its estimates have to be included in the general budget, which is introduced and defended in Parliament by the Minister for Finance and the Cabinet as a whole. In accepting the financial proposals of an 'Extern Minister' into the Estimates, the Executive Council implicitly assumes collective responsibility for them and for the policy which they embody.[100]

This again undermines the political versus non-political divide and the collective versus individual responsibility divide. This problem was exemplified by the fact that a dispute arose over finances between Lynch, Minister of Fisheries, and Cosgrave, where the latter publicly expressed his displeasure over the performance of the minister.[101]

As is evidenced by this episode, although the external ministers were Government nominees, they did not always conform to government policy. A serious dispute arose in 1927 between the government and Deputy J.J. Walsh, Minister for Posts and Telegraphs,[102] which led to Walsh's resignation.[103] The dispute centred on the issue of tariff protection, something which Walsh was strongly in favour of, and he argued publicly against the policy of the government in this area.[104]

The end of external ministers

In 1925, the Amendments to the Constitution Committee recommended amending the external ministers provision. The recommended amendment meant that all twelve ministers could be members of the Executive Council. In other words, it would now be the choice of the President whether or not to appoint any external ministers.[105] At this stage, the government expressly admitted that the scheme simply had not worked,[106] despite the fact that the amendment was being promoted as something which would 'provide greater elasticity for the President of

---

[100] Kohn, *Constitution of the Irish Free State*, 280.

[101] Ward, 'Challenging the British Constitution', 126.

[102] This was the old position of Postmaster General.

[103] He had also been Party Chairman of Cumann na nGaedheal. He later joined Fianna Fáil.

[104] He sent his letter of resignation to the press as well as to Cosgrave. In the letter he accused the government of allowing 'free trade civil servants' to sabotage the Tariff Commission. He also accused them of scrapping all of Griffith's economic doctrines 'without mercy'. See Ronan Fanning, *Independent Ireland* (Dublin, 1983), 101.

[105] Of course, under Article 55, the matter was always permissive. However, had the president previously chosen not to appoint any external ministers, he would have been restricted to seven ministers altogether, as per Article 51.

[106] 'It may be, too, that our experience of the working of the extern Minister idea has led us to think that it is not as valuable a constitutional idea as we once thought it would be.' *Dáil Debates*, vol 17, col 419, 1 December 1926 (Kevin O'Higgins).

the Executive Council than now exists'.[107] When presenting the amendment to the Dáil, O'Higgins admitted that the original limitation of between five and seven members of the Executive Council had been too small. He noted that the President was 'limited to [*sic*] the number of persons whom he can call into the political group, and which has collective responsibility before the Dáil and before the electorate'. The financial problems were also noted but, in general, the amendment was packaged so as to provide more 'flexibility' in relation to the appointment of ministers. The amendment came before the Dáil in November 1926 and was approved with minimal resistance.

The Constitution (Amendment No. 5) Act[108] was the death knell for the external ministers scheme, as after that time no further external ministers were appointed.

Doomed to failure?

Ward has summed up the external ministers scheme as naive:

> It had been naïve to suppose that the work of the ministry could be divided into two categories, the partisan and the non-partisan. It had also been naïve to suppose that the ministry could be divided into ministries with either individual or collective responsibility, and naïve to suppose that a prime minister, who could only come to power with the support of a majority in the Dáil, would not use that majority to form a cohesive ministry.[109]

However, this is a harsh conclusion. Had the original scheme been adopted and had the anti-Treaty side decided to co-operate, the story might have been different. Furthermore, the Civil War is a major factor which cannot be ignored in the analysis of the political experiments. Despite its failure, it cannot be denied that the scheme was an innovative experiment in the attempt to avoid party politics. Ward has conceded that it was 'a much more ambitious experiment with the executive than any other self-governing colonies or dominions in the British Commonwealth had ever dared attempt'.[110]

Nevertheless, the reality is that the scheme failed. Ironically enough, since the idea of the external ministers was to help eliminate party politics, Mansergh has blamed party politics for the failure of the scheme: '[P]arty feeling has been too strong for a serious attempt to give it practical or prolonged trial.'[111] The failure of the experiment can also partially be blamed on the political climate of the time and the irreconcilable split in Sinn Féin as well as the fact that the PR-STV experiment had failed to produce a multi-party Dáil. Of course, there were problems in

---

[107] *Ibid.*
[108] (No. 13 of 1927).
[109] Ward, 'Challenging the British Constitution', 127.
[110] *Ibid.*, 127.
[111] Nicholas Mansergh, *The Irish Free State: Its Government and Politics* (London, 1934), 56.

relation to the fact that the external ministries were never specified and the finance issues may not have been adequately thought through. The inherent defects in the scheme have already been mentioned but, what is more, there were never any truly 'external' ministers appointed. This was the true downfall of the scheme. The idea was that experts, who were not necessarily politicians, could be appointed and that these ministers would be above politics. However, all of the actual appointees were members of Cumann na nGaedheal and there does not seem to have been much of an attempt to ensure that the appointees were actually experts in the area. Thus, the crucial element in the scheme was ignored and by the time the scheme was put into practice it seems as if its original purpose had been forgotten.

Functional or vocational representation[112]

A further experiment which was intended to form part of the fight against British-style party politics was the idea of functional (sometimes called vocational) representation.[113] The Committee members wished to provide for the possibility of some measure of what they termed functional or vocational representation in the Irish Free State. The idea was to bring politics closer to the people by having ordinary people involved in politics. It was envisaged that councils based on trades, employment and other aspects of life could be established and gradually become directly involved in the political process.

The inspiration for the inclusion of functional representation in the Constitution

The source of the idea in the Irish Free State Constitution seems to have been Darrell Figgis's writings on the Gaelic state, in which he extolled the virtues of the corporate state of Ireland.[114] During meetings of the Constitution Committee, he spoke about the idea of functional representation but also expressed his opinion that Ireland was not yet ready for this experiment.[115] Other members of the Committee also expressed satisfaction with the idea of functional representation of some kind.[116]

---

[112] Both terms are used interchangeably by Committee members in drafting documentation and by the politicians, and this has been followed here.

[113] This is also sometimes referred to as corporatism. However, the term 'corporatism' now contains various fascist and religious connotations which do not apply to the original idea of functional representation.

[114] Figgis, *The Gaelic State*. However, Joe Lee has written that it was based on Article 165 of the Weimar Constitution. See Joe Lee, 'Aspects of Corporatist Thought in Ireland: The Commission on Vocational Organisation, 1939–43' in Art Cosgrave & Donal McCartney (eds), *Studies in Irish History* (Dublin, 1979), 324.

[115] See Stephens's Notebook, Papers of E.M. Stephens, MSS 4235, Trinity College Dublin Archives.

[116] *Ibid.*

Thus, the idea seems to have been inspired by ancient Ireland, where these sorts of councils played a major role in governance. Albert White has described the ancient system. He has written that the Gaelic state 'fully recognised the status of these various departments of the national life, and in the great assembly there was special provision made for consulting the various interests, each upon its own subject, the delegate poets and historians assisting in person'.[117] White described the scheme as 'the ideal business government'. He explained further that 'around the monarch were councils of historians, poets, and, in fact, representatives of every single department of the national life, each of which was supreme and expert in its own sphere, yet all correlated in the unity of Ireland'.[118]

Figgis has also elaborated on the ancient councils:

> In the old Irish State the elected monarch convened great councils charged with special functions and duties. There was a council of brehons, a council of administrative rulers, a council of historians, or public recorders, and a council of poets – all of them public officials, with their parts to play in their various stateships.[119]

Figgis believed that such a system would actually correct 'the modern weakness of parliaments, by bringing them into closer relation with the differing and special interests of the Nation'.[120] Kohn has noted that a suggestive model was already to be found in Ireland:

> The Council of Agriculture established under the Act of 1899, though merely advisory in scope, had attained a far greater reality in the lives of those affected by its labours than the organs of political representation at Westminster. It was not merely a new form, it embodied a new spirit. The new agricultural co-operativism fostered by the Irish Agricultural Organisation Society had evolved a new civic orientation … Gaelic romanticism invested it with the halo of ancient national ideals. It evolved the conception of an ancient Irish 'corporate state' which, however mythical its foundations, offered a potent incentive at a moment when the new liberty would seem all the more real if inspired by the traditions and moulded by the forms of the ancient national culture.[121]

Figgis felt that surrounding a modern assembly with these councils would prevent arbitrary and theoretical actions and encourage practicality by a 'definite relation to the life of the nation'. The idea was that the government would

---

[117] Albert White, *The Irish Free State: Its Evolution and Possibilities* (London, 1920), 33.
[118] *Ibid.*
[119] Figgis, *The Gaelic State*, 61.
[120] *Ibid.*, 62.
[121] Kohn, *Constitution of the Irish Free State*, 248. The Irish Agricultural and Technical Instruction Act 1899 set up a 'council consisting of two persons appointed by the county council of each county and a number of persons equal to the number of counties in each province, nominated for each province by the Agricultural Department'. Sir T.E. May, *The Constitutional History of England Since the Accession of George the Third – 1860–1911 – Vol III*, ed. Francis Holland (London, 2007), 188.

not lose touch with the people. Figgis envisaged that, instead of a few councils representing 'the comparatively simple texture of the life in the first millennium', there would, in the 1920s, have to be a number of different specialist councils representing 'the proportionately greater complexity of the life of to-day'.[122] He explained why and how this system would be applicable to modern government:

> There would thus be two different kinds of representation gathered together. There would be the direct representation of the Nation, and there would be the representation of the special interests, the union and pattern of which create the national life. Both would meet in the Government ... Each council would be formed by the direct vote of all those in the country engaged in that branch of work ... each council would control its own affairs by the direct representation of all the people in the country engaged in its practical conduct and these special interests would meet the direct representation of the Nation by Assembly in the Government of the day ... But the Ministers of Government would be presidents of various councils, and would reflect their desire.[123]

It is ironic that Figgis opposed the external ministers scheme proposed by Draft B, when what he proposed in this work is very similar. He describes how ministers would be elected from the representative councils but he also notes that certain parts of government 'belong so essentially to the business of the whole that they would not come under the review of any special council'.[124] He gives the Minister for Finance as an example. But essentially, what he has described is very similar to the external ministers scheme, as later proposed by Douglas.

Another member of the Committee vigorously promoted the idea of vocational representation, but for different reasons. Alfred O'Rahilly advocated the principles espoused in *Rerum Novarum*, an encyclical written by Pope Leo XIII in 1891. Among the ideas enunciated in that document was the principle of subsidiarity, under which lay the idea that government should not generally become involved in local issues and should interfere only when the issue exceeded the capacity of individuals, private groups or associations acting independently. Don O'Leary has written that O'Rahilly's advocacy of vocational councils was inspired by this principle of subsidiarity.[125] Although many of O'Rahilly's ideas were too radical for the Committee, this was one area where there was a consensus.

Conversely, Lee has written that Article 165 of the Weimar Constitution was the inspiration for the idea in the Irish Free State Constitution.[126] The relevant parts of Article 165 provide the following:

> For the protection of their social and economic interests, workers and salaried employees shall have legal representation in Workers' Councils for individual

---

[122] Figgis, *The Gaelic State*, 62.

[123] *Ibid.*, 65–6.

[124] *Ibid.*, 69.

[125] Don O'Leary, *Vocationalism & Social Catholicism in Twentieth-Century Ireland: The Search for a Christian Social Order* (Dublin, 2000), 28.

[126] Lee, 'Aspects of Corporatist Thought', 324.

undertakings and in District Workers' Councils grouped according to economic districts and in a Workers' Council of the Reich.

The District Workers' Council and the Workers' Council of the Reich shall combine with representatives of the employers and other classes of the population concerned so as to form the District Economic Councils and an Economic Council of the Reich, for the discharge of their joint economic functions and for co-operation in the carrying-out of laws relating to socialization. The District Economic Councils and the Economic Council of the Reich shall be so constituted as to give representation thereon to all important vocational groups in proportion to their economic and social importance.

All Bills of fundamental importance dealing with matters of social and economic legislation shall, before being introduced, be submitted by the Government of the Reich to the Economic Council of the Reich for its opinion thereon. The Economic Council of the Reich shall have the right itself to propose such legislation.[127]

There may be some truth in Lee's analysis as Figgis was notoriously enamoured with that particular document. However, Figgis, writing in 1917, two years before the enactment of the Weimar Constitution, had already described the genesis of the provision in his book on the Gaelic state. Thus, while the German Constitution may have had an influence, it seems more likely that it was the inspiration for Mortished's scheme[128] rather than the one inserted into the 1922 Constitution. The original inspiration for that provision came from the research of Figgis into the Gaelic state.[129]

A further source of inspiration for this provision may have been Article 68 of the Polish Constitution of 1921. That provision states:

In addition to territorial autonomy, a special law shall provide for autonomy in the various branches of economic life by the establishment of councils representing agriculture, commerce, industry, skilled labour, salaried employment, etc., which shall form together the Supreme Economic Council of the Republic. The co-operation of the Supreme Economic Council with the State in common control of economic affairs and in legislation shall be determined by law.[130]

In March 1922, Figgis brought this provision to the attention of Collins in order to demonstrate his idea in relation to functional representation.[131]

Although the scheme may have had various different sources of inspiration, the strength of the idea can be seen in each of the three Drafts and it was evidently felt that this device would satisfy a number of different interests including the Southern Unionists (because it would help to limit the powers of central government and encourage the involvement of the councils in governance), those with socialist ideals, the Trade Unions and the Catholic Church.

---

[127] *Select Constitutions of the World*, 238–9.
[128] See below.
[129] Figgis admitted as much in his book *The Irish Constitution Explained* (Dublin, 1922), 59.
[130] See *Select Constitutions of the World*, 95.
[131] Hugh Kennedy Papers, P4/309, Trinity College Dublin Archives.

The result of all of these influences is Article 45, which states:

The Oireachtas may provide for the establishment of Functional or Vocational Councils representing branches of the social and economic life of the Nation. A law establishing any such Council shall determine its powers, rights and duties, and its relation to the government of the Irish Free State (Saorstát Éireann).

It was decided to make the activation of this provision optional rather than to provide for the establishment of such councils straight away. This was because it was felt that preparation had to be carried out first in order to create the councils, as, apart from the legal and medical professions, there was no other vocational group sufficiently organised to act as the basis for providing representation.

Alternative visions for implementing functional representation

There were two possible visions for the idea of functional representation in the Free State Constitution; one involving the executive and the other involving the legislature. The first, which was the one eventually adopted, was outlined by Kohn, who has written that the 'complex and ambitious' scheme was intended to complement the external ministers scheme:

Councils, if and when established, were to form part of the central machinery of the State. They were clearly designed not as advisory committees, but as representative bodies of such authoritative status as to be entrusted, if Parliament so decided, *with the recommendation of Extern Ministers* from among their members. When it is considered that Ministers were, under the terms of the Draft Constitution, to form a majority of the Cabinet and to enjoy a more permanent tenure of office than their parliamentary colleagues, the significance of that authorization may be inferred.[132]

So, under this scheme it was obviously envisaged that in a few years, following the enactment of the Constitution, the various different sections of society would have organised into their own representative groups. The Oireachtas would then pass the necessary legislation to activate Article 45 and the groups themselves would either become or elect the vocational councils. The councils would then elect the external ministers.

However, the idea of functional representation was alternatively proposed for the Seanad. Mortished, one of the secretaries to the Constitution Committee, wrote a memorandum on this subject.[133] In his memorandum he describes how parliaments 'are having to devote increasing amounts of time to industrial questions' and that 'the parliamentary machinery does not secure to the individual a proper share in the consideration of these matters'. He decided that there were two possible solutions to this problem. The first would be to set up a chamber

---

[132] Kohn, *Constitution of the Irish Free State*, 248, emphasis added.
[133] R.J.P. Mortished, Memorandum on Functional Representation, document 7, in Hugh Kennedy Papers, P4/320, Trinity College Dublin Archives.

especially qualified by the methods of its election to deal with vocational questions as part of Parliament itself. This method was entirely experimental as it had not been adopted in any country. The second solution would set up machinery outside Parliament but connected to it. This is the system which was adopted in the German Constitution.

He admitted that there would be great difficulty in establishing a functional chamber as part of ordinary Parliament. He noted the problems of overlapping employment categories or having electoral categories which would be too broad. He suggested the use of indirect elections by Trade Unions and employers' federations in order to simplify the problem of election.

Ultimately, he suggested functional representation be provided for, along German lines, by establishing separate economic machinery. However, he acknowledged that German councils had already existed before their Constitution was enacted, unlike Ireland where there were no such councils. He reached the conclusion therefore that the best view would be for the Parliament to have power to give statutory recognition to bodies outside of Parliament as being competent to advise the legislature as to framing of laws and assist the executive in administration of them. Powers and scope of bodies could be left to the legislature.

Executive scheme chosen

The Constitution Committee ultimately decided on Figgis's original idea of functional representation in the Executive. The original Article 54a[134] stated:

> Citizens engaged in any function, vocation, or industry have the right to establish representative councils, deriving their sanction and authority from the persons engaged in such functions, vocations, or industries for the regulation and control of all matters directly affecting them in that capacity, provided that such right shall not be used in a manner prejudicial to other citizens, or the common weal. The deliberations of such Councils may be presided over by the Minister of Dáil Éireann concerned with such functions vocations or industries. Dáil Éireann may grant charters to such Councils recognising their rights and defining their liberties and duties.[135]

In a newspaper article, Douglas gave his views on vocational councils:

> I am strongly in favour of the creation of vocational councils, and believe that Ministers should be members of such councils, and be nominated with their approval. Some such system will do more to curb an autocratic executive than any I can conceive of, and I contend that it will only be really workable if Ministers acting in conjunction with such councils are chosen without regard to party and have no party in the House dependent on their votes.[136]

[134] This was before the Committee had decided on separate Drafts. This Article did not make it into any of the final drafts.

[135] Hugh Kennedy Papers, P4/323, Trinity College Dublin Archives.

[136] Newspaper clipping (27 June 1922), with name of paper missing. Alfred O'Rahilly Papers, P178, University College Dublin Archives.

Kennedy expressed a similar view in putting forward the argument for the adoption of the external ministers scheme:

> Another important point is that the provision for a number of ministers who shall not be actual members of the House will make the development of vocational councils much more likely to be effective. It will then be possible, as is referred to in Art 53 for the vocational councils to nominate the ministers.[137]

So the executive scheme was incorporated into the Free State Constitution by Article 45[138] along with Article 56 (which was referred to above by Kennedy at the drafting stage as Article 53). The latter Article provided that 'should arrangements for Functional or Vocational Councils be made by the Oireachtas these [external] Ministers or any of them may, should the Oireachtas so decide, be members of, and be recommended to Dáil Éireann by, such Councils'.

However, whether it was felt that society was still insufficiently organised or whether the government lost interest in the idea, Article 45 was never activated. Thus, it is pointless to speculate on whether or not the scheme would have been successful had it been implemented or whether it could have improved the external ministers scheme. Despite this, its inclusion in the Constitution has shown the commitment of the Committee and the Constituent Assembly in 1922 to the idea of involving the people in government and finding alternatives to traditional party politics. The failure of successive governments to implement the scheme is indicative of the weakness of their commitment to the same ideal.

Alternative adoption in Bunreacht na hÉireann

The provision was retained in 1937, although it was essentially Mortished's scheme which was adopted; Article 15.3 states:

> The Oireachtas may provide for the establishment or recognition of functional or vocational councils representing branches of the social and economic life of the people.
> A law establishing or recognizing any such council shall determine its rights, powers and duties, and its relation to the Oireachtas and to the Government.[139]

Article 19 of Bunreacht na hÉireann makes it clear that these councils, if established, would have been involved in the legislature:

> Provision may be made by law for the direct election by any functional or vocational group or association or council of so many members of Seanad Éireann as may be

---

[137] Hugh Kennedy Papers, P4/308, University College Dublin Archives.

[138] 'The Oireachtas may provide for the establishment of Functional or Vocational Councils representing branches of the social and economic life of the Nation. A law establishing any such Council shall determine its powers, rights and duties, and its relation to the government of the Irish Free State (Saorstát Éireann).'

[139] Article 15.3.1 and 15.3.2 of Bunreacht na hÉireann.

fixed by such law in substitution for an equal number of the members to be elected from the corresponding panels of candidates constituted under Article 18 of this Constitution.

That the provision was written into the 1937 Constitution almost as an after-thought to the Seanad provisions is indicative of a lack of intent to ever use the provision. Although it is difficult to imagine why the provision was included if there was no real intention behind it, J.M. Kelly has suggested that 'it may have been wished not to drop a provision which had proved harmless'.[140] Either way, as with its predecessor in 1922, there was never any attempt made to activate the provision. In fact Lee has described de Valera's reluctance even to acknowledge the idea.[141]

The Seanad[142]

Like the PR-STV experiment, the Seanad was originally included in the Constitution in order to satisfy the terms of an agreement reached between Griffith and the Southern Unionists. The Committee was originally apprehensive about the creation of a second House. However, this being one of the only stipu-lations given to them by Collins, the Committee commenced an intense study of second chambers. While the original motivation behind the inclusion of a second Chamber may have had little to do with anti-party politics, it soon became clear that a second House not devised on party lines but composed of senatorial persons of high integrity would be another check on the party system and would provide another boost to the anti-party theme.

The first Seanad

As seen in Chapter 1, there were disagreements in relation to the powers and com-position of the proposed second Chamber, and this led to slightly different plans being presented in the three Drafts. There were few significant changes made to the Seanad provisions in the Constituent Assembly[143] and the scheme envisaged

---

[140] J.M. Kelly, *The Irish Constitution* (Dublin, 2003), 267.

[141] Pius XI had published a papal encyclical, *Quadragesimo Ano*, on corporatist prin-ciples, and the Commission on the Second House of the Oireachtas recommended the incorporation of a vocational element into Senate elections in 1936. Because of these, de Valera had to show interest in the idea. Moreover, he could not appear to reject papal teaching but, despite many opportunities to introduce the concept, he failed to do so. Lee explains that this was due to his fear of losing his powerful majority. See Lee, 'Aspects of Corporatist Thought', 325.

[142] For an excellent account of the Seanad during the Irish Free State years, see O'Sullivan, *The Irish Free State and Its Senate*.

[143] The most significant change was the movement of the University representatives from the Seanad to the Dáil. The result was a Seanad of 56 members but this was

in the final document was as follows. Article 30 stated that the Seanad would be composed of 'citizens who shall be proposed on the grounds that they have done honour to the Nation by reason of useful public service or that, because of special qualifications or attainments, they represent important aspects of the Nation's life'. The House would comprise 60 members of at least 35 years of age who would serve for a term of 12 years.[144] A quarter of the members would be elected on the basis of PR every three years with the state as one constituency and an electorate of all citizens of 30 years and over.[145] Members would be elected from a panel, which would contain three times as many qualified persons as vacancies. Two-thirds of the panel would be nominated by the Dáil and one-third by the Seanad.[146] John Coakley has noted that 'it was intended that these would have an important filter effect, ensuring that candidates of an appropriate quality were put forward'.[147] Article 33 also provided that the method for proposal and selection of nominees would be decided by each House but special reference was to be had 'to the necessity for arranging for the representation of important interests and institutions in the country'.

In order to simplify matters and rather than providing for the immediate direct election of 60 senators, a special procedure was provided for the composition of the very first Seanad: 30 members would be nominated by the President of the Executive Council[148] and 30 would be elected by the Dáil. On 6 December 1922, President Cosgrave announced his nominations for the Seanad.[149] Donal O'Sullivan has commented in relation to the list of names that 'Anyone with a knowledge of Ireland must agree that this was a remarkable list'.[150] He notes further that 16 of the 30 were Southern Unionists and among them were men who had given distinguished service to their country in different ways; and commerce, administration and regional interests were well represented among the

then restored to 60 members during the Report stage. In addition, the original Bill had given 14 days for the consideration of a money bill and this was later changed to 21 days. A new Article (57) was also inserted which gave the ministers the right to be heard in the Seanad.

144   Article 31.
145   Article 32 and Article 14.
146   Article 33.
147   John Coakley, 'Ireland's Unique Electoral Experiment: The Senate Election of 1925' (2005) 20 (3) *Irish Political Studies* 231, 236.
148   Donal O'Sullivan has noted that 'it had been agreed with the Southern Unionists that the President's nominations were to be made "in a manner calculated to represent minorities or interests not represented adequately in the Dáil" and on the advice of certain named bodies'. A resolution was then passed in accordance with that agreement on 25 October 1922. The 'certain named bodies' were listed as the Chamber of Commerce, the Royal College of Physicians of Ireland, the Royal College of Surgeons in Ireland, the Benchers of the Honourable Society of King's Inns, the Incorporated Law Society of Ireland and Councils of the County Boroughs of the Irish Free State. See O'Sullivan, *The Irish Free State and Its Senate*, 89–90.
149   For the list of nominees, see *ibid.*, 90.
150   *Ibid.*

remaining 14.[151] O'Sullivan also points out a curious omission in that not a single lawyer appeared on the list. The election of the final 30 members was somewhat more chaotic due to the fact that the electorate had been reduced from 128 Dáil members to 86 by the refusal of the anti-Treaty delegates to take their seats. Furthermore, there were 113 candidates for the 30 seats.[152] The 30 elected were assigned three- or nine-year terms by lot, the first 30 having been nominated to either six- or 12-year terms by Cosgrave.[153]

O'Sullivan has remarked that

> In view of all of the circumstances, the result was better than might have been anticipated ... Taking the Senate as a whole, and apart from the absence of adequate legal representation, we see it as a body admirably qualified for the task of expert revision which was to be its main function under the Constitution. It was much more truly a microcosm of the country than was the Dáil, comprising as it did representatives of the professions, commerce, agriculture, letters, organized labour, banking, and the landlord interest.[154]

It was a religiously diverse House in that it consisted of 36 Catholics and 24 non-Catholics including Protestants, one Jew and three Quakers. It has also been noted that there were no organised political parties in the Seanad except for the small group of five Labour Party members.[155] During the early debates, W.B. Yeats declared: 'We do not represent constituencies; we are drawn together to represent certain forms of special knowledge, certain special interests, but we are just as much passionately concerned in these great questions as the Dáil.'[156] Senator Jameson also remarked: 'We have our own individual opinion about things. I do not believe there is any member of the Senate ... who is belonging to a party, or in any way shaping his actions or votes in the interest of any party.'[157] Furthermore, O'Sullivan has commented that 'a rigid alignment of parties can hardly be said to have taken place until December 1928, when the election of a number of Mr De Valera's supporters, new to the Senate and its traditions, made that course inevitable'.[158] Thus, in the beginning, the Seanad appears to have been successful in its role as a senatorial House without the influence of party but again it seems that Civil War politics distorted this development.

The first Seanad met on 11 December 1922, and from then on members of the Seanad worked on the large blocks of legislation which were often sent from

---

[151] *Ibid.*, 91.

[152] *Ibid.*, 93. For the list of elected senators, see 94.

[153] The staggering of terms was originally necessary in order to achieve the situation envisaged in the Constitution whereby a quarter of the Senate would retire every three years, requiring triennial elections.

[154] O'Sullivan, *The Irish Free State and Its Senate*, 94–5.

[155] *Ibid.*, 117.

[156] *Seanad Debates*, vol 1, col 167, 24 January 1923.

[157] *Ibid.*, col 155.

[158] O'Sullivan, *The Irish Free State and Its Senate*, 117–18.

the Dáil. In the first eight months, 47 Acts covering almost every aspect of the national life were passed,[159] and Tom Garvin has commented that the Seanad took 'an active, independent and effective role in public affairs'.[160] Soon, a quarter of the Seanad terms had expired and, in 1925, the first and only popular election for the Seanad took place. This has been described as 'possibly the most complex election ever carried out by the Single Transferrable Vote'.[161] This was because 76 candidates ran for 19[162] places with an electorate of about 1,345,000.[163]

The 1925 election

The Constitution had not specified the details involved in the nomination process and so these had been provided by the Electoral Act 1923, and Coakley has commented that: 'The legislators of 1923 underestimated the potential difficulty of the election'.[164] This is because the system of nomination was quite complex: the outgoing senators were all automatically eligible for re-election, then the Seanad had to select another 19 candidates by PR-STV from a list of 29 and the Dáil then had to select 38 candidates from a possible 57 by the same process. The large numbers involved meant that many of the candidates did not have the senatorial characteristics desired by Article 30 and the Article was interpreted rather broadly.[165] Furthermore, the fact that the outgoing senators were eligible to participate in the nomination of their opponents in the election led to the failure of some very desirable candidates.[166]

Once the nomination process was completed, the 26 counties now had to vote as one constituency, and voters faced a ballot-paper with 76 names on it. Nicholas Whyte has commented that '[P]arty politics were ... not a strong feature of the campaign' and he has noted in particular that 'Cumann na nGaedheal declined to run a party political campaign for its candidates'.[167] Coakley has noted similarly

---

[159] *Ibid.*, 123.

[160] Tom Garvin, *The Irish Senate* (Dublin, 1969), 1.

[161] Nicholas Whyte, 'The Irish Senate Elections of 1925: An Exceedingly Severe Test' (17 February 2002), available on the Northern Ireland Social and Political Archive 'Ark' at www.ark.ac.uk/elections/h1925.htm

[162] The 15 original three-year senators now had to run for re-election and four vacancies had also been filled by co-option in the interim and these also had to run, which made a total of 19 vacancies.

[163] Whyte, 'Irish Senate Elections', 1.

[164] Coakley, 'Ireland's Unique Electoral Experiment', 234.

[165] Whyte gives examples such as one candidate who was a teacher who 'for many years has taken [a] deep interest in public affairs'. See Whyte, 'Irish Senate Elections', 1.

[166] O'Sullivan lists Lady Gregory, John J. Horgan and L. Grattan Esmonde among others, and he notes that 'it is perhaps not cynical to assume that some of them [the outgoing senators] might not be over-anxious that candidates should be returned who would prove formidable rivals at the election'. See O'Sullivan, *The Irish Free State and Its Senate*, 154.

[167] Whyte, 'Irish Senate Elections', 2.

that 'The election campaign contrasted most obviously with a Dáil election campaign in the enormous size of the constituency and the subdued role of the political parties'.[168] However, Kohn has remarked that this fact made it a more difficult choice for the electorate.[169]

The election was held on a very wet day on 17 September 1925, and less than a quarter of the electorate turned out to vote.[170] It took nearly a week to check and count the ballot-papers and, although the official count started on 25 September, it did not end until 19 October. Of the 19 outgoing senators, only eight were re-elected. O'Sullivan felt that this was a good result in that '[n]ot a single candidate of the "professional politician" type was successful, and none of the new Senators could be described as an extreme party man'.[171] While the election itself was a complicated process, the PR Society termed it 'a triumph for PR'[172] and Whyte has pointed out that while 'few modern supporters of STV would be totally enthusiastic about a nationwide constituency to elect so many representatives from so many candidates, ... in fact this was the system envisaged by Thomas Hare, the originator of STV, for electing the entire Westminster Parliament'.[173] Furthermore, Coakley has commented: 'In principle, though, the process of vote counting should not present an insuperable barrier to the effective conduct of an election of this kind'[174] and Kohn admitted: 'The single instance in which the elaborate scheme embodied in the Constitution was applied offers insufficient material for an appreciation of its merits.'[175]

However, critics considered the method to be impractical, and a joint committee of both Houses was set up, which recommended the abolition of the system. The government had spent £100,000 of public money on the election and, as Whyte has noted, saw 'little political reward for doing so'.[176] Thus, a number of amendments were made to the Constitution[177] with the result that, by 1928, direct

---

[168] Coakley, 'Ireland's Unique Electoral Experiment', 241.

[169] 'Election on grounds of personal merit is not practical politics in the diversified conditions of a modern democracy.' See Kohn, *Constitution of the Irish Free State*, 194.

[170] Coakley, 'Ireland's Unique Electoral Experiment', 244.

[171] O'Sullivan, *The Irish Free State and Its Senate*, 156.

[172] Whyte, 'Irish Senate Elections', 3.

[173] *Ibid.*

[174] Coakley, 'Ireland's Unique Electoral Experiment', 255.

[175] Kohn, *Constitution of the Irish Free State*, 194.

[176] Whyte, 'Irish Senate Elections', 3.

[177] Constitution (Amendment No. 1) Act (11 July 1925), which made changes relating to the terms of office of senators and to the date on which senatorial elections were to be held; Constitution (Amendment No. 10) Act (12 July 1928), which removed a number of provisions for direct democracy from the constitution such as the right of the Senate to force a referendum on certain bills; Constitution (Amendment No. 6) Act (23 July 1928), which replaced the direct election of the Senate with the system of indirect election; Constitution (Amendment No. 13) Act (23 July 1928), which extended the Senate's power of delay over legislation from nine to 20 months; Constitution (Amendment No. 8) Act (25 October 1928), which reduced the age

elections for the Seanad had been removed from the Constitution; it was provided instead that the number of nominees would be equal to twice the number of seats to be filled and that half would be elected by the Dáil and the other half by the Seanad. The right of outgoing senators to nominate themselves was also removed. Sircar and Hoyland have remarked that these changes benefited party politics:

> The effect of these changes not only benefited Fianna Fáil, but also members of Cosgrave's party. By contrast, independent Senators could not gain from support from vocational or other non-party organizations as they had in the direct elections of 1925 ... The changes in the selection rules reflected the preferences of the members of the Joint Committee. For both Fianna Fáil and the Government party, an Upper House populated with loyal party members would result in a more compliant Seanad versus a chamber filled with non-partisan independents. Adherence and loyalty to the party could be rewarded with a nomination to the Seanad. Since the 'electorate' for the Seanad was the same as the nominating body, this led to a partisan Seanad.[178]

It was at this stage also that Fianna Fáil members entered the Seanad and the House necessarily became more party-orientated. As Garvin has noted, from 1928 onwards the Seanad became more and more dominated by party and Fianna Fáil, in particular, espoused contempt for the House.[179] Thus, in response to attempts by the Seanad to oppose certain of his proposals, de Valera decided to abolish the institution. This was effected on 25 May 1936.[180]

Anti-party politics and the Seanad

Many people would consider the Seanad of the Irish Free State a complete failure, and perhaps the long list of amendments to the Seanad provisions and the eventual abolition of the House is evidence of that. The system was unnecessarily complicated, perhaps because of the fact that the original proposal, whereby the whole state would vote as one constituency envisaged a senate of only 40 members. As a result of the agreement with the Southern Unionists the number was increased

of eligibility for senators from 35 to 30; Constitution (Amendment No. 9) Act (25 October 1928), which removed the existing provisions for the nomination of Senate candidates and empowered the Oireachtas to make alternative arrangements by law. The new system of nomination was then introduced by the Seanad Electoral Act, 1928 (enacted on the same day); Constitution (Amendment No. 7) Act (30 October 1928), which reduced the term of office of senators from 12 years to nine years.

[178] Indraneel Sircar & Bjorn Hoyland, 'Get the Party Started: Development of Political Party Legislative Dynamics in the Irish Free State Seanad (1922–36)' (2010) 16 *Party Politics* 89, 107.

[179] De Valera was particularly contemptuous towards the Seanad. Sircar & Hoyland, 'Get the Party Started', 91: 'The Fianna Fáil party had been hostile towards the existence of the Seanad and promised to abolish or reduce its membership.' Also see Garvin, *The Irish Senate*, 5, 9.

[180] For detail on how the Seanad was abolished, see Sircar & Hoyland, 'Get the Party Started', 97.

to 60 but no changes were made to the election system. During the debates in the Constituent Assembly, Figgis spoke out against the impracticality of the system when the numbers had increased.[181] Unfortunately, the system remained unchanged.

However, in relation to anti-party politics, for a while at least the Seanad was quite effective. A general perusal of the members of the early Seanad will show that persons of high standing were elected and there was very little party influence. O'Sullivan wrote of the first Seanad:

> This new Senate was in a position to realize, in microcosm, [Thomas] Davis's dream of a united Ireland wherein all men of goodwill would work together in a self-respecting, self-governing motherland: and, given the conditions, a spirit of co-operation there engendered and fostered might in time infuse the whole polity.[182]

He also mentioned the election of Lord Glenavy as chairman of the House when, despite the fact that he had been 'Edward Carson's right-hand man in the campaign of opposition to Home Rule', the nationalists 'made it clear that these things belonged to the dead past'. O'Sullivan felt that 'the fostering of this spirit was made easier by the fact that there were no organized political parties'.[183] Moreover, using a sophisticated data collection methodology, Sircar and Hoyland have demonstrated that there was no significant block voting in the early Seanad and have concluded that 'Members of the Seanad were largely non-partisan from 1922 until 1928'.[184] Accordingly, there is much evidence of the fact that party was not an element of the Seanad before 1928 and therefore, until that time, the institution functioned along the lines of what was intended.

However, somewhat ironically, as Sircar and Hoyland have noted: 'The establishment of disciplined parties also sealed the fate of the legislature when the Fianna Fáil party, hostile to the Free State Seanad, became an organized force inside the institution.'[185] It was not until 1928 that the Seanad became dominated by party and Sircar and Hoyland have commented that 'The onset of party political dynamics continued through the remaining two elections in the life of the Seanad ... The relative strengths of the political parties in the Dáil over the next two general elections sealed the fate of the Seanad'.[186] Thus, like the external ministers experiment, to a certain extent, party politics (facilitated by the technical changes made in 1928) helped to destroy the device which had been intended as a component in the anti-party theme.

Whatever about the Seanad as an institution generally, as a device which was intended to prevent the domination of party politics, the Seanad was relatively

---

[181] *Dáil Debates*, vol 1, col 1155, 4 October 1922.
[182] O'Sullivan, *The Irish Free State and Its Senate*, 116.
[183] *Ibid.*, 117.
[184] Sircar & Hoyland, 'Get the Party Started', 101. However, the analysis showed that Labour Party members did sometimes vote together.
[185] *Ibid.*, 90.
[186] *Ibid.*, 96.

successful until Civil War politics again intervened. If heed had been taken of Figgis's warning perhaps it would have been even more successful with a less confusing system. In fact, in recent times it has been praised as 'a House which was not divided along party lines' and one which 'fundamentally influenced the guiding principles, legislative foundations and institutional structures of the Irish State'.[187] Thus, this was one area in which the anti-party experiment was relatively successful for a time.

Conclusion

The anti-party theme was introduced into the Constitution in order to prevent domination by parties and to bring politics closer to the people. The devices of the referendum and initiative were also intended to complement the anti-party theme by encouraging the participation of the people in the political process and thus limit the involvement of dominant parties. The anti-party theme was also intended to strengthen the theme of popular sovereignty as it envisaged the involvement of the people in functional councils and it was hoped to inspire the people with an interest in politics by the use of further devices such as PR-STV, expert external ministers and an independent Seanad.

Each of these devices constituted a brave step towards the goal of complete political reform. The fact that they did not succeed cannot take away from the enormous significance of the experiment. It would have been much safer to follow, without question, the traditional British system, as other Dominions had done previously. However, the ambitious members of the Constitution Committee and the Irish government wanted to achieve something greater and set themselves apart. They wanted to avoid the shame and corruption of past experiences[188] and to prove to the Irish people that this Constitution truly belonged to them and that the people should be involved in running the country. The anti-party theme was, initially, quite strong and a commendable effort was made to ensure that the Constitution would promote that theme.

Unfortunately, Civil War tensions, poor forecasting, failure to follow through completely with the experiments and a general waning of enthusiasm all meant that none of these novel departures succeeded. The Treaty split meant that PR-STV could not have the effect of spawning smaller political groupings. Fear and laziness possibly contributed most to the failure of the external ministers scheme, the functional representation scheme failed because it was simply

---

[187] Elaine Byrne, 'Do Not Ditch the Seanad but Finesse It as a Political Dynamo', *The Irish Times*, 27 October 2009.

[188] Ireland's Parliament of 1789 came to an end with the Act of Union in 1800. This involved much bribery and corruption and remained a point of shame for the Irish people even a decade later. See Laura Cahillane, 'Ireland's Forgotten Constitutions' (2009) 27 *Irish Law Times* 243.

ignored or forgotten and, while the Seanad resisted party politics for a time, Civil War politics eventually overcame this. The entry of de Valera and his supporters into parliamentary politics marked the end of a certain mind-set. Party lines began to harden and the original enthusiasm for anti-party politics disappeared as opinion now favoured strong parties for political stability.[189] The reasons for the reassertion of party politics cannot be stated definitively but the assassination on 10 July 1927 of O'Higgins, which revived fears of revolutionary violence and the apparent weakness of coalition governments, added to the growing strength of the Fianna Fáil party, all contributed.[190]

So these experiments failed to impact upon the Irish constitutional and political system, at least in the way intended, but their inclusion in the 1922 Constitution demonstrates what was originally envisaged for the Irish state and, under different conditions, they might have proved more successful.

[189] O'Leary, *Irish Elections*, 25–6.
[190] *Ibid.*, 24.

9

The legacy of the Irish Free State Constitution

Introduction

Opinions diverge on the success of the Irish Free State Constitution. While some highlight positively the liberal democratic nature and experimental features of the Constitution,[1] others concentrate on the number of amendments and the short lifespan of the document. The most extreme criticism is that the Constitution was 'a deeply flawed project which ended in almost total failure'.[2] However, that the 1937 Constitution retained and reused most of its predecessor is a testament to the earlier document. To John Kelly, the 1937 Constitution 'was very largely a re-bottling of wine most of which was by then quite old and of familiar vintages'. He went so far as to conclude that 'it is quite possible that the State might have developed, within the 1922 framework, in much the same way as it ultimately did within that of 1937'.[3] Garret FitzGerald has commented similarly that a 'very large part' of the 1937 Constitution was 'in fact the Constitution

---

[1] Professor Dermot Keogh has commented that the document was exceptional in a number of ways: 'Firstly, it was a constitution for a new dominion which was an integral part of the United Kingdom of Great Britain and Ireland. That set a precedent. Secondly, it was written in less than ideal circumstances but, notwithstanding the difficulties, the Irish drafting team were a match professionally for their British counterparts ... The Free State Constitution was concise, clear and unadorned with the detail of the 1937 Constitution. It was a fine example of how Irish revolutionary nationalists – of the Collins way of thinking – could craft a document based on the idea that Dominion status was not fixed and that in an evolving British Commonwealth of Nations the freedom to achieve freedom could be utilised to the full – and it was by both W.T. Cosgrave and by Eamon de Valera.' He opined that it was superior in many ways to the 1937 document. Interview with Professor Keogh, University College Cork, 13 January 2011.

[2] Richard Humphreys, 'Review of Kelly: The Irish Constitution, Third Edition' (1994) 16 *Dublin University Law Journal* 222.

[3] J.M. Kelly, preface to the first edition, in J.M. Kelly, *The Irish Constitution*, eds Gerard Hogan & Gerry Whyte (Dublin, 2003).

of 1922, with the language in many cases unchanged'.[4] While, in 1922, the Constitution Committee started from scratch to build up a new legal and political system rather than 'simply turning to any existing Dominion Constitutions for a model',[5] the 1937 Constitution includes many provisions from the 1922 document word for word or restates older provisions[6] and even material discarded from early drafts of the 1922 Constitution.[7] As the principal additions to Bunreacht na hÉireann are the introduction of the President and the associated institutions and a more comprehensive Bill of Rights, Kelly's view that the 1937 document was a stabilising and reforming continuation of that of 1922 is fair comment. Although the 1922 Constitution was replaced within 15 years of its enactment, a significant number of its provisions live on in its replacement, and

---

[4] Garret Fitzgerald, 'The Irish Constitution in its Historical Context' in Tim Murphy & Patrick Twomey, *Ireland's Evolving Constitution 1937–1997: Collected Essays* (Oxford, 1998), 32.

[5] Hugh Kennedy, 'Character and Sources of the Constitution of the Irish Free State', An Address delivered at the meeting of the American Bar Association at Seattle, Washington, 25 July 1928, 1928 14 (8) *American Bar Association Journal* 443.

[6] Article 6 of 1937 is the same as Article 2 of 1922. Article 8 of 1937 is fundamentally the same as Article 4 of 1922. Article 10 of 1937 is like Article 11 of 1922. Article 15.2 of 1937 is comparable with Article 12 of 1922. Article 15.2.1 of 1937 is similar to Article 44 of 1922. Article 15.3 of 1937 is substantially similar to Article 45 of 1922. Article 15.5.1 of 1937 is the same as Article 43 of 1922. Article 15.6 of 1937 is quite similar to Article 46 of 1922. Many of the provisions on the Oireachtas are the same. Article 16.1 of 1937 reproduces the substance of Articles 14 and 15 of 1922. Article 16.2 of 1937 reproduces most of Article 26 of 1922. Article 17 of 1937 is based substantially on Articles 36 and 37 of 1922. Article 20 of 1937 uses material from Articles 38, 39 and 40 of 1922. Article 21 of 1937 reproduces part of Article 38 of 1922. Article 25 of 1937 corresponds to Articles 41 and 42 of 1922. The provision involved in Article 27 of 1937 is similar to Article 48 of 1922. The first two subsections of Article 28.3 of 1937 substantially reproduce Article 49 of 1922. Article 28.4 of 1937 reuses much of Article 54 of 1922. Articles 28.4 to 28.12 of 1937 contain similar material to Articles 51-59 of 1922. Article 33 of 1937 is quite similar to Articles 62 and 63 of 1922. The majority of the provisions on the judiciary are in a different order but are taken word for word from 1922. Article 34.3.2 of 1937 is the same as Article 65 of 1922. Article 38.1 of 1937 echoes Article 70 of 1922. Article 38.2 of 1937 contains the substance of Article 72 of 1922. Article 40.2.1 of 1937 is the same as Article 5 of 1922. Article 40.4 of 1937 contains the same sentiments as Article 6 of 1922. Article 40.5 of 1937 contains the exact wording of Article 7 of 1922. Article 40.6 of 1937 corresponds to Article 9 of 1922. Article 44.2 of 1937 takes the beginning of Article 8 of 1922. Articles 49 and 50 of 1937 contain more or less the same wording as Article 73 of 1922.

[7] For example, the Preamble of 1937 is very similar to the draft preamble of 1922, which was taken out before the draft was sent to London. Article 1 of 1937 is very like the preliminary Articles in the early drafts of 1922. Article 5 of 1937 is the same as a draft Article of 1922. Also, many of the provisions in relation to the family, education and religion in 1937 are based on O'Rahilly's Draft C. See letter from de Valera to O'Rahilly on 27 March 1934, returning O'Rahilly's drafts of the 1922 Constitution and thanking him 'for the lend' of them; Alfred O'Rahilly Papers, P178, University College Dublin Archives.

other provisions of the 1937 Constitution were influenced by the experience of their 1922 predecessors.

When assessing the successes and failures of the 1922 Constitution and exploring whether the failures of the document are attributable to its drafting or to circumstances which arose later, two areas are worth examining. The amendment procedure is of relevance because it was a controversial aspect of the 1922 Constitution and one which 'ultimately proved to be the means whereby the entire 1922 Constitution was undone'.[8] In addition the judicial review provision requires consideration because it was a surprising inclusion in 1922 but one which was never truly set in motion during the Constitution's lifespan.

Lessons learned: amendment

The method of amendment of the 1922 Constitution has plagued public memory of the document. It contained two methods of constitutional amendment.[9] The method which was originally intended and which was the only one included in the Drafts, as provided for in Article 50, was the referendum. To pass, a constitutional amendment had to be favoured by a majority of registered voters or two-thirds of the votes recorded, after having already passed through the Oireachtas. This contrasts with a referendum for ordinary legislation where only a majority of the votes actually recorded was needed.

Significantly, the second method of amendment, which allowed the Oireachtas to amend the Constitution by ordinary statute, was added as a qualification to Article 50 during the debates in the Constituent Assembly. It felt that, while the referendum was an important democratic device, it was a process which would become cumbersome if the need for minor changes to the Constitution became evident following promulgation. Kevin O'Higgins recognised that the Constitution was being debated with 'undue haste' and that only when the Constitution was in operation would any 'latent defects' become apparent.[10]

It was decided during the Committee stage to introduce a clause allowing the Constitution to be amended by ordinary legislation for a specified period in order to facilitate teething problems. All parties were satisfied with this arrangement. O'Higgins had originally suggested a five-year transitional period. However, Thomas Johnson, leader of the Labour Party, felt that this was not adequate and suggested seven or 10 years 'because it is obvious, that constitutional matters will not be in the minds of the people if these other legislative demands are being

---

[8] Gerard Hogan, 'A Desert Island Case Set in the Silver Sea: The State (Ryan) v. Lennon (1934)' in Eoin O'Dell (ed.), *Leading Cases of the Twentieth Century* (Dublin, 2000), 96–7.

[9] The initiative could potentially have been a third, if it had been activated.

[10] *Dáil Debates*, vol 1, col 1237, 5 October 1922 (Kevin O'Higgins).

attended to in the Parliament'.[11] O'Higgins agreed to eight years, or the life of two parliaments. Deputies voiced their approval and it is clear that all sides felt that this was an improvement.[12] However, as the next section will show, as a result of careless drafting the qualification had an effect which was never intended.

The final version of Article 50 reads:

> Amendments of this Constitution within the terms of the Scheduled Treaty may be made by the Oireachtas, but no such amendment, passed by both Houses of the Oireachtas, after the expiration of a period of eight years from the date of the coming into operation of this Constitution, shall become law, unless the same shall, after it has been passed or deemed to have been passed by the said two Houses of the Oireachtas, have been submitted to a Referendum of the people, and unless a majority of the voters on the register shall have recorded their votes on such Referendum, and either the votes of a majority of the voters on the register, or two-thirds of the votes recorded shall have been cast in favour of such amendment. Any such amendment may be made within the said period of eight years by way of ordinary legislation and as such shall be subject to the provisions of Article 47 hereof.

So in essence, the Article provided that, for the first eight years of the Irish Free State, the Constitution could be amended by ordinary legislation. However, no procedure was specified and it was not provided that any bill which purported to amend the Constitution must do so expressly. Moreover, there was nothing to prevent what eventually happened, namely the amendment of the amendment provision itself. The lack of detail on the method of parliamentary amendment led to some confusion, and questions arose over whether the Constitution could be amended implicitly.

Implicit amendment

Discussing the amendment provision, Kohn considered the question of implicit amendment. He argued that 'If, during the initial period, the Constitution is not invested with higher authority than any act passed by the Oireachtas, the question inevitably arises whether it may not be regarded as implicitly amended by the enactment of any law which contravenes its provisions'. This was a question of 'basic importance' to Kohn because he saw that 'any law passed during the initial period may, if repugnant to the Constitution, be construed as an effective amendment of the latter, a position of grave insecurity must inevitably arise'.[13] Nevertheless, Kohn concluded, citing statements from the Dáil, that the Constitution could not be amended implicitly, although he recommended a constitutional amendment to that effect just to remedy the confusion.[14]

---

[11] *Ibid.*, col 1238.

[12] In particular, Gavan Duffy congratulated the minister and, significantly, Figgis also expressed approval. See *ibid.*, col 1238.

[13] Leo Kohn, *The Constitution of the Irish Free State* (London, 1932), 254.

[14] *Ibid.*, 256.

In July 1923, during the debates on the first Public Safety Act, Gavan Duffy warned the government that the interpretation could be taken that anything which offended against the Constitution must have been meant as an amendment. However, Cosgrave dismissed this statement. He maintained that all legislation must be construed as being in accordance with the Constitution.[15] When Gavan Duffy suggested an amendment to ensure that the adverse interpretation could not be taken, the Ceann Comhairle[16] ruled it out of order. Cathal O'Shannon[17] then asked what would happen if certain sections of the Public Safety Act did contravene the Constitution. The Ceann Comhairle referred him to Article 65, explaining that the High Court could declare them null and void. This appeared to be the end of the discussion.

The case of *R (Cooney) v. Clinton*,[18] an appeal from the judgment of the King's Bench Division in relation to a writ of *habeas corpus*, showed that the discussion had not ended. Cooney was being held under the Indemnity Act 1923. This Act retrospectively validated the decisions of the military courts which had been established to try the anti-Treaty offenders. The case challenged the Act's validity. O'Connor MR considered the validity of passing the Act without an amendment to the Constitution. He decided that the Act itself could be held to be a constitutional amendment:

> It was urged that any Act of Parliament purporting to amend the Constitution should declare that it was so intended, but I cannot accede to that argument in view of the express provision that any amendment made within the period may be made by ordinary legislation.[19]

Most significantly, he added that it was 'difficult to see how, during the period of eight years, any Act passed by the Oireachtas can be impeached as *ultra vires* so long as it is within the terms of the Scheduled Treaty'.[20]

Following this unexpected result the matter was raised again in the Dáil. In June 1924, Tomás Mac Eoin[21] asked Cosgrave whether his attention had been called to the *Cooney* case.[22] He asked the President whether he proposed to amend Article 50 to ensure its interpretation in accordance with the intention of the Constituent Assembly or whether he would take other action to remedy the situation. Cosgrave answered that the late Court of Appeal was not competent to interpret the Constitution and that certain judges of that court were reluctant to recognise the position of Dáil Éireann as a Constituent Assembly. He noted that

---

15 *Dáil Debates*, vol 4, col 420, 10 July 1923.
16 Michael Hayes of Cumann na nGaedheal.
17 Labour Party member.
18 This case was reported in [1935] IR 245 but the case was actually heard on 23 May 1924. It was heard jointly with *R (Corcoran) v. Clinton*.
19 *Ibid*, 247.
20 *Ibid*.
21 Labour Party member.
22 He refers to the case as *Corcoran*.

the late Attorney General had advised the government that the Constitution could not be amended implicitly and that any amendment must be directed expressly to that purpose. Thomas Johnson suggested putting a proviso in every bill that the bill must be read subject to the Constitution. However Cosgrave felt that this would imply that there was a foundation to the judges' contention.

In deciding that the Constitution could not be amended implicitly, Kohn cited Cosgrave's contention that the Court of Appeal was not competent to interpret the Constitution. The government passed all further constitutional amendments, except one,[23] expressly as Acts to amend the Constitution and Kohn felt that this satisfied the matter. It is strange that Kohn failed to mention *Cooney* as, although the case was unreported until 1935, it was referred to in the Dáil in the very passage he cited. The situation appeared to have been clarified by Cosgrave but the Cosgrave government was naive to think that the position was resolved simply because the Attorney General had given advice which contradicted the opinion of the Court of Appeal. It would have been easier to follow the advice of Gavan Duffy or Johnson and clarify the matter by amendment, rather than allow the courts to give an unintended interpretation of an Article which was originally included as a safeguard of democracy and popular sovereignty. However the problem is that *Cooney* was accepted as law and subsequently cited in a number of cases.[24]

Cooney was confirmed four years later by the new High Court in *Attorney General v. McBride*.[25] The background to this case was the Public Safety Act 1927, which had been passed in response to the murder of Kevin O'Higgins.[26] Section 3 of the Act provided that 'every provision of this Act which is in contravention of any provision of the Constitution shall to the extent of such contravention operate and have effect as an amendment for so long only as this Act continues in force of such provision of the Constitution'. The Act was passed through the Oireachtas despite rigorous protests but the validity of the Act was then questioned in *McBride*.

In that case, Justice Hanna asked himself: 'Is it a sufficient compliance in law with Art. 50 to insert in an Act of Parliament, in vague and general terms, a clause such as this – a drag-net – without specifying either any Article, or part of an Article, of the Constitution that is to be amended or whether in fact any amendment is made?'[27] He stated that the Constitution is a sacred charter, not to

---

[23] See below. While the Public Safety Act 1927 did not purport to amend the Constitution by its title, it contained an amendment clause in Section 3.

[24] For example, *Halpin v. Attorney General* [1936] IR 226 and, notably, in *State (Ryan) v. Lennon* [1935] IR 170, 241, Murnaghan J relied on the judgment of O'Connor MR in *Cooney*.

[25] [1928] IR 451.

[26] Following the assassination of O'Higgins by the IRA, Cosgrave felt that it was necessary to introduce harsh measures in an attempt to crush that organisation. The Act provided for special courts, the imprisonment of members of proscribed organisations and detention of suspects for up to three months. It also provided for the death penalty.

[27] [1928] IR 451, 456.

be 'lightly, vaguely, or equivocally tampered with', and conceded that the section 'leaves the subjects of the State, who have rights under the Constitution and rights to exercise against amendments of the Constitution, in the dark as to what is really altered in the Constitution, instead of enlightening them as to any change in their status'. However, he then comes to the following conclusion: '[B]ut, having regard to the wording of Art. 50, that the amendment can be made "by way of ordinary legislation", I feel compelled, but with great hesitation, to come to the conclusion that this sect. 3 comes within that term; but it is a precedent that should not be followed.'[28]

So, as a result of *Cooney* and *McBride*, the Constitution could be amended by ordinary legislation without specifying the provisions to be amended and without even specifying any intention to amend the Constitution.[29] That the section at issue in *McBride* was intended to be temporary does not make the situation any less serious. Despite what he said, Justice Hanna gave an interpretation which created an incredible precedent. Granted, rather oddly, he advised it was something not to be repeated but it was the law nonetheless.

It is interesting to consider whether the idea of implicit amendment which arose in these cases was in any way influenced by the UK doctrine of implied repeal. The concept, which is a creation of the common law[30] and is expressed in the Latin phrase *leges posteriores priores contrarias abrogant*, states that, where an Act of Parliament conflicts with an earlier one, the later Act takes precedence. The conflicting parts of the earlier Act are then repealed. The doctrine is based on the doctrine of parliamentary sovereignty and the idea that Parliament cannot bind its successors. In *Vauxhall Estates v. Liverpool Corporation*[31] it was argued that the Acquisition of Land (Assessment of Compensation) Act 1919 was immune from implied repeal because section 7 had stated: 'so far as inconsistent with this Act [other] provisions shall cease to have or shall not have effect'. However, this argument was rejected. Similarly, in *Ellen Street Estates v. Minister of Health*,[32] Lord Justice Maughan held: 'The legislature cannot, according to our constitution bind itself as to the form of subsequent legislation, and it is impossible for Parliament to enact that in a subsequent statute dealing with the same subject matter there can be no implied repeal.'[33]

However, it has been recognised that it is possible to have exceptions to this posi-

---

[28] *Ibid.*

[29] Even though, in *McBride*, the legislation in question did expressly state that it was intended to amend the Constitution.

[30] See the dictum of Lord Langdale in *Dean of Ely* v. *Bliss* (1842) 5 Beau 574, 582: 'If two inconsistent Acts be passed at different times, the last must be obeyed, and if obedience cannot be observed without derogating from the first, it is the first which must give way ... [the] operation ... [of an Act] is not to be impeded by the mere fact that it is inconsistent with previous enactments.'

[31] [1934] 1 KB 733.

[32] [1934] 1 KB 590.

[33] [1934] 1 KB 597.

tion without rejecting the doctrine itself. In the recent case of *Thoburn v. Sunderland City Council*[34] Lord Justice Laws held that there were exceptions to the doctrine of implied repeal and outlined a new constitutional framework which included a hierarchy of laws. This meant that certain statutes were, because of their constitutional importance, to be protected from implied repeal and, while not entrenched in English law, could be repealed only by the express intervention of Parliament. Thus, even in Britain it is recognised that certain legal instruments are of such fundamental importance that they should not lightly be contradicted. This fact makes the Irish decisions even more surprising in that, even if the judges were influenced by the doctrine of implied repeal in holding that legislation could amend the Constitution implicitly, perhaps they should have considered the fact that the Constitution is a document of such importance that it should have constituted an exception.

More to the point, the doctrine of implied repeal would have been incompatible with the Irish Free State Constitution because of its basis in parliamentary sovereignty. As has been emphasised in earlier chapters, the Irish Free State Constitution was drafted around the principle of popular sovereignty and many of its provisions were included with this in mind. Thus, the implementation of a doctrine which was designed to complement parliamentary sovereignty, in a system based on popular sovereignty, would have been contradictory.

Modern views

The view in *Cooney* was not rejected until 1965, when the matter had become rather academic. In *Conroy v. Attorney General*,[35] the modern Supreme Court summarily rejected a submission that the Constitution of the Irish Free State must have been automatically amended by any provision of the Road Traffic Act 1933, which was in conflict with the Constitution. Similarly and at greater length, in *Laurentiu v. Minister for Justice*,[36] Justice Barrington severely criticised the *Cooney* decision:

---

[34] (2003) QB 151, (2002) 3 WLR 247, (2002) 4 All ER 156.
[35] [1965] IR 411. This case involved the interpretation of the words 'minor offences' in Article 38 of the 1937 Constitution. The plaintiff, who had been charged with driving while intoxicated, argued that his case did not come under the meaning of 'minor' and so should not be tried by the District Court. It was submitted that the above-mentioned Act changed the meaning of the word 'minor' in the 1922 Constitution. Walsh J held at 443 that 'the Court rejects the submission that the Constitution of Saorstát Éireann was amended by the Road Traffic Act, 1933'.
[36] [1999] 4 IR 26. This case involved the constitutionality of the Aliens Act 1935. Barrington J decided that, since Article 15.2 of the 1937 Constitution is so similar to Article 12 of the 1922 Constitution, if the Act could be presumed not to be in conflict with Article 12 of 1922 then the same could be held in relation to Article 15.2 of 1937. The above quotation is the answer to the 'assumption' that the 1922 Constitution was incidentally amended by any piece of ordinary legislation which conflicted with it. This allowed Barrington J to hold that the Act could be presumed to be constitutional and the onus of disproving the presumption lay on the applicant.

For many years it was assumed that, because the Constitution of the Irish Free State could be amended during all of its life by 'ordinary legislation' that any piece of legislation which, incidentally, conflicted with the Constitution amended it *pro tanto* even though it was not expressed to be an Act to amend the Constitution ... But if one looks at Article 50 of the Constitution of the Irish Free State it seems quite clear that the Article uses the term 'ordinary legislation' to distinguish amendments which may, for a limited period, be made by the Oireachtas itself from amendments which must be submitted to the people by way of referendum.

To derive from this distinction a doctrine that the Constitution could be amended by ordinary legislation which need not even be expressed to be a constitutional amendment showed scant respect to the Constitution. It also assumed that the Oireachtas had so little respect for the Constitution that they would amend it without thinking of what they were doing. It also had the practical disadvantage that one could not find out what the Constitution of the Irish Free State provided without reading the whole body of statute law passed since 1922.[37]

Barrington's reasoning seems so logical that it makes the decisions in *Cooney* and *McBride* seem incredible and one wonders how the judges in those cases could have possibly felt justified in their reasoning. As Justice Barrington cogently indicates, the decision in *Cooney* was based on an erroneous interpretation of Article 50 and it was detrimental to the whole spirit of the Constitution but *Conroy* and *Laurentiu* came much too late to be of any assistance.

Amending the amendment provision

To compound matters further, in 1929 it was decided to amend the amendment provision itself in order to provide for a further eight years of amendment by the Oireachtas. This was affected by the Sixteenth Amendment in May 1929.[38] There was little opposition to the move, despite a warning from T.J. O'Connell,[39] who pointed out that 'if the government or governments who will be in power for the next eight years are as prolific in amendments as the [present] Government ... there will not be much of the original Constitution left at the end of the eight years'.[40] However, the constitutionality of the amendment was questioned in *State (Ryan) v. Lennon*.[41]

The *Ryan* case involved an examination of the constitutionality of two amendments. The first was the Constitution (Amendment No. 17) Act 1931. This amendment introduced the radical Article 2A which required every Article of the Constitution to be read and construed subject to its own provisions. It also established a military court which had jurisdiction to impose the death penalty. The validity of this Act was the key issue in *Ryan*, but its validity depended on the

---

[37] [1999] 4 IR 26, 69.
[38] Constitution (Amendment No. 16) Act 1929 (No. 10 of 1929).
[39] Labour Party deputy.
[40] *Dáil Debates*, vol 28, col 1317, 13 March 1929.
[41] [1935] IR 170.

validity of the earlier Sixteenth Amendment, mentioned above.[42] This is because, if the Sixteenth Amendment was held to be unconstitutional, the Seventeenth Amendment would automatically fall. Thus, what is relevant here is that the Court had to adjudicate on the validity of extending the original eight-year period of legislative amendment in Article 50. While Chief Justice Kennedy dissented in the Supreme Court, Justices Murnaghan and Fitzgibbon upheld the judgment of Justices O'Sullivan, Meredith and O'Byrne in the High Court and, consequently, the validity of the amendment.

The majority judgment was based on a positivist interpretation of the Constitution whereby the Oireachtas was a totally unfettered institution and it was within its power to pass such amendments. However, it could have been argued that the amendment effectively violated popular sovereignty, an argument which Chief Justice Kennedy acknowledged in the Supreme Court.[43] This would have been a chance for the judiciary to ignite the judicial review provision by protecting the Constitution from the unrestrained acts of the Oireachtas and avoid so much of the criticism of the Sixteenth Amendment.

In response to the argument in the High Court that the Sixteenth Amendment was *ultra vires* the Oireachtas, Justice Meredith commented:

> That argument asserts a legal principle, adopted in the form of a principle of constitutional law, which looks outside the four corners of the Constitution itself, and, accordingly, this Court has no authority to pay regard to it in exercising its jurisdiction under Art. 65. The power of amendment conferred by Art. 50 is, in terms [*sic*], general. Power to amend Art. 50 itself could have been expressly excepted, but it was not. This Court cannot then declare an amendment of Art. 50 itself to be invalid on a principle extraneous to the Constitution. If this Court had authority to look outside the Constitution to extraneous principles of law to determine the validity of any law 'having regard to the provisions of the Constitution' it could build up a body of judge-made law standing alongside the Constitution.[44]

In effect, Meredith, in a positivist stance, decided he could only look to the words of the Constitution itself when interpreting it. His reasoning is valid in that he was expressing concern about the possibility of endless judicial amendments. Although this possibility would have been fatal to the idea of popular sovereignty, the result of this case effectively meant endless amendments by the Oireachtas, which was arguably just as detrimental. The effect of this decision was to restrict the power of judicial review as, when the Sixteenth Amendment was declared

---

[42] The case was brought by four prisoners who challenged the legality of their detention and the constitutionality of the tribunal (which had been set up under Article 2A) which was to try them.

[43] See below. This argument was never raised during legal argument: it was simply argued that the Seventeenth Amendment was invalid because it was passed following the Sixteenth Amendment which was also invalid. Arguments for the invalidity of the Sixteenth Amendment were not given.

[44] [1935] IR 170, 179.

valid, this meant the Oireachtas would continue to amend the Constitution arbitrarily and this power could have been potentially infinite.

However, Kennedy, the dissentient in the Supreme Court, summed up the need for judicial review, which protects popular sovereignty and individual rights, when he stated:

> Our trust is for the people, our duty and responsibility to the people, and, while bowing inevitably to lawful amendment, when established to have been properly and duly made, we must be watchdogs to protect against unlawful encroachment and to maintain intact, so far as in us lies, the principles and provisions embodied in the Constitution for the protection of the liberties of the citizens in mass and individually.[45]

He also pointed out the absurdity of the amendment:

> In my opinion ... the Constituent Assembly cannot be supposed to have in the same breath declared certain principles to be fundamental and immutable, or conveyed that sense in other words, as by a declaration of inviolability, and at the same time to have conferred upon the Oireachtas power to violate them or to alter them. In my opinion, any amendment of the Constitution, purporting to be made under the power given by the Constituent Assembly, which would be a violation of, or be inconsistent with, any fundamental principle so declared, is necessarily outside the scope of the power and invalid and void.[46]

Gerard Hogan has compared Kennedy's reasoning to the modern judgments of Chief Justice Hamilton in *Re Article 26 and the Information (Termination of Pregnancies) Bill*[47] and *Hanafin v. Minister for Environment*[48] and of Justice Barrington in *Riordan v. An Taoiseach (No. 1)*.[49] In each of these judgments, the Court 'affirmed the supremacy of popular sovereignty as the key principle of the [1937] Constitution' and acknowledged 'the supremacy of the Constitution and the referendum process'.[50]

The architects of the Constitution had always intended the people to be sovereign and to have a role in constitutional amendment. The provision which brought in amendment by ordinary legislation was only a last-minute addition, intended to give effect to minor changes and alterations without having to have resort to the more cumbersome method of submitting the changes to the people. Because of this, it could be argued that the provision was intended to be transitory and that, by extending it, the Oireachtas was, in effect, taking away from the sovereignty of the people.

However, Murnaghan and Fitzgibbon agreed with the literal interpretation given in the High Court and held that

---

[45] *Ibid.*, 203.
[46] *Ibid.*, 213.
[47] [1995] 1 IR 1.
[48] [1996] 2 IR 321.
[49] [1999] 4 IR 325.
[50] Hogan, 'A Desert Island Case', 96–7.

The enactments (16th and 17th Amendments to the Constitution) were within the power of amendment conferred on the Oireachtas by Article 50 and were valid amendments of the Constitution; and that, consequently, an amendment of the Constitution enacted after the expiry of the original period of eight years was not invalid by reason only of not having been, or having been, capable of being submitted to a Referendum of the people under Article 50 or Article 47, respectively, as originally enacted.[51]

This result in this case is deserving of criticism, both of the government which decided to circumvent the right of the people to constitutional amendment by referendum and of the Supreme Court which allowed it to happen despite the obvious contrary intention of the provision.

The bulk of the criticism of the 1922 Constitution is directed at the fact that it was so easily amendable by the Oireachtas. And rightly so, for the actions of the government, reinforced by the decision in *Ryan*, undermined the original intention of the Constitution as a rigid constitution amendable only with the direct consent of the people. These actions conflicted with the notion of the 'people's Constitution' and the idea that the people should have a direct say on fundamental matters rather than having decisions imposed on them by government (even a popularly elected one). Thus the entire tone of the Constitution was changed. A harmonious, purposive or originalist approach to interpreting the amendment provision would have made it obvious that implicit amendment was not intended and neither was extension of the introductory period. Unfortunately, none of those approaches was taken and the result was fatal to the 1922 Constitution. The result of the *Ryan* case meant that the period of legislative amendment could now be potentially infinite. Furthermore, it meant that successive governments could make autocratic changes, contrary to the original spirit of the Constitution and without consulting the people. Because of the various changes which were subsequently effected, the Constitution was left in tatters and it was for this reason that it was replaced in 1937.

How Article 50 was used to deconstruct the Constitution

The Constitution was first amended in July 1925, and those early amendments were minor matters dealing mostly with election dates.[52] However, by 1927 and 1928 a series of more significant amendments had been carried out. These included: extending the maximum term of the Dáil;[53] increasing the

---

[51] [1935] IR 170.

[52] Amendment No. 1 (11 July 1925) made changes relating to the terms of office of senators, and the date on which senatorial elections were to be held. Amendment No. 2 (19 March 1927) introduced a system of automatic re-election of the Ceann Comhairle of the Dáil in a general election. Amendment No. 3 (4 March 1927) removed the requirement that the day of any general election would be declared a public holiday.

[53] Amendment No. 4 (4 March 1927).

membership of the Executive Council;[54] the removal of direct democracy from the Constitution;[55] and a string of changes in relation to the Seanad.[56] The most crucial amendment, which extended the period of legislative amendment and which was discussed above, took place in 1929. After this date, many more amendments were effected which left the Constitution 'a thing of shreds and patches'.[57] Those amendments were as follows: Amendment No. 17[58] which introduced Article 2A; The Constitution (Removal of Oath) Act[59] which abolished the oath of allegiance and removed requirements that the Constitution and laws of the Free State be compatible with the Anglo-Irish Treaty; Amendment No. 20[60] which removed the Governor-General's role in recommending appropriations of money to the Dáil; Amendment No. 21[61] which removed provisions granting the Governor-General the theoretical right to both veto bills and reserve them 'for the King's pleasure'; Amendment No. 22[62] which abolished the right of appeal to the Privy Council; Amendment No. 26[63] which made a technical change to Article 3, which dealt with citizenship; Amendment No. 23[64] which abolished the two university constituencies in the Dáil; Amendment No. 24[65] which abolished the Seanad; and Amendment No. 27[66] which abolished the

---

[54] Amendment No. 5 (5 May 1927).

[55] Amendment No. 10 (12 July 1928).

[56] Amendment No. 6 (23 July 1928), which replaced the direct election of the Seanad with a system of indirect election; Amendment No. 13 (23 July 1928), which extended the Seanad's power of delay of legislation; Amendment No. 8 (25 October 1928), which reduced the age of eligibility for senators from 35 to 30; Amendment No. 9 (25 October 1928), which altered provisions relating to the procedure for nominating candidates to stand in senatorial elections; Amendment No. 7 (30 October 1928), which reduced the term of office of senators from 12 to nine years; Amendment No. 14 (14 May 1929), which clarified a technical matter relating to the relationship between the two Houses of the Oireachtas; and Amendment No. 15 (14 May 1929), which permitted one member of the Executive Council to be a senator.

[57] Diana Mansergh (ed.), *Nationalism and Independence: Selected Irish Papers by Nicholas Mansergh* (Cork, 1997), 113.

[58] 17 October 1931. This Article provided that every other Article of the Constitution be construed according to its provisions. It established the Constitution (Special Powers) Tribunal, which had the power to impose the death penalty. It conferred special powers on the police, including powers of arrest and detention on suspicion in certain cases, examination of persons detained on suspicion or in custody, power to bring detained persons before the Tribunal, and power to stop and search vehicles. It defined 'unlawful associations' and provided penalties for membership of, or possession of documents relating to, such associations. It also conferred miscellaneous powers on the Executive Council, the Tribunal and the Garda Siochána.

[59] 3 May 1933. Strangely, this amendment was not given a number.

[60] 2 November 1933.

[61] 2 November 1933.

[62] 16 November 1933.

[63] 5 April 1935.

[64] 24 April 1936.

[65] 29 May 1936.

[66] 11 December 1936.

office of Governor-General and removed all references to the King from the Constitution.

Admittedly, the root cause of all of the confusion in relation to Article 50 and the legislative amendment provision originated in the careless drafting of a sentence added to Article 50 in the Constituent Assembly. It was something which could have been avoided with more careful wording. However, this error alone did not lead to the downfall of the Constitution.

Originally, the Constitution was supposed to be entrenched so as to protect the rights of the people against the unrestrained actions of the Oireachtas. However, the original plan was never even given a fair trial. It was agreed in the Constituent Assembly that a temporary period of legislative amendment would be useful to remedy any teething problems but this method became too useful to the government in an era of turmoil and division. Furthermore, the government was aware of the problems with implicit amendment – yet chose to ignore them. While the wording error is forgivable, the actions of the politicians may not be. By dismissing the warnings about implicit amendment, they allowed for a questionable interpretation of the Constitution and, by extending the temporary amendment period, they offended the spirit of the Constitution, prevented entrenchment and ultimately, opened the door to the destruction of the Constitution. Thus, the blame is partly attributable to drafting and partly to subsequent events, although the drafting fault was a technical one rather than a more serious case of flawed vision. At least this provided a valuable lesson for the drafting team of 1937.

Amendment in the 1937 Constitution

The problems which occurred under the 1922 document resulted in very careful drafting in relation to Article 51 of the 1937 Constitution,[67] which provided for a temporary amendment arrangement. Justice Barrington, in the case of *Finn v. Attorney General*,[68] noted that the problems with Article 50 of the 1922 Constitution would most certainly have been in the minds of the drafters in 1937:

> Article 50 of the Constitution of Saorstát Éireann,1922, provided simply for 'amendments of this Constitution.' In *The State (Ryan) v. Lennon* the contention was put forward by counsel that the power of 'amendment' in article 50 of the Constitution of 1922 did not extend to a power of repeal but meant merely a power

---

[67] Section 1 of Article 51 provided the following: 'Notwithstanding anything contained in Article 46 hereof, any of the provisions of this Constitution, except the provisions of the said Article 46 and this Article, may, subject as hereinafter provided, be amended by the Oireachtas, whether by way of variation, addition or repeal, within a period of three years after the date on which the first President shall have entered upon the office.'

[68] *Finn v. The Attorney General* [1983] IR 154. This case involved a claim that the terms of the Eighth Amendment of the Constitution Bill 1982 were repugnant to the Constitution and a request for an injunction restraining the Minister for the Environment from holding a referendum in connection with the proposal.

to improve, to vary in detail or to remedy defects. While that submission was rejected by the former Supreme Court of Justice, the case and the problem would have been present to the minds of the drafters of the present Constitution and probably account for the wording of s. 1 of Article 46 of the Constitution. That *The State (Ryan) v. Lennon* was present to the minds of the drafters of the present Constitution is illustrated by Article 51 of the transitory provisions to the Constitution which stated that the provision therein contained enabling the Constitution to be amended by simple legislation for a period of three years could not itself be amended under the provisions of that article. In other words, Article 51 of the Constitution was not to be amended in the way in which the Oireachtas had amended Article 50 of the Constitution of 1922 – an amendment which the Supreme Court of Justice had held to be valid in *The State (Ryan) v. Lennon*.[69]

The drafting committee of the 1937 Constitution was not going to fall into the 1922 trap and so, while the 1937 Constitution provided for a transitional period whereby minor amendments could be affected by ordinary legislation until June 1941, it was also provided that this provision itself could not be amended.[70] The provision in the 1937 Constitution had the advantage of creating an entrenched constitution with the benefit of a simple amendment procedure for early minor problems.

Of course, the major advantage of an entrenched Constitution was that it provided the essential basis for the development of judicial review. As outlined above, one of the problems with the 1922 Constitution was that, since it could be amended at the whim of the Oireachtas, the judiciary had no real power of judicial review, even if they had been inclined to use it. How could the judiciary act as guardians of the Constitution if the executive had a limitless power of amendment? The judiciary needed the security of an entrenched Constitution before more use could be made of the judicial review provision.

Provisions maintained: judicial review

Because it was never put into practice on a major scale, it is not widely known that the 1922 Constitution contained a judicial review provision. Yet, in fact, Article 65 of the Irish Free State Constitution conferred the power of judicial review of the validity of laws on the High Court: 'The judicial power of the High Court shall extend to the question of the validity of any law having regard to the provisions of the Constitution. In all cases in which such matters shall come into question, the High Court alone shall exercise original jurisdiction.' This has been described as

[69] *Ibid.*, 163 (citations omitted).
[70] Articles 51 to 63 contained transitory provisions (which are no longer included in official texts of the Constitution) which permitted the Oireachtas to amend the Constitution for a period of three years after the first President took office. This meant up until 25 June 1941. Article 51 also prevented the transition period from being extended by the Oireachtas. John Coakley & Michael Gallagher (eds), *Politics in the Republic of Ireland* (Dublin, 1993), 78.

'the most arresting provision in the Irish Free State Constitution'.[71] The reason it was described as such was that it constituted a massive break with the British tradition whereby Parliament was supreme and judges could not question the actions of Parliament. Popular sovereignty had already been proclaimed in Article 2 but this was an even further extension of that.[72] Nothing like this had ever been seen in a Dominion constitution.[73]

However, the problem with this provision, as Kohn has stressed, was , as long as the Constitution could be amended by ordinary legislation, judicial review would not be of any great import in Ireland.[74] This is because any piece of legislation conflicting with a constitutional provision could be deemed to have amended the provision. However, Kohn also realised the significance that judicial review could have, when the period of ordinary legislation ran out and the Constitution assumed 'a greater measure of rigidity'. It was taken for granted that this would happen when the eight-year period set out in Article 50 lapsed and the more formal procedure would then apply. However, as we have seen, on 14 May 1929, the Sixteenth amendment to the Constitution was passed which extended the period of amendment by ordinary legislation from eight to 16 years.[75]

The far-sighted Kohn felt that judicial review would have most significance in relation to the interpretation of the fundamental rights provisions.[76] Although it did not exercise this role during the Free State years, judicial review was to play a most important part later in securing the doctrine of unenumerated rights under the 1937 Constitution. In recent years, the power of judicial review has been

---

[71] Letter from Professor Felix Frankfurter from Harvard University to Lionel Curtis. According to Gerard Hogan, Frankfurter was enquiring as to whether this Article was based on the American experience of judicial review and also whether this was insisted upon by the Irish or the British. Curtis apparently passed the letter on to Kennedy but tantalisingly, owing to the difficulties which the state was experiencing at the time, the letter apparently went unanswered. See Gerard Hogan, *Development of Judicial Review of Legislation and Irish Constitutional Law 1929–1941* (unpublished PhD Thesis, Trinity College Dublin, 2001), 1, citing a letter written on 10 August 1922 to Lionel Curtis.

[72] The people could now ensure that their rights would be protected and could check the actions of the Oireachtas by having recourse to the judicial review procedure.

[73] However, it seems judicial review may have been in the air in some of the Home Rules plans for Ireland. Before the second Home Rule Bill, there was some limited discussion of the American system with its entrenched rights and mechanism for court action. However, it seems these discussions mainly took place at an academic level and were not reflected in the Westminster debates. See Donal O'Donnell, '"The Most Curious Forerunner" to the Fundamental Rights Provisions in the 1937 Constitution' in Bláthna Ruane, Jim O'Callaghan & David Barniville, *Law and Government: A Tribute to Rory Brady* (Dublin, 2014).

[74] Kohn, *Constitution of the Irish Free State*, 352.

[75] Kohn's work was published in 1932 but much of it was actually written before 1927, when it was submitted as a thesis. When writing this part, it is likely that he was anticipating that the ordinary legislation period would run out in 1930.

[76] Kohn, *Constitution of the Irish Free State*, 352.

crucial in vindicating important rights and in modernising the law. However, if judicial review had never been included in the 1922 Constitution it is highly likely that it would not have appeared in 1937.[77]

We have very little information on the origin and intent of this fascinating provision in the Irish Free State Constitution. One major question, to which there may be no satisfactory answer, is why did the architects of the 1922 Constitution decide to specify this power in the Constitution and where did their inspiration come from? In order to try and answer that question it is necessary to look at the status of the doctrine at the time.

Judicial review internationally

The concept of judicial review was not seen as internationally accepted at the time.[78] Traditionally in Europe, the principal objection to judicial review was that it violated the separation of powers principle. One contemporary commentator remarked that 'Whereas the doctrine of judicial review of legislation is regarded in the United States as a necessary requirement in the application of the theory of the separation of powers, in Europe such a doctrine is generally thought to involve a confusion, and not a separation, of powers'.[79] For in many European jurisdictions the legislature, as the voice of the people, was supreme, and to give the judiciary a power over the legislature was to make the judicial power supreme, which in turn violated their strict interpretation of the tripartite doctrine.[80] Britain did not recognise the doctrine either as it would have been in conflict with its doctrine of parliamentary sovereignty.[81] So it was in the United

---

[77] The argument could be made that, like the functional councils provision, the judicial review provision was retained in 1937 only because it was harmless. There is no evidence in relation to what was intended by the judicial review provision in 1937. Kelly has opined that the drafters never envisaged such rigorous use of the provision. See 'Statements on the 70th Anniversary of the Constitution in Seanad Éireann' available at www.inis.gov.ie/en/JELR/Pages/Statements%20on%20the%2070th%20 Anniversary%20of%20the%20Constitution%20in%20Seanad%20%C3%89ireann. Furthermore, Kelly has written that, in 1937, the fundamental rights provisions were intended to be mere headlines for the Oireachtas and that 'a situation in which judicial review of statutes in the light of these Articles would become common was far from [the Government's] mind'. See J.M. Kelly, *Fundamental Rights in Irish Law* (Dublin, 1967), 18. However, Hogan disagrees with this: see Gerard Hogan, *The Origins of the Irish Constitution 1928–1941* (Dublin, 2012), 335, 353.

[78] See, for example, Kohn, *Constitution of the Irish Free State*, 350.

[79] C.G. Haines, 'Some Phases of the Theory and Practice of Judicial Review of Legislation in Foreign Countries' (1930) 24 (3) *The American Political Science Review* 583, 588–9.

[80] Ultimately, however, this did not prevent the development of the doctrine in some jurisdictions. See below.

[81] A.L. Bendor & Zeev Segal, 'Constitutionalism and Trust in Britain: An Ancient Constitutional Culture, a New Judicial Review Model' (2002) 17 *American University International Law Review* 683, 683–4.

States that the idea of legislative Acts being reviewed by the judiciary came into being.

There is no express provision in the Constitution of the United States which gives this power to the judiciary. In fact, the suggestion of the inclusion of a power of judicial review arose three times during the debates on the draft constitution in Philadelphia but each time it was rejected.[82] However, the power was established by precedent in the famous case of *Marbury v. Madison*[83] and widely accepted by the American legal community. It is now based on the idea of the Supremacy of the Constitution.[84]

Despite the fact that it was not generally accepted, the doctrine had begun to emerge in Europe in some form by the 1920s.[85] The German (Weimar) Constitution of 1919 allowed for judicial review in a very narrow realm. Article 13 s 2 provided that the Reichsgericht[86] was empowered to review the validity of state statutes which were alleged to be in conflict with the federal law.[87] However, on the question of whether the courts could adjudicate on the constitutionality of federal statutes the Constitution remained silent. This meant that judicial review in the broad sense was neither prohibited nor sanctioned.[88] In the Austrian Constitution of 1920, judicial review was specifically provided for and a constitutional court (Verfassungsgerichtshof)[89] was established to exercise this function.[90] Although not included in its Constitution, a constitutional court was

---

[82] Barra O'Briain, *The Irish Constitution* (Dublin, 1929), 113.

[83] 5 US (1 Cranch) 137 (1803). Some dispute this as the very first case in which judicial review was established but it is the one most often cited.

[84] At this stage, it was still being used in a fairly restrained way in the US. See n. 95 below.

[85] It should also be noted that, although the Australian Constitution (The Commonwealth of Australia Act 1900) did not expressly confer a power of judicial review upon the High Court, the doctrine developed years later and is said to be based on a number of provisions in the Constitution. See Anthony Mason, 'The Role of a Constitutional Court in a Federation: A Comparison of the Australian and the United States Experience' (1986) 16 *Federal Law Review* 1, and K.E. Foley, 'Australian Judicial Review' (2007) 6 *Wash U Global Studies Law Review* 281.

[86] Federal Supreme Court.

[87] See *Select Constitutions of the World*, 211.

[88] The debate as to constitutional review raged on into the mid-1920s. However, in 1925 the Reichsgericht decided that it did have authority to question federal statutes (111 RGZ 320 (1925)) and in 1929 it declared a statute unconstitutional (124 RGZ 173 (1929)). For more on judicial review under the Weimar Constitution, see Gerhard Casper, 'Guardians of the Constitution' (1979–80) 53 *S Cal L Rev* 773; Heinrich Nagel, 'Judicial Review in Germany' (1954) 3 (2) *American Journal of Comparative Law* 233; B.J. Hartman, 'The Arrival of Judicial Review in Germany under the Weimar Constitution of 1919' (2003–4) 18 *BYU J Pub L* 107, and Michael Stolleis, 'Judicial Review, Administrative Review, and Constitutional Review in the Weimar Republic' (2003) 16 (2) *Ratio Juris* 266.

[89] Articles 137–48 and law of 4 April 1930, Bundesgesetzblatt, No. 112.

[90] For more see J.A.C. Grant, 'Judicial Review of Legislation under the Austrian Constitution of 1920' (1934) 28 (4) *The American Political Science Review* 670.

also established in Czechoslovakia by statute on 9 March 1920 on the authority of an earlier statute (29 February 1920), which governed the introduction of the Constitution.[91] However, while the idea of judicial review was widely debated at the time, it was not widely adopted.[92] The next country to adopt the doctrine was the Irish Free State.

Judicial review in Ireland

Drafts A and B of the Irish Free State Constitution both contained the judicial review provision but Draft C did not. This is because O'Rahilly, author of Draft C, was a great admirer of the Swiss Constitution whereby the people were sovereign and so they, rather than the judiciary, would be the ultimate interpreter of the Constitution. O'Rahilly envisaged that this system would work concurrently with the referendum and initiative proposals. However, both of the other Drafts included the judicial review provision without discussion. Kelly has referred to the origin of the provision as 'obscure', pointing out that the records of the Committee 'give no hint as to whose idea it was, or whether any debate took place within the committee on the wisdom of making so large a modification of common constitutional law'.[93]

Although this was quite a novel idea, surprisingly there was comment on only one aspect of it during the debates in the Constituent Assembly[94] and it was generally accepted by the Provisional Government as well as the British government without discussion.

So why was the provision written into the Constitution and what was intended by it? It is evident that the idea came from the American doctrine of judicial review. At this stage, the doctrine was well recognised and accepted in the United States, although it had not yet developed to the extent that was later seen in the 1960s.[95] The Irish educated and legal community would also have been very

---

[91] See S.L. Paulson, 'Constitutional Review in the United States and Austria: Notes on the Beginnings' (2003) 16 (2) *Ratio Juris* 223, who also recommends the following; Franz Weyr, 'Der Tschechoslowakische Staat' (1922) 11 *Jahrbuch des öffentlichen Rechts der Gegenwart* 351.

[92] See David Deener, 'Judicial Review in Modern Constitutional Systems' (1952) 46 (4) *The American Political Science Review* 1079, 1085.

[93] J.M. Kelly, 'Grafting Judicial Review on to a System Founded on Parliamentary Supremacy: The Irish Experience' (Paper given at the European University Institute Florence, June 1978) in Papers of J.M. Kelly, P147/4, University College Dublin Archives. Kelly also notes that, although the earliest commentators on the Constitution all pointed out the judicial review provision, 'they displayed a strange lack of historian's curiosity as to the spirit responsible for this conspicuous and potentially crucial feature of the new Irish polity'.

[94] See Gavan Duffy's point below. Perhaps the lack of discussion indicates that deputies understood what was intended.

[95] Judicial review developed to its modern scope only in the 1950s and 1960s when Earl Warren was Chief Justice of the United States Supreme Court. The Irish

aware of the development of the doctrine in the United States.[96] The Constitution Committee had studied the American Constitution and was obviously impressed with this practice which had developed. The constitutions of Germany, Austria and Czechoslovakia were also examined by the Committee and may have had an influence.

Another possibility (and perhaps the main motivation) is that it was an attempt to move further away from the doctrine of parliamentary sovereignty. In Britain, judges would not interfere in legislative decisions because of the fact that Parliament was supreme. So if the Irish were to introduce a clause whereby the judiciary would actually be supervising the actions of the Oireachtas this would constitute a huge leap from the previous system. Perhaps owing to this and because of the American system, the power of judicial review was seen as a necessary facet of a republican (or at least quasi-republican) state.

The fact that judicial review would provide another mechanism for the protection of people's rights must also have been a strong motivational factor. The Irish people did not trust the power of Parliament, which, in the past, had only limited the rights of the Irish people. So, providing the people with an additional method of protection in the form of judicial review was further proof that the architects intended the document to truly be a Constitution for the people.

These are all possible answers as to why it was felt necessary to include this provision in the Constitution but it is still unclear as to what was intended by the provision. Was it hoped that the judges would become actively involved in supervising the actions of the Oireachtas and vindicating personal rights or was it simply put there as a symbol of independence or even republicanism? Unfortunately, we are no closer to answering this question.

Form of judicial review

Again, there was little discussion in Ireland on the form judicial review should take. Kohn has explained that 'the question of the constitutionality of any law can in America be raised only as an incidental issue in an ordinary judicial proceeding, the Court adjudging on the question merely in so far as it is essential to, and as part of, the decision of the case'.[97] In other words there is no possibility of simply referring a piece of legislation to the courts for a decision on its validity: it must arise as part of a judicial proceeding. Kohn also expressed the opinion that the Irish High Court would be likely to treat the issue in the same way; that due to the phrasing of Article 65 it would seem the constitutionality of a law could

---

Supreme Court soon followed suit (see below). It would be interesting to consider whether either jurisdiction would have established the institution if it had been known how significant it would become.

[96] 'The Irish practitioner would at least have heard in general terms of the US Supreme Court and of the judicial review which it practised in the heart of a system of pure common law descent.' Kelly, 'Grafting Judicial Review'.

[97] Kohn, *Constitution of the Irish Free State*, 351.

only be raised as part of a case. However, he also notes that the case could 'centre exclusively on the issue and be instituted expressly as a test case'.[98]

During the debates in the Constituent Assembly, Gavan Duffy questioned the fact that only the High Court and no inferior court had the power to determine the validity of laws.[99] In America, the power belongs to all of the courts rather than just the Supreme Court. This system is sometimes referred to as a decentralised *intra partes*[100] system.[101] The idea is that every court has the power of judicial review 'as long as the constitutionality of the statute was decisive for the case at hand'.[102] However, in practice, lower courts are reluctant to pronounce on the validity of laws. This is in contrast with the Irish situation in which the High Court alone was conferred with such a power and a finding of unconstitutionality would mean that the legislation would be struck down.[103] This would be described as a centralised *inter omnes*[104] system. Presumably Gavan Duffy felt that the American system should be followed. However, O'Higgins, in pointing out the need for uniformity, remarked that, if inferior judges were also to have this power, 'you might have as many views of the validity of a particular law as Judges'.[105] While Gavan Duffy persisted, his amendments were without support and the centralised *inter omnes* system was retained.

Case law

The first case involving the constitutionality of a law passed without controversy. In *R (O'Brien) v. the Military Governor of the Military Internment Camp & Ors*[106] the formal requirements regarding the enactment of legislation had been ignored in the passing of the Public Safety (Emergency Powers) Act 1923. According to Article 47, a period of seven days had to elapse before an Act could be effective, so as to allow time for the possibility of a referendum.[107] However, in this case, the Act had been passed and signed into law the day before the case was heard and

---

[98] *Ibid.*, 352.
[99] *Dáil Debates*, vol 1, col 1400, 10 October 1922.
[100] If the effect of a court's decision is that it is binding *intra partes* this means that it is binding on the parties involved.
[101] Hartman, 'Judicial Review in Germany', 109.
[102] *Ibid.* Theoretically then, the verdict should be binding only with respect to the parties before the court. However, a hierarchy of courts together with the doctrine of *stare decisis* means that *inter partes* decisions often become *inter omnes* by precedent.
[103] There was appeal to the Supreme Court.
[104] *Inter omnes* means a decision is binding 'among all'.
[105] *Dáil Debates*, vol 1, col 1400, 10 October 1922.
[106] (1924) 1 IR 32. This case is also dealt with in Chapter 7, 113–15.
[107] Article 47 allowed for a seven-day period during which time the Bill could be suspended on the written demand of two-fifths of the members of Dáil Éireann or of a majority of the members of Seanad Éireann in order to allow for the possibility of a referendum.

without waiting for the elapse of the seven days. An order of detention was then made under the Act. The Court held that the Act was not immediately applicable due to the non-observance of time limit but it was not held to be invalid. This was because there was nothing unconstitutional contained in the Act; it was simply the non-observance of the time limit which was unconstitutional. In other words, the Act would have been perfectly valid after the seven days. However, the order which had been made by the Minister for Defence[108] under the Act was held to be null and void.[109]

There were few other cases involving the constitutionality of laws during the Free State years and those that did occur mostly involved, like the previous case, issues of internment and *habeas corpus*.[110] So, despite this innovative power which had been conferred upon them and would have allowed them to develop the new civil and political constitutional rights significantly, the Irish judiciary failed to make much use of Article 65. One quite obvious reason for this is that members of the Irish legal profession were all trained in the British tradition, which did not recognise such a power, and for this reason they may have been reluctant to use it. Of course, the judiciary could hardly make strides in relation to judicial review if the cases were not brought before them. Donal Barrington has alluded to this point:

> [T]he fact is that the general body of the Irish legal profession – both judges and practitioners – appear to have been slow to appreciate the significance of having a written constitution with a charter of rights and judicial review of legislation. Their training was in the British tradition of parliamentary sovereignty and legal positivism and, with some significant exceptions, they did not believe that lawyers should seriously concern themselves with natural rights and the validity of acts of Parliament.[111]

Kelly commented similarly: 'This Constitution, with its politically revolutionary background, and these legally revolutionary contents, was committed to the interpretation of a completely non-revolutionary judiciary and bar.'[112]

---

[108] Richard Mulcahy had detained Nora O'Brien under the Act and the case arose when a writ of *habeas corpus* was sought.

[109] The Oireachtas decided to pass a new Act, Public Safety (Emergency Powers) (No. 2) Act 1923, incorporating the first, and the time limit was avoided this time as it was declared necessary for public peace and safety. See Chapter 7.

[110] In *R (O'Connell) v. Military Governor of Hare Park Camp* [1924] 2 IR 104, the court held that the Public Safety (Powers of Arrest and Detention) Temporary Act 1924 was *intra vires* the Constitution. In *Attorney General v. McBride* [1928] 62 ILTR 145, Hanna J held that section 3 of the Public Safety Act 1927 was a valid amendment to the Constitution. In the *State (Ryan) v. Lennon* [1935] IR 170, although Chief Justice Kennedy dissented, it was held that the Seventeenth Amendment which inserted Article 2A into the Constitution was valid. See below.

[111] Donal Barrington, 'Private Property under the Irish Constitution' (1973) 8 *Irish Jurist* 1, 6.

[112] Kelly, 'Grafting Judicial Review'.

Another reason often given for the failure of judicial review under the Irish Free State Constitution is one Kohn also touched upon: that the power of the Oireachtas to amend the Constitution by ordinary legislation effectively prevented the exercise of any effectual sort of judicial review. However, as previously noted, this period was only intended to last until 1930 and, when the Sixteenth Amendment, which extended the period, was inserted in 1929, the courts had a chance to exercise their power of judicial review and declare the amendment invalid.

This issue arose in *State (Ryan) v. Lennon*[113] but, as we have already seen, the majority in the Supreme Court upheld the amendment. However, Chief Justice Kennedy, the dissentient, made significant statements in relation to judicial review and also set the scene for later cases where, under the 1937 Constitution, the judiciary would use general constitutional principles, including Natural Law, in order to vindicate fundamental rights:

> [I]t seems clear that, if any legislation of the Oireachtas (including any purported amendment of the Constitution) were to offend against that acknowledged ultimate Source from which the legislative authority has come through the people to the Oireachtas, as, for instance, if it were repugnant to the Natural Law, such legislation would be necessarily unconstitutional and invalid, and it would be, therefore, absolutely null and void and inoperative.[114]

Kennedy did not draw on any 'extraneous principles'[115] but instead drew a distinction between the permanent power of the people to amend the Constitution, which is inalienable, and the temporary power of the Oireachtas to pass amendments by ordinary legislation, which was transitory.[116] In relation to the amendment of Article 50, he opined: 'If this was lawful it can be continued indefinitely in time and scope of amendment, ultimately even to the exclusion of the people from all voice in legislation and administration and the open mockery of Article 2 of the Constitution.'[117] He held therefore that the Sixteenth Amendment to the Constitution was invalid. However, his colleagues on the Supreme Court bench did not agree and, in holding the amendment valid, effectively prevented any measure of judicial review.

While this episode could have signalled the beginning of the major period of judicial review which was to occur some 30 years later, it seems the judiciary was simply not ready for this innovative, unfamiliar power which required perhaps a little more creativity than it was used to.

---

[113] [1935] IR 170.

[114] *Ibid.*, 205.

[115] In the High Court, Meredith J had commented that the Court could not take into consideration principles extraneous to the Constitution. [1935] IR 170, 179.

[116] *Ibid.*, 213.

[117] *Ibid.*, 212.

Judicial review under the 1937 Constitution

The notion of judicial review in the 1922 Constitution has traditionally been either ignored or criticised. However, those views have given an unfair impression of the provision. Séamus O'Tuama wrote of the 1937 Constitution:

> [It] made a move away from the British constitutional model of parliamentary primacy. Its predecessor the Irish Free State Constitution was a child of the British parliament and was framed in the context of the British experience ... However the Irish Constitution [1937] contains explicit measures for judicial review in Articles 26 and 34, thus the seeds were sown by de Valera, which would allow for the emergence of a strong judicial review along American lines ... However, as stated above the Irish system migrated from a clearly weak model under the ... Irish Free State Constitution, which model initially continued under the 1937 Constitution, but given the strength of Article 34 in particular the emergence of a stronger model was always a possibility.[118]

The impression given by this writer is that the Irish Free State Constitution was simply a carbon copy of Britain's unwritten constitution. It is implied that it contained a weak judicial review provision and the provision contained in the 1937 Constitution was of such strength that it sparked the emergence of a tradition of judicial review along American lines. This is not an accurate representation.

We have already looked at the reasons for the failure of judicial review under the Irish Free State Constitution and it is clear that the provision itself was not a factor. On the contrary, it was due to the ease with which the Constitution could be amended by the Oireachtas and the fact that the legal community had not yet emerged from the British tradition. Furthermore, Article 34 of the 1937 Constitution reproduces substantially the wording of the earlier provision. Article 34.3.2 provides:

> Save as otherwise provided by this Article, the jurisdiction of the High Court shall extend to the question of the validity of any law having regard to the provisions of this Constitution and no such question shall be raised ... in any court established under this or any other Article of this Constitution other than the High Court or the Supreme Court.

This does not strengthen the 1922 position. Article 15.4 also provides:

> 1° The Oireachtas shall not enact any law which is in any respect repugnant to this Constitution or any provision thereof.
> 2° Every law enacted by the Oireachtas which is in any respect repugnant to this Constitution or to any provision thereof, shall, but to the extent only of such repugnancy, be invalid.

---

[118] Seamus O'Tuama, 'Judicial Review under the Irish Constitution: More American than Commonwealth' (2008) 12 (2) *Electronic Journal of Comparative Law* 1.

In 1922, before the Article 50 controversy, it was already assumed that the Oireachtas could not enact any law which would be repugnant to the Constitution, since the Constitution was intended to be the superior source of law.[119] Furthermore, because of the fact that the 1922 Constitution did not have entrenchment for reasons outlined above, this provision would have been of no effect in 1922.

Thus, the blossoming of judicial review in the 1950s and 1960s was down not to the strength of the 1937 provision but rather to the rigidity of that Constitution and, as Ronan Keane has noted, due to 'the arrival of a new generation of Irish judges who did not share their predecessors' lack of enthusiasm for crafting a new Irish constitutional jurisprudence'.[120] As for the reason for including judicial review in the new Constitution, Kelly has commented: 'It is of course quite likely that mere inertia, mere unwillingness to scrap provisions which had shown themselves harmless (though under a quite different constitution in point of flexibility), may have led to the incorporation of judicial review in the 1937 document.'[121]

Where the 1937 Constitution did improve on its predecessor was with the creation of abstract review in Article 26.[122] That Article provides:

> The President may, after consultation with the Council of State, refer any Bill to which this Article applies to the Supreme Court for a decision on the question as to whether such Bill or any specified provision or provisions of such Bill is or are repugnant to this Constitution or to any provision thereof.[123]

Thus, the constitutionality of a Bill can be tested before it ever becomes law. Kelly has suggested that, although Article 26 was 'a relative innovation', its inspiration may have been drawn 'from other pre-1922 legislative models'.[124] Here he

---

[119] See comments of Cosgrave in *Dáil Debates*, vol 7, col 2022, 6 June 1924. In view of what happened, it is submitted that it would have been better to clarify this position. With entrenchment, this provision might have helped to prevent the development of implicit amendment under the 1922 Constitution.

[120] Ronan Keane, 'Judges as Lawmakers: The Irish Experience' (2004) *JSIJ* 1, 9. In addition, David Gwynn Morgan has commented that 'Sean Lemass consciously initiated the era of judicial activism as part of his project of modernizing Ireland, by his selection of Ó Dálaigh CJ and Walsh J and by his private admonition to each of them, on appointment … that he 'would like the Supreme Court to become more like the United States Supreme Court'. See D.G. Morgan, *A Judgment Too Far: Judicial Activism and the Constitution* (Cork, 2001), 12.

[121] Kelly, 'Grafting Judicial Review'.

[122] However, there are arguments as to whether or not this is actually a beneficial procedure. One disadvantage is that a piece of legislation which has been declared constitutionally valid under the Article 26 procedure can never again be questioned even in the case of technological advancements. See the judgment of O'Higgins CJ in *Re Article 26 and the Housing (Private Rented Dwellings) Bill 1981* [1983] IR 181. For a discussion on the Article 26 procedure, see Niamh Howlin, 'Shortcomings and Anomalies: Aspects of Article 26' (2005) 13 *Irish Student Law Review* 26.

[123] Article 26.1.1 of 1937.

[124] Kelly, *The Irish Constitution*, 399.

gives the example of the Judicial Committee of the Privy Council and the reference procedure contained in Section 51 of the Government of Ireland Act 1920.

Whatever its inspiration, the Article 26 procedure has been a successful addition to ordinary judicial review and has enhanced and improved the whole process of constitutional interpretation. Even taking the abstract review provision aside however, judicial review has proved to be one of the most significant aspects of our current Constitution. It is interesting to consider whether it would ever have made it into the 1937 Constitution were it not for the decision of the 1922 Constitution Committee to include it in the Irish Free State Constitution.

Conclusion

In examining certain aspects of the Irish Free State Constitution which failed to function as intended, it is clear that, for the most part, these provisions did not fail as a result of defective drafting but rather the original intention and spirit of the Constitution were distorted by outside factors. The mistake made in Article 50 was an error of omission but it could not be considered a major drafting error in the sense that it was not any particular vision which had failed but rather it was simply something which was not quite stated correctly and was then given an unintended interpretation. The failure to adhere to the original spirit of the Constitution was much more serious. The original method of constitutional amendment could still have been activated but a political choice was made not to do so. This failure to implement the original intentions of the drafters had further consequences for judicial review as that doctrine could never flourish without entrenchment. Both provisions concentrated upon here could quite possibly have succeeded as originally drafted but under different conditions.

However, the underlying lesson here is that it is important not to focus on the negative aspects of the 1922 document because, as was made clear by Kelly, the success of the 1922 Constitution is that it essentially lives on in the Constitution of 1937. Even elements such as the judicial review provision, which might otherwise have been deemed a failure, were kept on in 1937, something which shows the prescience of both drafting teams.

Furthermore, we still have much to learn from the 1922 document. We will never know whether a more settled atmosphere might have led to a more successful trial of the experiments in the 1922 document or whether the true spirit of the Constitution might have been realised with proper management of the document. However, many of the experimental provisions originally contained in the document are now being considered once again as possible reforms to our current legal and political system. Many of the problems which we are confronted with today and which have prompted the discussions on constitutional reform – issues such as complete governmental control of the Dáil, lack of interest in politics, petty party politics, no voice for the people, no real role for the people and no way for the people to implement the reforms that they want – these are the issues which the 1922 Committee was so anxious to avoid and the reason why the innovative provisions such as the legislative referendum, the initiative, functional councils, external ministers, judicial review and so on were included in the document. So in searching for solutions to these problems today perhaps we should take another look at the 1922 document and not at the politics surrounding it but at what was originally intended.

Reflections

A new page of Irish history is beginning. We have a rich and fertile country – a sturdy and intelligent people. With peace, security and union, no one can foresee the limits of greatness and well-being to which our country may not aspire.[1]

It was in the spirit of the above quotation from Collins that the first Constitution of the modern Irish State was drafted. There was hope and enthusiasm for the future of the fledgling state. Now that the Irish people had finally gained the freedom to construct their own political and legal institutions, it was important that the Constitution should both reflect Ireland's ancient heritage and provide the pathway to creating a new, strong and successful Irish state.

When the 1922 Committee sat down to draft such a document, it carried out an intense study of foreign constitutions but also of Irish history and the philosophy of the ancient Gaelic state. It was inspired by the ideas of popular sovereignty and democracy and enthusiastically (some may say naively) believed that it could draft a constitution based on those ideals.

However, the path to promulgation was not straight-forward. Owing to differences of opinion on various matters, the Committee could not produce a unanimous document. Despite this, the three Drafts which were produced in such a brief period of time were of such quality that any one of them would have made a suitable model. Although a final draft was produced from the original Draft B, with additions and modifications from the other Drafts, there was much more revision to come in London. The Irish wanted to incorporate Dominion practice into the document but the British demanded rigid adherence to the unwritten tradition and the inclusion of British symbols. The Irish were forced to accept these controversial provisions under threat of war and, while it was recognised that they were largely symbolic, the inclusion of these elements was nevertheless a feature in the spiral to Civil War. However, while the Draft now contained many theoretical superfluities, included in order to make the Draft look more like that of

---

[1] Michael Collins, *The Path to Freedom* (Dublin, 1922), 19.

a Dominion, it had still managed to retain much of its inspiration and the internal matters and important themes remained as before. The passage of the Constitution Bill through the Constituent Assembly was difficult at times, though constructive; and apart from the amendment to Article 50, which would have a profound effect on the future of the document, the Constitution which emerged had still retained much of the spirit and inspiration of the original Drafts and the work of the Committee still shone through.

The document contained many important and innovative provisions in order to create a new Irish state in which the people could place their trust. Such features included: popular sovereignty, the referendum and initiative, PR-STV, external ministers, functional councils, the Seanad, amendment and judicial review. Unfortunately, apart from popular sovereignty, for the most part these devices never functioned as originally intended.

The referendum was undermined early on with the evasion of the time limit which was put in place in order to allow for a referendum to be brought. This was because the government wished to implement unpopular measures without worrying about the opposition appealing to the people. The referendum and initiative were then removed from the Constitution because of the realisation that de Valera and his supporters would otherwise use the devices to their advantage.

The PR-STV experiment was expected to cause the emergence of many small parties but the issue of the Civil War prevented this, as people generally stood on one side or the other, and essentially a two-party system materialised.

The reasons for the failure of the external ministers scheme are manifold. First, because PR-STV had not created a multiplicity of parties, a key ingredient had already been removed. Second, the changes made in London and in the Constituent Assembly reduced much of the appeal of the scheme. There were also certain problems in relation to the fact that the ministries which would be external were never agreed upon and also the details in relation to finance had the potential to cause confusion. Finally and most importantly, there were never any truly 'external' ministers appointed. Because the government party held a majority in the Dáil, the appointees were all members of that party and none could have been considered experts in the relevant field, as originally envisaged by the plan. Ironically, party politics prevented the operation of the scheme which had been devised to combat party politics.

Like the referendum and initiative, the functional councils experiment was never even given a chance because it was simply never implemented. The reasons for this are unclear but it is possible that the government was too preoccupied with post-Civil War concerns to turn its attention to the implementation of such a scheme.

The Seanad was originally successful as a defence against party politics but, again, the Civil War legacy intervened and party lines developed and eventually came to dominate the House.

The original amendment procedure is another provision which was never given a fair trial. The legislative amendment loophole was too useful a tool for the government to surrender in the midst of the ongoing political conflict and because entrenchment never came into effect, this effectively prevented the exercise of judicial review, along with the fact that the legal community had still not emerged from the British tradition of parliamentary sovereignty.

From this analysis, it is apparent that many of the experiments included in the Irish Free State Constitution were never truly given a fair trial, and external elements, such as the Civil War legacy, prevented the operation of others. The Irish Free State Constitution was envisaged, drafted, created, debated, amended and finally promulgated within 12 months, despite the outbreak of Civil War in the interim. But the unrest that both led up to and followed that war was to have a profound significance in the life of the Constitution. As we have seen, the split on the issue of the Treaty was on the minds of the drafters, and the Constitution was designed to try and reconcile all sides. Discussions on the unrest also punctuated the talks with the British and undoubtedly influenced the direction of those talks. The threat of war also forced the Irish to accept provisions which they knew would further distance the anti-Treaty side. We have also observed how the unrest which continued after the close of the Civil War effectively contributed to the failure of some aspects of the constitutional design, since the government was too preoccupied with stabilising the country to concentrate on the true ideals of the Constitution. Owing to these and more reasons, many of the experiments originally included in the Constitution were never put into action and others were treated in a manner not originally intended.

Accordingly, it is submitted that there were three main contributory factors in the failures of the Constitution. First, the changes demanded under threat of war by the British played a significant role in the rejection of the Constitution by the anti-Treaty side. In addition, the Civil War split and subsequent political atmosphere contributed enormously to the failures of the Constitution, through the non-use and amendment of various important aspects such as referendum and initiative, external ministers and the Seanad provisions. Finally, careless last-minute drafting in the Constituent Assembly also played a role, particularly in the amendment provision.

Therefore the eventual failures of the Constitution can be attributed to all three of these factors. The first is directly linked to the second and these are major factors. The third is simply failure of detail rather than one of vision, and so less serious. Thus, the drafters themselves bear by far the least blame for the failures and, while it is impossible to say whether or not the Constitution might have proved more successful in a more stable environment, it is certainly clear that it was a victim of its period in time.

The Irish Free State Constitution was a remarkably strong document, something which becomes evident when one realises that the spine of the 1937 Constitution is actually based on its predecessor. From a technical point of view, de Valera could quite reasonably have carried on with the original document once he had removed those provisions which offended certain parts of the population, but for political reasons he had decided that the document had been tainted by its association with the British; something which demonstrates that, while symbolism may be of no constitutional or legal import, it can be exceedingly significant nonetheless. But although the decision was taken to draft a completely new constitution, most of the 1922 Constitution was actually retained; something which demonstrates the far-sightedness of those involved in 1922. It cannot be denied that there were failures in the Irish Free State Constitution but the whole constitutional project cannot be considered a failure; its retention in the 1937 Constitution confirms an enduring legacy.

The Irish Free State Constitution was intended to be a document which would work for the people of the new Irish state. It was supposed to unite the people with a sense of trust in the State; the people would have rights and these would be protected by an independent judiciary; the people would choose their own form of government and become directly involved in it; the people would have a say in legislation and constitutional amendment; the government would be responsible to the Dáil, which would be responsible to the people; the members of the Oireachtas would be patriotic and conscientious people who would not be ruled by a party whip. This was the vision of those who drafted the Constitution and this was how it was supposed to function. Unfortunately, for all of the various reasons touched upon above, the original spirit of the Constitution evaporated and now it has been all but forgotten.

This period in history has been overly rigidly interpreted and the Irish Free State Constitution has been underestimated by historians and by anti-Treatyite commentary. Over 90 years later and in the midst of the decade of commemorations, perhaps now is the time to appreciate the immensity and foresight of the 1922 project.

Appendix 1*

Selected provisions from the Irish Free State Constitution Act

DÁIL ÉIREANN sitting as a Constituent Assembly in this Provisional Parliament, acknowledging that all lawful authority comes from God to the people and in the confidence that the National life and unity of Ireland shall thus be restored, hereby proclaims the establishment of The Irish Free State (otherwise called Saorstát Éireann) and in the exercise of undoubted right, decrees and enacts as follows: –

1. The Constitution set forth in the First Schedule hereto annexed shall be the Constitution of The Irish Free State (Saorstát Éireann).

2. The said Constitution shall be construed with reference to the Articles of Agreement for a Treaty between Great Britain and Ireland set forth in the Second Schedule hereto annexed (hereinafter referred to as 'the Scheduled Treaty') which are hereby given the force of law, and if any provision of the said Constitution or of any amendment thereof or of any law made thereunder is in any respect repugnant to any of the provisions of the Scheduled Treaty, it shall, to the extent only of such repugnancy, be absolutely void and inoperative and the Parliament and the Executive Council of the Irish Free State (Saorstát Éireann) shall respectively pass such further legislation and do all such other things as may be necessary to implement the Scheduled Treaty.

Article 1
The Irish Free State (otherwise hereinafter called or sometimes called Saorstát Éireann) is a co-equal member of the Community of Nations forming the British Commonwealth of Nations.

---

* A number of typographical errors have been corrected in this and the other Appendices.

Article 2

All powers of government and all authority, legislative, executive, and judicial, in Ireland are derived from the people of Ireland, and the same shall be exercised in the Irish Free State (Saorstát Éireann) through the organisations established by or under, and in accord with, this Constitution.

Article 3

Every person, without distinction of sex, domiciled in the area of the jurisdiction of the Irish Free State (Saorstát Éireann) at the time of the coming into operation of this Constitution, who was born in Ireland or either of whose parents was born in Ireland or who has been ordinarily resident in the area of the jurisdiction of the Irish Free State (Saorstát Éireann) for not less than seven years, is a citizen of the Irish Free State (Saorstát Éireann) and shall within the limits of the jurisdiction of the Irish Free State (Saorstát Éireann) enjoy the privileges and be subject to the obligations of such citizenship: Provided that any such person being a citizen of another State may elect not to accept the citizenship hereby conferred; and the conditions governing the future acquisition and termination of citizenship in the Irish Free State (Saorstát Éireann) shall be determined by law.

Article 4

The National language of the Irish Free State (Saorstát Éireann) is the Irish language, but the English language shall be equally recognised as an official language. Nothing in this Article shall prevent special provisions being made by the Parliament of the Irish Free State (otherwise called and herein generally referred to as the 'Oireachtas') for districts or areas in which only one language is in general use.

Article 5

No title of honour in respect of any services rendered in or in relation to the Irish Free State (Saorstát Éireann) may be conferred on any citizen of the Irish Free State (Saorstát Éireann) except with the approval or upon the advice of the Executive Council of the State.

Article 11

All the lands and waters, mines and minerals, within the territory of the Irish Free State (Saorstát Éireann) hitherto vested in the State, or any department thereof, or held for the public use or benefit, and also all the natural resources of the same territory (including the air and all forms of potential energy), and also all royalties and franchises, within that territory shall, from and after the date of the coming into operation of this Constitution, belong to the Irish Free State (Saorstát Éireann), subject to any trusts, grants, leases or concessions then existing in respect thereof, or any valid private interest therein, and shall be controlled and administered by the Oireachtas, in accordance with such regulations and provisions as shall be from time to time approved by legislation, but the same shall not, nor shall any part thereof, be alienated, but may in the public interest be from time to time granted by way of lease or licence to be worked or enjoyed under the authority and subject to the control of the Oireachtas: Provided that no such lease or licence may be made for a term exceeding ninety-nine years, beginning from the date thereof, and no such lease or licence may be renewable by the terms thereof.

Article 12
A Legislature is hereby created, to be known as the Oireachtas. It shall consist of the King and two Houses, the Chamber of Deputies (otherwise called and herein generally referred to as 'Dáil Éireann') and the Senate (otherwise called and herein generally referred to as 'Seanad Éireann'). The sole and exclusive power of making laws for the peace, order and good government of the Irish Free State (Saorstát Éireann) is vested in the Oireachtas.

Article 14
All citizens of the Irish Free State (Saorstát Éireann) without distinction of sex, who have reached the age of twenty-one years and who comply with the provisions of the prevailing electoral laws, shall have the right to vote for members of Dáil Éireann, and to take part in the Referendum and Initiative. All citizens of the Irish Free State (Saorstát Éireann) without distinction of sex who have reached the age of thirty years and who comply with the provisions of the prevailing electoral laws, shall have the right to vote for members of Seanad Éireann. No voter may exercise more than one vote at an election to either House, and the voting shall be by secret ballot. The mode and place of exercising this right shall be determined by law.

Article 15
Every citizen who has reached the age of twenty-one years and who is not placed under disability or incapacity by the Constitution or by law shall be eligible to become a member of Dáil Éireann.

Article 17
The oath to be taken by members of the Oireachtas shall be in the following form: –

I .... do solemnly swear true faith and allegiance to the Constitution of the Irish Free State as by law established, and that I will be faithful to H. M. King George V., his heirs and successors by law in virtue of the common citizenship of Ireland with Great Britain and her adherence to and membership of the group of nations forming the British Commonwealth of Nations.

Such oath shall be taken and subscribed by every member of the Oireachtas before taking his seat therein before the Representative of the Crown or some other person authorised by him.

Article 26

Dáil Éireann shall be composed of members who represent constituencies determined by law. The number of members shall be fixed from time to time by the Oireachtas, but the total number of members of Dáil Éireann (exclusive of members for the Universities) shall not be fixed at less than one member for each thirty thousand of the population, or at more than one member for each twenty thousand of the population: Provided that the proportion between the number of members to be elected at any time for each constituency and the population of each constituency, as ascertained at the last preceding census, shall, so far as possible, be identical throughout the country. The members shall be elected upon principles of Proportional Representation. The Oireachtas shall revise the constituencies at least once in every ten years, with due regard to changes in distribution of the population, but any alterations in the constituencies shall not take effect during the life of Dáil Éireann sitting when such revision is made.

Article 27

Each University in the Irish Free State (Saorstát Éireann), which was in existence at the date of the coming into operation of this Constitution, shall be entitled to elect three representatives to Dáil Éireann upon a franchise and in a manner to be prescribed by law.

Article 30

Seanad Éireann shall be composed of citizens who shall be proposed on the grounds that they have done honour to the Nation by reason of useful public service or that, because of special qualifications or attainments, they represent important aspects of the Nation's life.

Article 31

The number of members of Seanad Éireann shall be sixty. A citizen to be eligible for membership of Seanad Éireann must be a person eligible to become a member of Dáil Éireann, and must have reached the age of thirty-five years. Subject to any provision for the constitution of the first Seanad Éireann the term of office of a member of Seanad Éireann shall be twelve years.

Article 32

One-fourth of the members of Seanad Éireann shall be elected every three years from a panel constituted as hereinafter mentioned at an election at which the area of the jurisdiction of the Irish Free State (Saorstát Éireann) shall form one electoral area, and the elections shall be held on principles of Proportional Representation.

Article 33

Before each election of members of Seanad Éireann a panel shall be formed consisting of: –

(a) Three times as many qualified persons as there are members to be elected, of whom two-thirds shall be nominated by Dáil Éireann voting according to principles of Proportional Representation and one-third shall be nominated by Seanad Éireann voting according to principles of Proportional Representation; and

(b) Such persons who have at any time been members of Seanad Éireann (including members about to retire) as signify by notice in writing addressed to the President of the Executive Council their desire to be included in the panel.

The method of proposal and selection for nomination shall be decided by Dáil Éireann and Seanad Éireann respectively, with special reference to the necessity for arranging for the representation of important interests and institutions in the country: Provided that each proposal shall be in writing and shall state the qualifications of the person proposed and that no person shall be proposed without his own consent. As soon as the panel has been formed a list of the names of the members of the panel arranged in alphabetical order with their qualifications shall be published.

Article 35
Dáil Éireann shall in relation to the subject matter of Money Bills as hereinafter defined have legislative authority exclusive of Seanad Éireann …

Article 38
Every Bill initiated in and passed by Dáil Éireann shall be sent to Seanad Éireann and may, unless it be a Money Bill, be amended in Seanad Éireann and Dáil Éireann shall consider any such amendment; but a Bill passed by Dáil Éireann and considered by Seanad Éireann shall, not later than two hundred and seventy days after it shall have been first sent to Seanad Éireann, or such longer period as may be agreed upon by the two Houses, be deemed to be passed by both Houses in the form in which it was last passed by Dáil Éireann: Provided that every Money Bill shall be sent to Seanad Éireann for its recommendations and at a period not longer than twenty-one days after it shall have been sent to Seanad Éireann, it shall be returned to Dáil Éireann which may pass it, accepting or rejecting all or any of the recommendations of Seanad Éireann, and as so passed or if not returned within such period of twenty-one days shall be deemed to have been passed by both Houses. When a Bill other than a Money Bill has been sent to Seanad Éireann a Joint Sitting of the Members of both Houses may on a resolution passed by Seanad Éireann be convened for the purpose of debating, but not of voting upon, the proposals of the Bill or any amendment of the same.

Article 39
A Bill may be initiated in Seanad Éireann and if passed by Seanad Éireann shall be introduced into Dáil Éireann. If amended by Dáil Éireann the Bill shall be considered as a Bill initiated in Dáil Éireann. If rejected by Dáil Éireann it shall

not be introduced again in the same session, but Dáil Éireann may reconsider it on its own motion.

Article 44

The Oireachtas may create subordinate legislatures with such powers as may be decided by law.

Article 45

The Oireachtas may provide for the establishment of Functional or Vocational Councils representing branches of the social and economic life of the Nation. A law establishing any such Council shall determine its powers, rights and duties, and its relation to the government of the Irish Free State (Saorstát Éireann).

Article 47

Any Bill passed or deemed to have been passed by both Houses may be suspended for a period of ninety days on the written demand of two-fifths of the members of Dáil Éireann or of a majority of the members of Seanad Éireann presented to the President of the Executive Council not later than seven days from the day on which such Bill shall have been so passed or deemed to have been so passed. Such a Bill shall in accordance with regulations to be made by the Oireachtas be submitted by Referendum to the decision of the people if demanded before the expiration of the ninety days either by a resolution of Seanad Éireann assented to by three-fifths of the members of Seanad Éireann, or by a petition signed by not less than one-twentieth of the voters then on the register of voters, and the decision of the people by a majority of the votes recorded on such Referendum shall be conclusive. These provisions shall not apply to Money Bills or to such Bills as shall be declared by both Houses to be necessary for the immediate preservation of the public peace, health or safety.

Article 48

The Oireachtas may provide for the Initiation by the people of proposals for laws or constitutional amendments. Should the Oireachtas fail to make such provision within two years, it shall on the petition of not less than seventy five thousand voters on the register, of whom not more than fifteen thousand shall be voters in any one constituency, either make such provisions or submit the question to the people for decision in accordance with the ordinary regulations governing the Referendum. Any legislation passed by the Oireachtas providing for such Initiation by the people shall provide (1) that such proposals may be initiated on a petition of fifty thousand voters on the register, (2) that if the Oireachtas rejects a proposal so initiated it shall be submitted to the people for decision in accordance with the ordinary regulations governing the Referendum; and (3) that if the Oireachtas enacts a proposal so initiated, such enactment shall be subject to the provisions respecting ordinary legislation or amendments of the Constitution as the case may be.

Article 50

Amendments of this Constitution within the terms of the Scheduled Treaty may be made by the Oireachtas, but no such amendment, passed by both Houses of the Oireachtas, after the expiration of a period of eight years from the date of the coming into operation of this Constitution, shall become law, unless the same shall, after it has been passed or deemed to have been passed by the said two Houses of the Oireachtas, have been submitted to a Referendum of the people, and unless a majority of the voters on the register shall have recorded their votes on such Referendum, and either the votes of a majority of the voters on the register, or two-thirds of the votes recorded shall have been cast in favour of such amendment. Any such amendment may be made within the said period of eight years by way of ordinary legislation and as such shall be subject to the provisions of Article 47 hereof.

Article 51

The Executive Authority of the Irish Free State (Saorstát Éireann) is hereby declared to be vested in the King, and shall be exercisable, in accordance with the law, practice and constitutional usage governing the exercise of the Executive Authority in the case of the Dominion of Canada, by the Representative of the Crown. There shall be a Council to aid and advise in the government of the Irish Free State (Saorstát Éireann) to be styled the Executive Council. The Executive Council shall be responsible to Dáil Éireann, and shall consist of not more than seven nor less than five Ministers appointed by the Representative of the Crown on the nomination of the President of the Executive Council.

Article 52

Those Ministers who form the Executive Council shall all be members of Dáil Éireann and shall include the President of the Council, the Vice-President of the Council and the Minister in charge of the Department of Finance.

Article 53

The President of the Council shall be appointed on the nomination of Dáil Éireann. He shall nominate a Vice-President of the Council, who shall act for all purposes in the place of the President, if the President shall die, resign, or be permanently incapacitated, until a new President of the Council shall have been elected. The Vice-President shall also act in the place of the President during his temporary absence. The other Ministers who are to hold office as members of the Executive Council shall be appointed on the nomination of the President, with the assent of Dáil Éireann, and he and the Ministers nominated by him shall retire from office should he cease to retain the support of a majority in Dáil Éireann, but the President and such Ministers shall continue to carry on their duties until their successors shall have been appointed: Provided, however, that the Oireachtas shall not be dissolved on the advice of an Executive Council which has ceased to retain the support of a majority in Dáil Éireann.

Article 54

The Executive Council shall be collectively responsible for all matters concerning the Departments of State administered by Members of the Executive Council. The Executive Council shall prepare Estimates of the receipts and expenditure of the Irish Free State (Saorstát Éireann) for each financial year, and shall present them to Dáil Éireann before the close of the previous financial year. The Executive Council shall meet and act as a collective authority.

Article 55

Ministers who shall not be members of the Executive Council may be appointed by the Representative of the Crown, and shall comply with the provisions of Article 17 of this Constitution. Every such Minister shall be nominated by Dáil Éireann on the recommendation of a Committee of Dáil Éireann chosen by a method to be determined by Dáil Éireann, so as to be impartially representative of Dáil Éireann. Should a recommendation not be acceptable to Dáil Éireann, the Committee may continue to recommend names until one is found acceptable. The total number of Ministers, including the Ministers of the Executive Council, shall not exceed twelve.

Article 56

Every Minister who is not a member of the Executive Council shall be the responsible head of the Department or Departments under his charge, and shall be individually responsible to Dáil Éireann alone for the administration of the Department or Departments of which he is the head: Provided that should arrangements for Functional or Vocational Councils be made by the Oireachtas these Ministers or any of them may, should the Oireachtas so decide, be members of, and be recommended to Dáil Éireann by, such Councils. The term of office of any Minister, not a member of the Executive Council, shall be the term of Dáil Éireann existing at the time of his appointment, but he shall continue in office until his successor shall have been appointed, and no such Minister shall be removed from office during his term otherwise than by Dáil Éireann itself, and then for stated reasons, and after the proposal to remove him has been submitted to a Committee, chosen by a method to be determined by Dáil Éireann, so as to be impartially representative of Dáil Éireann, and the Committee has reported thereon.

Article 64

The judicial power of the Irish Free State (Saorstát Éireann) shall be exercised and justice administered in the public Courts established by the Oireachtas by judges appointed in manner hereinafter provided. These Courts shall comprise Courts of First Instance and a Court of Final Appeal to be called the Supreme Court. The Courts of First Instance shall include a High Court invested with full original jurisdiction in and power to determine all matters and questions whether of law or fact, civil or criminal, and also Courts of local and limited jurisdiction, with a right of appeal as determined by law.

Article 65

The judicial power of the High Court shall extend to the question of the validity of any law having regard to the provisions of the Constitution. In all cases in which such matters shall come into question, the High Court alone shall exercise original jurisdiction.

Article 66

The Supreme Court of the Irish Free State (Saorstát Éireann) shall, with such exceptions (not including cases which involve questions as to the validity of any law) and subject to such regulations as may be prescribed by law, have appellate jurisdiction from all decisions of the High Court. The decision of the Supreme Court shall in all cases be final and conclusive, and shall not be reviewed or capable of being reviewed by any other Court, Tribunal or Authority whatsoever: Provided that nothing in this Constitution shall impair the right of any person to petition His Majesty for special leave to appeal from the Supreme Court to His Majesty in Council or the right of His Majesty to grant such leave.

Article 69

All judges shall be independent in the exercise of their functions, and subject only to the Constitution and the law. A judge shall not be eligible to sit in the Oireachtas, and shall not hold any other office or position of emolument.

Article 82

Notwithstanding anything contained in Articles 14 and 33 hereof, the first Seaned Éireann shall be constituted immediately after the coming into operation of this Constitution in the manner following, that is to say: –

(a) The first Seanad Éireann shall consist of sixty members, of whom thirty shall be elected and thirty shall be nominated.

(b) The thirty nominated members of Seanad Éireann shall be nominated by the President of the Executive Council who shall, in making such nominations, have special regard to the providing of representation for groups or parties not then adequately represented in Dáil Éireann.

(c) The thirty elected members of Seanad Éireann shall be elected by Dáil Éireann voting on principles of Proportional Representation.

(d) Of the thirty nominated members, fifteen to be selected by lot shall hold office for the full period of twelve years, the remaining fifteen shall hold office for the period of six years.

(e) Of the thirty elected members the first fifteen elected shall hold office for the period of nine years, the remaining fifteen shall hold office for the period of three years.

(f) At the termination of the period of office of any such members, members shall be elected in their place in manner provided by Article 32 of this Constitution.

(g) Casual vacancies shall be filled in manner provided by Article 34 of this Constitution.

Appendix 2

Draft A

Preamble

We, the people of Ireland, in our resolve to renew and re-establish our State and to found it upon principles of freedom and justice, take control of our destiny in order that Ireland may take her place among the Nations of the world as a free democratic State. In the exercise of our sovereign right as a free people and to promote the welfare and to preserve and develop the heritage and the spiritual aspirations of our people, we hereby declare Saorstát Éireann established and give it this Constitution.

Section1 – Fundamental Rights

Article1

The Nation's sovereignty extends not only to all men and women of the nation, but to all the material possessions of the nation, the nation's soil and all its resources and all the wealth and wealth-producing processes within the nation. All right to private property is subordinated to the public right and welfare of the nation. It is the duty of every man and woman to give allegiance and service to the commonwealth, and it is the duty of the nation to assure that every citizen shall have opportunity to spend his or her strength and faculties in the service of the people. In return for willing service it is the right of every citizen to receive an adequate share of the produce of the nation's labour.

Article 2

All powers of Government are derived from the people of Ireland and are based on their consent. All persons who exercise the authority of Saorstát Éireann, whether legislative, executive, or judicial, do so by virtue of the powers conferred on them by the people.

Article 3

Every person domiciled in Ireland at the time of the adoption of this Constitution who was born in Ireland or either of whose parents was born in Ireland or who has been so domiciled for not less than seven years is a citizen of Saorstát Éireann; Provided that any such person being a citizen of another State may elect not to accept the citizenship hereby conferred. The conditions governing the future acquisition and termination of citizenship in Saorstát Éireann shall be determined by law. All men and women have as citizens the same rights.

Article 4

The national language of Saorstát Éireann is the Irish language, but the English language shall be equally recognised as an official language. All records and proceedings of the Oireachtas may be kept in the Irish or in the English language or in both and all Acts and public announcements shall be issued in both languages. Nothing in this Article shall prevent special provisions being made by the Oireachtas for districts or areas in which only one language is in use.

Article 5

No dignity or title of honour may be conferred on any citizen of Saorstát Éireann and after a period to be prescribed by law no dignity or title of honour held by any citizen of Saorstát Éireann shall have hereditary effect.

Article 6

The liberty of the person is inviolable and no person shall be deprived of his liberty except in accordance with law. Upon complaint made by or on behalf of any person that he is being unlawfully detained, the Árd-Chúirt and every judge thereof shall forthwith enquire into the same and may make an order requiring the person in whose custody such person shall be detained to produce the body of the person so detained before such Court or Judge without delay and to certify in writing as to the cause of the detention and such Court or Judge shall thereupon order the release of such person unless satisfied that he is being detained in accordance with law.

Article 7

The dwelling of each citizen is inviolable and shall not be forcibly entered except in accordance with law.

Article 8

The free exercise and profession of conscience in respect of religious faith is an inviolate right of every citizen, and no law may be made either directly or indirectly to endow any religion, or to give any preference, or to impose any disability on account of belief.

Article 9

The right to free expression as well as the right to assemble peaceably and without arms, and to form associations or unions is guaranteed for purposes not opposed to public morality. Laws regulating the manner in which the right of forming associations and the right of free assembly may be exercised shall contain no political, religious or class distinction.

Article 10

Education is a primary duty of citizenship, and all citizens of Saorstát Éireann have the right to free elementary education.

Article 11

All estates and interests in the lands, waters, and natural resources of Ireland heretofore claimed to be vested in the King or Crown of Great Britain are reserved to and vested in Saorstát Éireann. The air of Ireland and all forms of potential energy and forces of nature which are unknown or not usable because of lack of scientific or technical knowledge are also reserved to and vested in Saorstát Éireann provided that the Oireachtas may make provisions for rewarding any persons making a scientific or technical discovery of general public utility.

Article 12

All estates and interests in the lands, waters, and natural resources of Ireland formally claimed to be vested in the King or Crown of Great Britain but alienated prior to the adoption of this Constitution to individuals or corporations which at the date of the adoption hereof were not developed or were not the subject of a mineral or development lease, and all wealth below the surface of the soil which was unknown or undeveloped at the date hereof, may be acquired by Saorstát Éireann acting on behalf of the people in such manner and on such basis of compensation as may be prescribed by law: Provided that in awarding compensation therefor account shall not be taken of the value occurring after the date of the adoption of this Constitution from any cause other than the industry of the individuals or corporations from which they were acquired, or their predecessors in title.

Section II – Legislative Provisions

A. The Legislature

Article 13

A Legislative Assembly is hereby created to be known as the Oireachtas. It shall consist of two Houses – Dáil Éireann (the Chamber of Deputies) and Seanad Éireann (the Senate). Subject to the limitations imposed in this Constitution, the Oireachtas has the power to make laws for the peace, order and good government of Saorstát Éireann.

Appendix 2

Article 14
The Oireachtas shall sit in or near the city of Dublin or in such other place as it may from time to time determine.

Article 15
All citizens of Saorstát Éireann without distinction of sex, who have reached the age of twenty years and who comply with the provisions of the prevailing electoral laws, shall have the right to vote for members of the Oireachtas and to take part in the Referendum or Initiative. No one voter may exercise more than one vote and the voting shall be by secret ballot. The mode and place of exercising this right shall be determined by law.

Article 16
No person may be elected or sit in the Oireachtas who is of unsound mind, and has been so declared according to law, or who is an undischarged bankrupt, or who holds any office of profit under Saorstát Éireann, or who is a member of the armed forces of Saorstát Éireann and wholly employed therein; but Ministers of State and persons in receipt of pensions from the State, and such subordinate civil officers in the service of the State as may be defined by legislation shall not be excluded from the Oireachtas by reason of their office. If a member of the Oireachtas shall become subject to any of the foregoing disabilities or shall cease to be qualified as required by the Constitution, his seat shall thereupon become vacant.

Article 17
No person may be a member of both Dáil Éireann and Seanad Éireann.

Article 18
Every Member of the Oireachtas shall except in case of treason, felony, or breach of the peace be privileged from arrest in going to and returning from, and while within the precincts of, either House, and shall not be amenable to any action or proceeding at law in respect of any utterance in either House.

Article 19
All reports and publications of the Oireachtas shall be privileged and utterances made in either House wherever published shall also be privileged.

Article 20
Each House of the Oireachtas shall make its own Rules and Standing Orders, with power to attach penalties for their infringement and shall have power to ensure freedom of debate, to protect its official documents and the private papers of its members, and to protect itself and its members against any person or persons interfering with, molesting or attempting to corrupt its members in the exercise of their duties.

Appendix 2

Article 21
Each House shall elect its own Chairman and Deputy Chairman, to be known respectively as Riaruidhe and Leas-Riaruidhe in the case of Dáil Éireann and as Treóruidhe and Leas-Treóruidhe in the case of Seanad Éireann. Their functions and terms of office shall be prescribed by Standing Orders.

Article 22
All questions in each House shall, save as otherwise provided by this Constitution, be determined by a majority of the votes of the members present other than the Chairman or presiding member, who shall have and exercise a casting vote in the case of an equality of votes. The number of members necessary to constitute a meeting of either House for the exercise of its powers shall be determined by its Standing Orders.

Article 23
The Oireachtas shall make provision for the payment of its members and may in addition provide them with free travelling facilities in any part of Ireland.

Article 24
The Oireachtas shall hold at least one session each year. Each House shall determine the date of the conclusion of each session and fix the date of re-assembly. If either House is not in session, the Chairman, or in his absence the Vice-Chairman, shall, on a requisition by one-fourth of the members of that House, summon it within fourteen days.

Article 25
Sittings of each House of the Oireachtas shall be public, but in cases of special emergency either House may hold a private sitting with the assent of two-thirds of the members present. In questions dealing with the relations of Saorstát Éireann with other States the assent of the majority of the members present shall be sufficient.

B. Dáil Éireann

Article 26
Dáil Éireann shall be composed of members who represent constituencies to be determined by law. The number of members shall be fixed from time to time by the Oireachtas, but shall not be fixed at less than one member for each thirty thousand of the population. The members shall be elected upon the principles of Proportional Representation. The Oireachtas shall revise the constituencies at least once in every ten years, with due regard to changes and distribution of the population, but any alteration in the constituencies shall not take effect during the life of the Dáil sitting when such revision is made. Every citizen who has reached the age of twenty years and is not otherwise disqualified shall be eligible for election to Dáil Éireann.

Article 27

Elections for a new Dáil Éireann shall be held on the same day throughout the country and that day shall be proclaimed a public holiday. The Dáil shall meet within one month of its election, and shall, unless earlier dissolved, continue for four years from the date of its first meeting and not longer. The Dáil may not at any time be dissolved except on its own motion and with the assent of a majority of its members. The Dáil shall provide on dissolution for the holding of a General Election within one month to elect a new Dáil.

Article 28

In the case of the death, retirement, or disqualification of a member of Dáil Éireann, the vacancy shall be filled by election in manner to be prescribed by law.

C. Seanad Éireann

Article 29

Seanad Éireann shall be composed of citizens who have done honour to the Nation by reason of useful public service or who because of special qualifications or attainments represent important aspects of the Nation's life.

Article 30

The number of members of Seanad Éireann shall be forty. A citizen to be eligible for membership of the Seanad must have reached the age of thirty years, and have been nominated by Dáil Éireann. Subject to the provisions hereinafter made for the constitution of the first Seanad the term of office of a member of the Seanad shall be twelve years.

Article 31

The first Seanad Éireann shall be elected from duly qualified persons by the members of Dáil Éireann voting on the principles of Proportional Representation. When the Seanad has been assembled the members shall be grouped into four classes of ten each. The first class shall consist of the first ten persons elected by Dáil Éireann, and they shall sit for the full term of twelve years. The next ten persons elected shall form the second class and shall sit for nine years; the third ten persons elected shall form the third class, and shall sit for six years; and the last ten persons elected shall form the fourth class and shall sit for three years. Thereafter ten members of Seanad Éireann shall retire in rotation every three years.

Article 32

As each ten persons shall retire the vacancies shall be filled by an election, for the holding of which the entire body of electors shall form one constituency, and the election shall be held on the principles of Proportional Representation. Prior to each election of members for Seanad Éireann, Dáil Éireann voting by

Proportional Representation shall nominate twice as many qualified persons as there are members to be elected. The method of selection for nomination shall be decided by the Dáil provided that each proposal shall be in writing, shall state the qualifications of the person proposed, and shall be published.

Article 33

In the case of the death, retirement, or disqualification of a member of Seanad Éireann, his place shall be filled by the vote of the Seanad.

D. Legislation

Article 34

Bills imposing taxation or appropriating revenues or moneys shall originate only in Dáil Éireann. A Bill shall not be deemed to impose taxation or to appropriate revenues or moneys by reason only of its containing provisions for the imposition or appropriation of fines or other money penalties, or for the payment or appropriation of fees for licences or fees for services under the Bill. A Bill which appropriates revenues or money for the ordinary annual services of Saorstát Éireann shall deal only with such appropriation; a Bill imposing taxation shall deal only with the imposition of taxation; and any provision in such Bills dealing with any other matter shall be of no effect.

Article 35

Dáil Éireann shall, as soon as possible after the commencement of each financial year, consider the Budget of receipts and expenditure of Saorstát Éireann for that year, and, save in so far as may be provided by specific enactment in each case, the legislation required to give effect to the Budget of each year shall be enacted within that year.

Article 36

A vote, resolution or proposed law for the appropriation of revenue or moneys shall not be passed unless the purpose of the appropriation has in the same session been recommended by the Aireacht (the Executive Council).

Article 37

Seanad Éireann shall have power to revise and suspend Bills passed by Dáil Éireann. A Bill imposing taxation or appropriating revenues or moneys may not be suspended by the Senanad for a longer period than one calendar month from the date on which it shall have been first sent forward by the Dáil. On the expiration of the month, or such longer period as may be determined by the Dáil, such Bills shall be deemed to have been passed by the Oireachtas in the form in which they were last passed by Dáil Éireann.

Article 38

A Bill passed by either House of the Oireachtas and accepted by the other House shall be deemed to be passed by the Oireachtas

Article 39

Except as otherwise provided in this Constitution any Bill passed by Dáil Éireann may be amended in Seanad Éireann. The Dáil shall consider such amendments and shall return the Bill to Seanad: a Bill passed by the Dáil and considered by the Seanad shall, not later than one hundred and eighty days after it shall have been first sent to the Seanad, or such longer period as may be agreed upon by the two Houses, be deemed to have been passed by the Oireachtas in the form in which it was last passed by the Dáil.

Article 40

A Bill may be initiated in Seanad Éireann and if passed by the Seanad shall be introduced into Dáil Éireann. If amended by the Dáil the Bill as so amended shall be considered as a Bill initiated in the Dáil. If rejected by the Dáil it shall not be sent forward again by the Seanad in the same session, but the Dáil may reconsider it on its own motion.

Article 41

The Oireachtas shall have no power to declare acts to be infringements of the law which were not so at the date of their commission.

Article 42

Estates and interests in the lands, waters, and natural resources of Ireland now or hereafter vested in the Saorstát Éireann shall not be alienated in perpetuity, but they may, in the interests of the general public, be leased under the authority and subject to the control of the Oireachtas: Provided that no such lease or leases may be made for a term exceeding ninety-nine years beginning from the date thereof nor shall any such lease or leases be renewable by the terms thereof. The right to acquire all easements and rights of way for public transportation, telephone lines, telegraph lines, wireless station and aerial navigation stations belongs exclusively to Saorstát Éireann and the same shall be controlled by the Oireachtas.

Article 43

The utilization of water power and the production of electrical energy is placed under the control of the Oireachtas, and the Oireachtas shall from time to time prescribe the manner in which this control shall be exercised so as to safeguard the public interest and to ensure proper development and use.

Article 44

The Oireachtas may create subordinate legislatures, but it shall not confer thereon any powers in respect of the Army, Navy, or Air Force, the making of peace and war, treaties or external relations, alienage, or naturalisation, coinage, legal tender, trade marks, designs, merchandise marks, copyright, patent rights, weights and measures, census, submarine cables, wireless telegraphy, post office, railways, customs and excise.

Article 45

The Oireachtas may provide for the establishment of Councils representing the functions of the national life, such as Education, Agriculture, Transport and Fisheries. A law establishing any such Council shall define its rights and duties and its relations to the government of Saorstát Éireann.

Article 46

The Oireachtas has the exclusive right of raising and maintaining armed forces in the territory of Saorstát Éireann, and every such force shall be subject to the control of the Oireachtas.

Article 47

No agreement or treaty with any other State shall have any validity unless and until it shall have been ratified by Dáil Éireann in public session.

E. Referendum and Initiative

Article 48

Any law passed or deemed to be passed by the Oireachtas may be suspended for a period of ninety days on the written demand of two-fifths of the members of Dáil Éireann or of a majority of the members of Seanad Éireann presented to the Uachtarán. Such a law shall be submitted by Referendum to the decision of the people if demanded before the expiration of the ninety days by a petition signed by not less than thirty thousand voters on the register. These provisions shall not apply to laws imposing taxation or appropriating revenues or moneys, or to such laws as may be declared by the Oireachtas to be necessary for the immediate preservation of the public peace, health or safety.

Article 49

After the expiration of five years from the date of the adoption of this Constitution the Oireachtas may provide for the initiation by the people of proposals for laws or constitutional amendments. Should the Oireachtas fail to make such provision, it shall, on the petition of not less than fifty thousand voters on the register of whom not more than twenty thousand shall be in one constituency, either make such provision or submit the question to the people for decision in accordance with the ordinary regulations governing the Referendum. Any legislation passed by the Oireachtas providing for such initiation by the people shall provide: (1) that such proposals may be initiated on a petition of fifty thousand voters on the register; (2) that if the Oireachtas rejects a proposal so initiated it shall be submitted to the people for a decision in accordance with the ordinary regulations governing the Referendum; and (3) that if the Oireachtas enacts a proposal so initiated such enactments shall be subject to the provisions respecting ordinary legislation.

Article 50
Save in the case of actual invasion, Saorstát Éireann shall not declare war upon any other State or Nation or be committed to participation in any way without the assent of a majority of the voters on the register obtained on a Referendum.

Article 51
Amendments of this Constitution may be made by the Oireachtas, but every such amendment must be submitted to a Referendum of the people and shall not be passed unless a majority of the voters on the register record their votes and either a majority of the voters on the register or two-thirds of the votes recorded are in favour of the amendment.

Section III – The Executive

A. The Aireacht

Article 52
The executive authority of Saorstát Éireann shall be vested in and exercised by the Aireacht (the Executive Council). Unless and until the Oireachtas shall otherwise enact the Aireacht shall consist of an Uachtarán (President) and not more than nine or less than four other Airidhe (Ministers). The Uachtarán and other Airidhe shall be responsible to and removable by Dáil Éireann.

Article 53
Dáil Éireann shall in the first instance elect the Uachtarán, and he shall appoint the other Airidhe with the assent of the Dáil in each case. The Dáil may by a vote of lack of confidence remove the entire Aireacht or any individual Aire.

Article 54
The Aireacht may appoint one of its members to act as Tánaiste (Vice-President). Should the Uachtarán die, resign, or be otherwise unable to act the Tánaiste shall discharge his duties until Dáil Éireann shall otherwise direct.

Article 55
Dáil Éireann may require any Aire to attend and answer questions, and an Aire who is not a member of the Dáil may speak therein by its leave. Any Aire who at the time of his appointment is a member of Seanad Éireann shall resign his membership. Any Aire may speak in the Seanad at its request.

Article 56

The members of the Aireacht shall receive such remuneration as may from time to time be prescribed by law.

Article 57

When a law has been passed or is deemed to have been passed by the Oireachtas and has been authenticated in such manner as may be provided by the Standing Orders of each House of the Oireachtas the Uachtarán shall sign the law and affix the seal of Saorstát Éireann thereto in the presence, and with the signature, of one other Aire. The law shall then be promulgated by publication in the Official Gazette, or in such other manner as may from time to time be prescribed by law, and every person shall be cognisant of the provisions of every such law after it has been promulgated.

Article 58

The seal of Saorstát Éireann shall be deposited with and remain in the custody of the Uachtarán who shall hand it to his successor on appointment. The seal shall not be attached to any document save by the Uachtarán acting under the authority of the Oireachtas and in the presence and with the signature of at least one other Aire.

Article 59

The Uachtarán shall summon the Oireachtas for each session. He may with the consent of the Aireacht summon the Oireachtas for a date prior to that fixed by the motion for adjournment, but in no circumstances may he summon it for a later date.

B. Financial Control

Article 60

The Aireacht shall prepare the Budget of receipts and expenditure of Saorstát Éireann for each financial year and shall present it to Dáil Éireann before the close of the previous financial year.

Article 61

All revenues of Saorstát Éireann from whatever sources arising, shall, subject to such exceptions as may be provided by law, form one fund, and shall be appropriated for the purpose of Saorstát Éireann in the manner and subject to the charges and liabilities imposed by law.

Article 62

A Mór-Mhaor shall be appointed by Dáil Éireann. He shall not be removed except for stated misbehaviour or incapacity, and then only on resolutions passed by Dáil Éireann and Seanad Éireann. His age for retirement, his remuneration, and his pension on retirement shall be fixed by law. His remuneration may not be diminished during his term of office. He shall not be a member of the Oireachtas, nor shall he hold any other office or position of emolument.

Article 63

The Mór-Mhaor shall control all issues of public money and shall audit all public accounts. No money shall be paid out by him accept for such purposes and to such amounts as may be authorised by law. He shall report annually to Dáil Éireann and his report shall be published. He shall answer any questions which may be addressed directly to him by, and he may be summoned to appear in person before, the Dáil.

Article 64

Notwithstanding anything here contained the Oireachtas may hereafter make other provision, whether by the establishment of a Court of Accounts or otherwise, for the effective control and audit of all public revenues and expenditure: Provided that the person or persons appointed to an office analogous to that of the Mór-Mhaor shall have a tenure not inferior to his.

Section IV – The Judiciary

Article 65

The judicial power of Saorstát Éireann shall be vested in and exercised by an Árd-Chúirt (High Court) and an Iar-Chúirt Eilimh (Court of Final Appeal) and by such inferior and other Courts as may from time to time be established by law.

Article 66

The Árd-Chúirt shall consist of such divisions as may be prescribed by law. It shall have original jurisdiction in all cases and such appellate jurisdiction whether from a judge of the Árd-Chúirt or from inferior Courts or tribunals as may be prescribed by law. The distribution of work between such divisions may be regulated by law.

Article 67

The Iar-Chúirt Eilimh shall, with such exceptions and subject to such regulations as may be prescribed by law, exercise appellate jurisdiction from decision of the Árd-Chúirt; and decisions of the Iar-Chúirt Eilimh shall in all cases be final and conclusive, and shall not be reviewed or capable of being reviewed by any other person, court, or tribunal whatsoever.

Article 68

The Árd-Chúirt and the Iar-Chúirt Eilimh shall respectively consist of so many Judges as may from time to time be prescribed by law.

Article 69

Judges of the Árd-Chúirt and the Iar-Chúirt Eilimh shall be appointed by the Aireacht. The age for the retirement of Judges may be fixed by law. Subject to any such law, they shall hold office during life, but may be removed for stated misbehaviour or incapacity on resolutions passed by Dáil Éireann and Seanad Éireann. They shall receive such remuneration and such pension on retirement as may be fixed by law. Such remuneration may not be diminished during their continuance in office.

Article 70

All Judges shall be independent in the exercise of their functions and shall be bound only by law. Before entering upon the duties of their office they shall, in such manner as may be prescribed by law, pledge themselves to abide by the law.

Article 71

Judges shall not be eligible to sit in the Oireachtas. They shall not perform any other paid functions except where permitted by law.

Article 72

The law shall be administered in public courts save in such cases and subject to such conditions as may be prescribed by law.

Article 73

No one shall be tried save in due course of law, and extraordinary courts shall not be established for any such purpose.

Article 74

The jurisdiction of Courts Martial may be extended to and exercised over the civil population only in time of war, and for acts committed in time of war, and in accordance with regulations to be prescribed by law. No such jurisdiction shall be exercised in any area in which the civil courts are open or are capable of being held, nor shall any person be removed from one area to another for the purpose of creating such jurisdiction.

Article 75

No military person not on active service shall be tried by any Court Martial for any offence cognisable by the Civil Courts.

Article 76

No person shall, save in any cases of summary jurisdiction prescribed by law for minor offences, be tried without a jury on any criminal charge.

Article 77

The judicial power shall extend to the interpretation of treaties and to the question of the validity of any law, having regard to the provisions of this Constitution. In all cases in which such matters shall come into question, the Árd-Chúirt shall exercise original jurisdiction, and in all such cases there shall be an appeal to the Iar-Chúirt Eilimh. When hearing such appeals the Iar-Chúirt Eilimh shall consist of at least five members, and for this purpose the President of that Court may require the attendance of not more than two Judges of the Árd-Chúirt. In the absence of a decision to the contrary by a Court of competent jurisdiction the validity of laws passed or deemed to have been passed by the Oireachtas shall not be questioned by any inferior Court or tribunal.

Article 78

Proceedings may be instituted against Saorstát Éireann in such manner and subject to such regulations as may be prescribed by law.

Section V – External Affairs

Article 79

So long as Saorstát Éireann shall by virtue of the Treaty between Great Britain and Ireland signed in London on the sixth day of December, 1921, continue to be in association with the Community of Nations known as the British Commonwealth of Nations, the following provisions shall have effect, that is to say: –

(1) The Said Treaty shall have the force of law in Saorstát Éireann and the Oireachtas shall pass the necessary legislation and the Aireacht shall do all other things necessary for executing the terms of the same.

(2) The representative in Saorstát Éireann of His Majesty King George the V, his heirs and successors, shall be styled Commissioner of the British Commonwealth, and shall be appointed only with the previous assent of the Aireacht of Saorstát Éireann.

(3) As soon as any act passed by the Oireachtas shall have been duly authenticated as hereinafter provided the Minister of External Affairs shall, if so requested by the Commissioner of the British Commonwealth for the time being, present the same to such Commissioner who shall thereupon set his hand to the same to signify the assent of His Majesty the said King or his successor for the time being.

Section VI – Transitory Provisions

Article 80

The laws in force in Saorstát Éireann at the date of the adoption of this Constitution shall, subject to this Constitution, continue to be of full force and effect until the same or any of them shall have been repealed or amended by enactment of the Oireachtas.

Article 81

The Constituent Assembly by which this Constitution had been adopted and passed into law shall be, and for a period not exceeding two years from the date of the adoption of this Constitution shall continue to be, the first Oireachtas for the purpose of this Constitution and shall have all the powers and authorities conferred on the Oireachtas by this Constitution, and the first election for Dáil Éireann under Articles 26 and 27 hereof shall take place as soon as possible after the expiration of such period.

Appendix 3

Draft B

Preamble

We, the people of Ireland, acknowledging that all authority comes from God, and in the exercise of our right as a free people, do hereby create Saorstát Éireann and give it this Constitution. Through it we shall endeavour to re-establish our national life and unity that Ireland may take her rightful place among the Nations of the earth.

Section I – Fundamental Rights

Article 1
The Nation's sovereignty extends not only to all men and women of the nation, but to all the material possessions of the nation, the nation's soil and all its resources and all the wealth and wealth-producing processes within the nation; and all right to private property is subordinated to the public right and welfare of the nation. It is the duty of every man and woman to give allegiance and service to the commonwealth, and it is the duty of the nation to ensure that every citizen shall have opportunity to spend his or her strength and faculties in the service of the people In return for willing service it is the right of every citizen to receive an adequate share of the produce of the nation's labour.

Article 2
All powers of Government are derived from the people in Ireland and are based on their consent. All persons who exercise the authority of Saorstát Éireann, whether legislative, executive or judicial, do so by virtue of the powers conferred on them by the people.

Article 3

Every person domiciled in Ireland at the time of the adoption of this Constitution who was born in Ireland or either of whose parents was born in Ireland or who has been so domiciled for not less than seven years is a citizen of Saorstát Éireann provided that any such person being a citizen of another State may elect not to accept the citizenship hereby conferred; and the conditions governing the future acquisition and termination of citizenship in Saorstát Éireann shall be determined by law. All men and women have as citizens the same rights.

Article 4

The national language of Saorstát Éireann is the Irish language, but the English language shall be equally recognised as an official language. All records and proceedings in the Oireachtas may be kept in the Irish or in the English language, or in both, and all Acts and public announcements shall be issued in both languages. Nothing in this article shall prevent special provisions being made by the Oireachtas for districts or areas in which only one language is in use.

Article 5

No dignity or title of honour may be conferred on any citizen of Saorstát Éireann and after a period to be prescribed by law no dignity or title of honour held by any citizen of Saorstát Éireann shall have hereditary effect.

Article 6

The liberty of the person is inviolable and no person shall be deprived of his liberty except in accordance with law. Upon complaint made by or on behalf of any person that he is being unlawfully detained, Cúirt Náisiúnta (the National Court) and every Judge thereof shall forthwith enquire into the same and may make an order requiring the person in whose custody such person shall be detained to produce the body of the person so detained before such Court or Judge without delay and to certify in writing as to the cause of the detention and such Court or Judge shall thereupon order the release of such person unless satisfied that he is being detained in accordance with law.

Article 7

The dwelling of each citizen is inviolable and shall not be forcibly entered except in accordance with law.

Article 8

The free exercise and profession of conscience in respect of religious faith is an inviolable right of every citizen, and no law may be made either directly or indirectly to endow any religion, or to give any preference, or to impose any disability on account of belief.

Article 9

The right of free expression of opinion as well as the right to assemble peaceably and without arms, and to form associations or unions is guaranteed for purposes not opposed to public morality. Laws regulating the manner in which the right of forming association and the right of free assembly may be exercised shall contain no political, religious or class distinction.

Article 10

Education is a primary duty of citizenship, and accordingly all citizens of Saorstát Éireann have the right to free elementary education.

Article 11

By the exercise of the sovereign powers which extend over all the natural resources and forces of nature within the territorial jurisdiction of Saorstát Éireann, the following property rights and natural wealth are reserved to and invested in Saorstát Éireann: – The remainders, reversions, rights, titles and interests of every kind whatsoever heretofore claimed to be vested in the King or Crown of Great Britain in all or any lands or waters; and also the air and water of Ireland and all forms of potential energy and forces of nature either in the sea, inland waters, the air, or beneath the soil which at the date hereof were either unknown or not usable because of lack of scientific knowledge; provided that due provision shall be made by law for reasonable compensation to the person making a scientific discovery of any unknown form of energy or force of nature, or making usable a known form.

Article 12

Any remainders, reversions, rights, titles or interests formerly claimed to be vested in the King or Crown of Great Britain in all or any of the lands, waters and natural resources of Ireland but alienated prior to the adoption of this Constitution to individuals or corporations, which at the date of the adoption hereof were not developed or were not the subject of a mineral or development lease, and also all wealth beneath the surface of the soil which was unknown or undeveloped at the date hereof, may be acquired by Saorstát Éireann acting on behalf of the people in such manner and on such basis of compensation as may be prescribed by legislation; provided that in awarding compensation therefor account shall not be taken of the value accruing after the date of the adoption of this Constitution from any cause other than the industry of the individual or persons from whom they were acquired, or from the industry of the predecessors in interest of such persons.

Section II – Legislative Provisions

A. The Legislature

Article 13

A Legislative Assembly is hereby created to be known as the Oireachtas. It shall consist of two Houses – Dáil Éireann (the Chamber of Deputies) and Seanad Éireann (the Senate). Subject to the limitations imposed in this Constitution and to the revisory and suspensory powers conferred on the Seanad, the power of making laws for the peace, order and good government of Saorstát Éireann shall be exercised by Dáil Éireann.

Article 14

The Oireachtas shall sit in or near the City of Dublin or in such other place as from time to time it may determine.

Article 15

All citizens of Saorstát Éireann without distinction of sex, who have reached the age of twenty years and who comply with the provisions of the prevailing electoral laws, shall have the right to vote for members of the Oireachtas and to take part in the Referendum or Initiative. No voter may exercise more than one vote and the voting shall be by secret ballot. The mode and place of exercising this right shall be determined by law.

Article 16

No person may be elected to, or sit in, the Oireachtas who is of unsound mind, and has been so declared according to law, or who is an undischarged bankrupt, or who holds any office of profit under Saorstát Éireann, or who is a member of the armed forces of Saorstát Éireann and wholly employed therein; but Ministers of State otherwise entitled to sit in the Oireachtas and persons in receipt of pensions from the State, and such subordinate civil officers in the service of the State as may be defined by legislation shall not be excluded from the Oireachtas by reason of their office. If a member of the Oireachtas shall become subject to any of these disabilities or shall cease to be qualified as required by the Constitution, his seat shall thereupon become vacant.

Article 17

No person may be at the same time a member of both Dáil Éireann and Seanad Éireann.

Article 18

Every member of the Oireachtas shall, except in case of treason, felony, or breach of the peace, be privileged from arrest in going to and returning from, and while within the precincts of either House, and shall not be amenable to any action or proceeding at law in respect of any utterance in either House.

Article 19
All reports and publications of the Oireachtas shall be privileged and utterances made in either House wherever published shall be privileged.

Article 20
Each House of the Oireachtas shall make its own rules and Standing Orders, with power to attach penalties for their infringement and shall have power to ensure freedom of debate, to protect its official documents and the private papers of its members, and to protect itself and its members against any person or persons interfering with molesting or attempting to corrupt its members in the exercise of their duties.

Article 21
Each House shall elect its own Chairman and Deputy Chairman to be known respectively as Riaruidhe and Leas-Riaruidhe in the case of Dáil Éireann and as Treóruidhe and Leas-Treóruidhe in the case of Seanad Éireann. Their functions and term of office shall be prescribed by Standing Orders.

Article 22
All questions in each House shall, save as otherwise provided by this Constitution, be determined by a majority of the votes of the members present other than the Chairman or presiding member, who shall have and exercise a casting vote in the case of an equality of votes. The number of members necessary to constitute a meeting of either House for the exercise of its powers shall be determined by its Standing Orders.

Article 23
The Oireachtas shall make provision for the payment of its members and may in addition provide free travelling facilities in any part of Ireland.

Article 24
The Oireachtas shall hold at least one session each year. Dáil Éireann shall fix the date of re-assembly of the Oireachtas and the date of the conclusion of the session of each House provided that the sessions of Seanad Éireann shall not be concluded without its consent.

Article 25
Sittings of each House of the Oireachtas shall be public. In cases of special emergency either House may hold a private sitting with the assent of two-thirds of the members present. In questions dealing with relations of Saorstát Éireann with other States the assent of the majority of the members present shall be sufficient.

B. *Dáil Éireann*

Article 26

Dáil Éireann shall be composed of members who represent constituencies to be determined by law. The number of members shall be fixed from time to time by the Oireachtas, but shall not be fixed at less than one member for each thirty thousand of the population. The members shall be elected upon the principles of Proportional Representation. The Oireachtas shall revise the constituencies at least once in every ten years, with due regard to changes and distribution of the population, but any alteration in the constituencies shall not take effect during the life of the Dáil sitting when such revision is made. Every citizen who has reached the age of twenty years, and is not otherwise disqualified shall be eligible for elections to Dáil Éireann.

Article 27

Elections for a new Dáil Éireann shall be held on the same day throughout the country and that day shall be proclaimed a public holiday. The Dáil shall meet within one month of its election, and shall, unless earlier dissolved continue for four years from the date of its first meeting, and not longer. The Dáil may not at any time be dissolved except on its own motion and with the assent of a majority of its members. The Dáil shall provide on dissolution for the holding of a General Election within one month to elect a new Dáil.

Article 28

In the case of the death, retirement or disqualification of a member of the Dáil, the vacancy shall be filled by election in a manner to be determined by law.

C. *Seanad Éireann*

Article 29

Seanad Éireann shall be composed of citizens who have done honour to the Nation by reason of useful public service or who because of special qualifications or attainments represent important aspects of the Nation's life.

Article 30

The number of members of Seanad Éireann shall be forty. A citizen to be eligible for membership of the Seanad must have reached the age of thirty years, and have been nominated by Dáil Éireann. Subject to any provision for the constitution of the first Seanad, the term of office of a member of the Seanad shall be twelve years.

Article 31

Ten members of Seanad Éireann shall be elected every three years at an election, at which Saorstát Éireann shall form one electoral area, and the election shall be held on the principles of Proportional Representation.

Article 32

Prior to each election of members for Seanad Éireann, Dáil Éireann voting by Proportional Representation shall nominate twice as many qualified persons as there are members to be elected. The method of selection for nomination shall be decided by the Dáil provided that each proposal shall be in writing, shall state the qualifications of the persons proposed and shall be published.

Article 33

In the case of the death, retirement or disqualification of a member of Seanad Éireann his place shall be filled by the vote of the Seanad.

D. Legislation

Article 34

Dáil Éireann shall have exclusive legislative authority in relation to the imposition of taxes and duties and the appropriation of revenues. A Bill shall not be deemed to impose taxation or to appropriate revenues or moneys by reason only of its containing provisions for the imposition or appropriation of fines or other money penalties, or for the payment or appropriation of fees for licences or fees for services under the Bill. A Bill which appropriates revenues or moneys for the ordinary annual services of the government shall deal only with such appropriation; a Bill imposing taxation shall deal only with the imposition of taxation; and any provision in such Bills dealing with any other matter shall be of no effect.

Article 35

Dáil Éireann shall as soon as possible after the commencement of each financial year consider the Budget of receipts and expenditures of Saorstát Éireann for that year, and, save in so far as may be provided by specific enactment in each case, the legislation required to give effect to the Budget of each year shall be enacted within that year.

Article 36

Money shall not be appropriated by vote, resolution or law, unless the purpose of the appropriation has in the same session been recommended by the Aireacht (the Executive Council).

Article 37

Any Bill, not being a bill imposing taxation or appropriating moneys, passed by Dáil Éireann may be amended in Seanad Éireann and the Dáil shall consider such amendment; but a Bill passed by the Dáil and considered by the Seanad shall, not later than one hundred and eighty days after it shall have been first sent to the Seanad, or such longer period as may be agreed upon by the two Houses, be deemed to be passed by the Oireachtas in its form as last passed by the Dáil.

Article 38

A Bill passed by either House and accepted by the other House of the Oireachtas shall be deemed to be passed by the Oireachtas.

Article 39

A Bill may be initiated in Seanad Éireann and if passed by Seanad shall be introduced into Dáil Éreann. If amended by the Dáil the Bill shall be considered as a Bill initiated by the Dáil. If rejected by the Dáil it shall not be introduced again in the same session, but the Dáil may reconsider it on its own motion.

Article 40

The Oireachtas shall have no power to declare acts to be infringements of the law which were not so at the date of their commission.

Article 41

The remainders, reversions, rights, titles and interests in the lands, waters and natural resources of Ireland now or hereafter vested in Saorstát Éireann shall not be alienated in perpetuity, but, they may, in the interests of the general public, be leased under the authority and subject to the control of the Oireachtas, but in no case for a term exceeding ninety-nine years beginning from the date on which such lease is made and such lease or leases shall not be renewable by the terms thereof. The right to acquire all easements and rights of way for public transportation, telephone lines, telegraph lines, wireless stations and aerial navigation stations belongs exclusively to Saorstát Éireann and the same shall be controlled by the Oireachtas.

Article 42

The utilization of water power and the production of electrical energy is placed under the control of the Oireachtas, and the Oireachtas shall from time to time prescribe the manner in which this control shall be exercised so as to safeguard the public interest and to ensure proper development and use.

Article 43

The Oireachtas may create subordinate legislatures, but it shall not confer thereon any powers in respect of the Army, Navy or Air Force, the making of peace and war, treaties or external relations, alienage or naturalisation, coinage, legal tender, trade marks, designs, merchandise marks, copyright, patent rights, weights and measures, submarine cables, wireless telegraphy, post office, railways, customs and excise.

Article 44

The Oireachtas may provide for the establishment of Functional or Vocational Councils representing branches of social and economic life, such as, Education, Agriculture, Transport, Labour and Industry, Fisheries, Co-operative development.

A law establishing any such Council shall determine its powers, rights and duties and its relation to the government of Saorstát Éireann and may provide for the introduction into the Oireachtas of Bills approved by such Council.

Article 45
The Oireachtas has the exclusive right of raising and maintaining armed forces in the territory of Saorstát Éireann, and every such force shall be subject to the control of the Oireachtas.

Article 46
No agreement or treaty with any other State shall have any validity unless and until it shall have been ratified by Dáil Éireann in public session.

E. Referendum and Initiative

Article 47
Any law passed or deemed to be passed by the Oireachtas may be suspended for a period of ninety days on the written demand of two-fifths of the members of Dáil Éireann or of a majority of the members of Seanad Éireann, presented to the Uachtarán. Such a law shall be submitted by Referendum to the decision of the people if demanded before the expiration of the ninety days by a petition signed by not less than thirty thousand persons then on the register of voters. These provisions shall not apply to laws imposing taxation or appropriating revenues or moneys, or to such laws as shall be declared by the Oireachtas to be necessary for the immediate preservation of the public peace, health or safety.

Article 48
After the expiration of five years from the date of the adoption of this Constitution the Oireachtas may provide for the initiation by the people of proposals for laws or constitutional amendments. Should the Oireachtas fail to make such provision, it shall, on the petition of not less than fifty thousand voters on the register of whom not more than twenty thousand shall be voters in any one constituency, either make such provision or submit the question to the people for decision in accordance with the ordinary regulations governing the Referendum. Any legislation passed by the Oireachtas providing for such initiation by the people shall provide (1) that such proposals may be initiated on a petition of fifty thousand voters on the register, (2) that if the Oireachtas rejects a proposal so initiated it shall be submitted to the people for decision in accordance with the ordinary regulations governing the Referendum; and (3) that if the Oireachtas enacts a proposal so initiated such enactments shall be subject to the provisions respecting ordinary legislation.

Article 49

Save in the case of actual invasion, Saorstát Éireann shall not declare war upon any other State or Nation or be committed to participation in any war without the assent of the majority of the voters on the register obtained on a Referendum.

Article 50

Amendments of this Constitution may be made by the Oireachtas, but every such amendment must be submitted to a Referendum of the people and shall not be passed unless a majority of the voters on the register record their votes and either a majority of the voters on the register or two-thirds of the votes recorded are in favour of the amendment.

Article 51

If any law should be declared unconstitutional by an Árd-Chúirt (the High Court of Appeal) the Oireachtas shall embody the principle of the law as a constitutional amendment and submit it by Referendum to the people unless the Oireachtas be able to meet the constitutional objection by an amendment of the law.

Section III – The Executive

A. The Aireacht

Article 52

The Executive Authority of Saorstát Éireann shall be an Aireacht (Executive Council) responsible to Dáil Éireann, consisting of four Airidhe (Ministers) who shall be members of the Dáil and a number of other Airidhe not exceeding eight chosen from all citizens eligible for election to the Dáil who shall not be members of the Oireachtas during their term of office, provided that the Dáil may from time to time determine that a particular Aire or Airidhe, not exceeding two, may be Members of that House in addition to the four above mentioned.

Article 53

The four Airidhe in Dáil Éireann shall be the Uachtarán (the President of Saorstát Éireann), the Tánaiste (the Vice President), the Minister of External Affairs, and the Minister of Finance The Uachtarán shall be the chief of the Aireacht and shall be elected by Dáil Éireann, and on election he shall appoint the Tánaiste, the Minister of External Affairs and the Minister of Finance The Uachtarán and the Airidhe appointed by him shall retire from office should he fail to be supported by a majority in the Dáil, but such Airidhe shall continue to carry on their duties until their successors are appointed.

Article 54

Airidhe who are not members of Dáil Éireann shall be nominated by a committee of members of the Dáil chosen by a method to be determined by the Dáil so as to be proportionally and impartially representative of the Dáil. Such Airidhe shall be chosen with due regard to their suitability for office and should as far as possible be generally representative of Saorstát Éireann as a whole rather than of groups or parties. Should a nomination not be acceptable to the Dáil, the Committee shall continue to propose names until one is found acceptable.

Article 55

Each Aire not a member of Dáil Éireann shall be the responsible head of an Executive Department or Departments and shall be elected to his office by the Dáil, provided that should arrangements for Functional or Vocational Councils be made by the Oireachtas these Airidhe or any of them may, should the Oireachtas so decide, be members of and be nominated on the advice of such Councils. The term of office of any such Aire shall be four years; or such other period as may be fixed by law, and shall not necessarily be affected by a dissolution of the Dáil; and no such Aire shall be removed from office during his term unless the proposal to remove him has been previously submitted to a committee chosen by a method to be determined by the Dáil, so as to be proportionately and impartially representative of the Dáil, and then only if the Committee shall have reported that such Aire has been guilty of malfeasance in office or has not been performing his duties in a competent and satisfactory manner, or has failed to carry out the lawfully expressed will of the Oireachtas.

Article 56

The four Airidhe who are members of the Dáil shall alone be responsible on all matters relating to external affairs whether policy, negotiations or executive acts. Subject to the foregoing provision the Aireacht shall meet and act as a single authority.

Article 57

Airidhe who are not members of the Dáil shall by virtue of their office possess all the rights and privileges of a member of the Dáil except the right to vote, and may be required by the Dáil to attend and answer questions.

Article 58

Should the Uachtarán die, resign, or be otherwise unable to act the Tánaiste shall discharge his duties until Dáil Éireann shall otherwise direct.

Article 59

The members of the Aireacht shall receive such salaries as shall from time to time be prescribed by law, but the salary of any Aire shall not be diminished during his term of office.

Article 60

Every law shall be authenticated by the signature of the Uachtarán and by the seal of Saorstát Éireann affixed thereto. It shall be the duty of the Uachtarán to promulgate every such law in the manner prescribed by the Oireachtas. Ignorance of the provisions of any law shall not be pleaded after the expiration of thirty days from the date of its promulgation.

Article 61

The seal of Saorstát Éireann shall be deposited with and remain in the custody of the Uachtarán who shall hand it to his successor on appointment. The seal shall not be attached to any document save by the Uachtarán acting on the authority of the Oireachtas and in the presence.

Article 62

The Uachtarán shall summon the Oireachtas for each session and may, should he deem it necessary, and shall, upon a written request of one-fourth of the members of the Dáil, summon it for a date earlier than that fixed at the time of adjournment.

Article 63

The Aireacht shall prepare the Budget of receipts and expenditure of Saorstát Eireann for each financial year and shall present it to Dáil Éireann before the close of the previous financial year.

B. Financial Control

Article 64

All revenues of Saorstát Éireann from whatever source arising, shall subject to such exceptions as may be provided by law, form one fund, and shall be appropriated for the purpose of Saorsát Éireann in the manner and subject to the charges and liabilities imposed by law.

Article 65

Dáil Éireann shall appoint a Mór-Mhaor to act on behalf of Saorstát Éireann. He shall control all disbursements and shall audit all amounts of moneys administered by or under the authority of the Oireachtas and shall report directly to the Dáil at stated periods to be determined by law. He may be summoned by the Dáil at any time to appear in person and answer questions with reference to the execution of his office.

Article 66

The Mór-Mhaor shall not be removed except for stated misbehaviour or incapacity on resolutions passed by Dáil Eireann and Seanad Éireann. Subject to this provision the terms and conditions of his tenure of office shall be fixed by law.

He shall not be a member of the Oireachtas, nor shall he hold any other office or position of emolument.

Article 67

Notwithstanding anything herein contained the Oireachtas may hereafter make other provision, whether by the establishment of a Court of Accounts, or otherwise, for the more effective control and audit of all public revenues and expenditures, provided that the person or persons appointed to an office analogous to that of the Mór-Mhaor shall have a tenure not inferior to his.

Section IV – The Judiciary

Article 68

The judicial power of Saorstát Éireann shall be exercised and justice administered by the judges appointed and in the public Courts established by the Oireachtas. These Courts shall comprise Courts of First Instance and a Court of Final Appeal to be called the Árd-Chúirt (the High Court of Appeal) of Saorstát Éireann. The Courts of First Instance shall include a Cúirt Náisiúnta (National Court) invested with full original jurisdiction in and power to determine all matters and questions whether of law or fact, civil or criminal, wherever arising in the territorial jurisdiction of Saorstát Éireann, and also Courts of local and limited jurisdiction with a right of appeal as determined by law to the Cúirt Náisiúnta.

Article 69

The Árd-Chúirt of Saorstát Éireann shall with such exceptions and subject to such regulations as may be prescribed by law have appellate jurisdiction from all decisions of the Cúirt Náisiúnta. The decisions of the Árd-Chúirt shall in all cases be final and conclusive, and shall not be reviewed or capable of being reviewed by any other person, court, or tribunal whatsoever.

Article 70

The judicial power of the Árd-Chúirt shall extend to the question of the validity of any law having regard to the provisions of the Constitution and to the interpretation of treaties. In all cases in which such matters shall come into question, the Árd-Chúirt shall exercise original jurisdiction.

Article 71

The number of judges, the constitution and organisation of and distribution of business and jurisdiction among the said courts and judges, and all matters of procedure shall be as prescribed by the laws for the time being in force and the regulations made thereunder.

Article 72

The judges of the Árd-Chúirt and of the Cúirt Náisiúnta shall be appointed by the Aireacht. They shall not be removed except for stated misbehaviour or incapacity and then only by resolutions passed by both Dáil Éireann and Seanad Éireann. The age for retirement, the remuneration and the pension of such judges on retirement and the declarations to be taken by them on appointment shall be prescribed by law. Such remuneration may not be diminished during their continuance in office. The mode and terms of appointment of the judges of such other courts as may be created shall be prescribed by law.

Article 73

All judges shall be independent in the exercise of their functions and subject only to the law. A judge shall not be eligible to sit in the Oireachtas and shall not hold any other office or position of emolument.

Article 74

No one shall be tried save in due course of law and Extraordinary Courts shall not be established. The jurisdiction of courts martial shall not be extended to or exercised over the civil population save in time of war, and for acts committed in time of war, and in accordance with the regulations to be prescribed by law. Such jurisdiction shall not be exercised in any area in which the civil courts are open or capable of being held, and no person shall be removed from one area to another for the purpose of creating such jurisdiction.

Article 75

A member of the armed forces of Saorstát Éireann not on active service shall not be tried by any Court Martial for an offence cognisable by the ordinary Courts.

Article 76

No person shall, save in case of summary jurisdiction prescribed by law for minor offences, be tried without a jury on any criminal charge. The penalty of death shall not be attached to any offence.

Article 77

Proceedings may be instituted against Saorstát Éireann only in such cases and in such manner and subject to such regulations as may be prescribed by law.

Section V – External Affairs

Article 78

So long as Saorstát Éireann shall by virtue of the Treaty between Great Britain and Ireland signed in London on the sixth day of December, 1921, continue to be in association with the Community of Nations known as the British

Commonwealth of Nations, the following provisions shall have effect, that is to say: – (1) The said Treaty shall have the force of law in Saorstát Éireann and the Oireachtas shall pass the necessary legislation and the Aireacht shall do all other things necessary for executing the terms of the same. (2) The representative in Saorstát Éireann of His Majesty King George V, his heirs and successors, shall be styled the Commissioner of the British Commonwealth, and shall be appointed only with the previous assent of the Aireacht of Saorstát Éireann. (3) As soon as any act passed by the Oireachtas shall have been duly authenticated as hereinafter provided the Minister of External Affairs shall, if so requested by the Commissioner of the British Commonwealth for the time being, present the same to such Commissioner who shall thereupon set his hand to the same to signify the assent of his Majesty the said King or his successor for the time being.

Section VI – Transitory Provisions

Article 79

The laws in force in Saorstát Éireann at the date of the adoption of this Constitution shall, subject to this Constitution, continue to be of full force and effect until the same or any of them shall have been repealed or amended by enactment of the Oireachtas.

Article 80

The Constituent Assembly by which this Constitution has been adopted and passed into law shall be, and for a period not exceeding two years from the date of this adoption shall continue to be, the first Dáil Éireann for the purposes of this Constitution and shall have all the powers and authorities conferred on Dáil Éireann by this Constitution, and the first election for Dáil Éireann under Articles 26 and 27 hereof shall take place as soon as possible after the expiration of such period.

Article 81

The first Seanad Éireann shall be constituted immediately after the adoption of this Constitution in a manner following, that is to say: Thirty members of the first Seanad shall be elected on the principles of Proportional Representation by Dáil Éireann and ten shall be nominated by the Uachtarán having special regard to providing representation for groups or parties not then adequately represented in Dáil Éireann. When the first Seanad so constituted has been assembled the members of the Seanad shall be grouped into four classes of ten each. The first class shall consist of the ten nominated members who shall hold office for the full period of twelve years. The first ten members elected shall form the second class who shall hold office for nine years. The next ten shall form the third class and shall hold office for six years. The last ten elected shall form the fourth class and shall hold office for three years.

Appendix 4

Draft C

Preamble

Chun Glóire Dé agus Ónora na hÉireann

We, the Irish people, acknowledging that political authority comes from God to the people, asserting our natural right to national independence and unity, and in pursuance of our claim to determine freely the forms of Irish Government, hereby vote and confirm this Constitution in the Constituent Assembly of the Irish Free State, in order to base the organisation and development of our country on the principles of justice and liberty.

I – Congress

Article 1

Legislative power resides directly in the people of Ireland and through them in Congress (Dáil Éireann), which consists of two Chambers, (Seomrai): a House of Representatives (Tig na dTeachtai), and a Senate (Seanaid).

Article 2

(1) Representatives and Senators exercise their function in person, they represent and act for the whole people according to their own judgment and not by the instructions of those who elected them. (2) They may resign at any time. A seat which has been casually vacated shall be filled by the same electoral body as previously elected thereto. (3) Their remuneration shall be determined by law and may include the provision of travelling facilities, special allowances for committees meeting during recess, and special deductions for absence.

Article 3

Each Chamber meets separately, regulates its own procedure, makes its own standing orders, appoints its own officials, has disciplinary and suspensory authority over its members, and has power to maintain and enforce its privileges and immunities.

Article 4

At the beginning of each regular session, each chamber elects out of its own number its own Chairman (Cathaoirleach) and Deputy Chairman (Leas-Chathaoirleach), who remain in office even beyond the session or elective period until their successors are appointed.

Article 5

(1) Any person who – (a) is not an Irish citizen qualified to take part in elections for the House of Representatives; or (b) has been sentenced and is under sentence, or subject to be sentenced, for any offence punishable under the law of the Irish Free State for one year or longer; or (c) is an undischarged bankrupt; or (d) is certified as mentally deficient; or (e) holds any office of profit under the Irish or any other government; or (f) has a pecuniary interest in any agreement with the public service of Ireland otherwise than in virtue of membership of an incorporated company consisting of more than twenty-five persons; shall be incapable of being chosen or sitting as Representative or Senator, or of being appointed a member of the Executive Council.

(2) But subsection (e) of the preceding section shall not apply to the following – (a) the Members of the Executive Council; (b) a person in receipt of a pension from the Irish Free State; (c) an officer or member of the Irish armed forces on retired or half-pay or not wholly employed in such forces; (d) a civil servant or public official of the Irish Free State not directly appointed by Congress or by the Executive Council, as may be specified by legislation.

(3) Civil servants or public officials, eligible to Congress, shall have the right to obtain leave pending their term as members of Congress or of the Executive Council.

(4) Members of Congress or of the Executive Council cannot enter the Civil Service or Judiciary until after the expiration of one year from the time they cease to be members. This time-limit shall not affect Representatives, Senators or Ministers who were civil servants or public officials before they became members of Congress or of the Executive Council, provided that they return to the same department.

Article 6

If a Representative or Senator or Minister becomes subject to any of the disabilities enumerated in the first section of the preceding article; or ceases to be qualified as required by this Constitution or by law; or fails for a whole ordinary session to attend, without the special leave of the House or Senate as the case may be; his membership or seat shall thereupon become vacant.

Article 7

No person may be at the same time a member of both Chambers, or a member of either Chamber and a member of a local public body such as a corporation or county council or subordinate parliament.

Article 8

The consent of the House or Senate as the case may be is requisite for any limitation of personal liberty which might prejudice a member in the exercise of his functions during the session. Members shall not be prosecuted for the exercise of their functions as members. No person shall be amenable elsewhere for any statement made in either Chamber, or in any Committee thereof. All publications authorised by either Chamber, and all accurate reports of the proceedings therein, shall be privileged.

Article 9

A simple majority is required for decisions in either Chamber, where no other proportion of votes or method of voting is prescribed by this Constitution or by Standing Orders. The Chairman or presiding member shall not have a vote except in case of equality of votes when he shall have a casting vote. The number or proportion required to form a quorum is determined by Standing Orders.

Article 10

(1) The House and Senate assemble annually in regular session, at the seat of government, on the first Wednesday of November or on such a date as is fixed by Standing Orders. (2) The House and Senate are convened, in regular session at an earlier date than that appointed or in extra session by the respective Chairmen, upon the request of the Executive Council or of one-third of the members of the House of Representatives. (3) The House of Representatives determines the conclusion of the session and the date of re-assembly. The sessions of the House and Senate begin and end together.

Article 11

The debates of the House and Senate are public. The public may be excluded from either House or Senate upon the motion of one-third of the members supported by a two-thirds majority.

II – The House of Representatives

Article 12

(1) The House of Representatives is composed of representatives of the Irish People, chosen, upon the principles of proportional representation, by the universal, equal and secret suffrage of all Irish citizens, without distinction of sex, who have completed their twenty-first year and who possess full civic rights. Details

and conditions shall be settled by electoral laws. (2) The electoral areas and constituencies shall, as far as possible, be compact and contiguous; they shall be chosen and arranged, and when necessary rearranged, by some judicial process to be prescribed by law. (3) The Representatives shall be chosen in the ratio of one member for each thirty thousand persons of the total population, fractions of upwards of fifteen thousand persons being reckoned as thirty thousand. (4) If, during the first seven years after the enactment of this Constitution, the mode of election and voting herein prescribed is impracticable in any part of Ireland, Congress shall decide the method whereby the citizens of these areas may be represented in the House of Representatives.

Article 13
Every citizen of Ireland who has attained the age of twenty-five years and has for the preceding five years resided in Ireland, and is not subject to any of the disqualifications enumerated in Article 5, is eligible for election to the House of Representatives. For the purpose of this article, residence either in Ireland prior to the enactment of this Constitution or outside Ireland in the service of Ireland, shall be treated as residence in Ireland.

Article 14
(1) The House is chosen for three years and is entirely renewed at each general election. (2) The general election must take place on one day which shall not be later than sixty days after dissolution. (3) The House shall assemble not later than thirty days after the election, either on a day fixed before dissolution or at a date fixed by the Chairman in accordance with article 10, or else of full right on the thirtieth day after the general election.

Article 15
The House has the right – which, on the motion of one-third of its members becomes an obligation – to appoint Committees of Inquiry. Details as to election, number and procedure of such Committees shall be determined by standing orders or special resolution. The courts and administrative authorities are bound to produce evidence and documents before such Committees, as is provided in article 48.

Article 16
The House shall out of its own members select, by a method of proportional voting, a Finance Committee (Coiste an Airgid) and by some method of voting to be determined, a Committee for External Affairs (Coiste na nGnothai Eachtranach), the membership of each of which must not exceed one-tenth of the total number of Representatives. Each Committee shall select its own chairman, shall make its own rules of procedure; it may sit even when Congress is not in session, and continues until a new Committee is selected; it decides if its sittings shall be public or private; and it has the same power as a Committee of Inquiry.

III – The Senate

Article 17

The Senate shall consist of fifty persons of national achievement, merit or eminence. They shall be chosen, with the advice of outside bodies if considered desirable, by the House of Representatives voting by proportional representation. (2) Each Senator is chosen for a period of ten years; and one-tenth of the whole Senate retire every year. (3) The first Senate shall be nominated beforehand by the Constituent Assembly. At the first meeting of this first Senate the senators shall be divided by lot into ten equal consecutive classes; and the seats of the Senators of each class shall be vacated at the expiration of successive years.

Article 18

Every citizen of Ireland who has attained the age of thirty-five years, and has for the preceding ten years resided in Ireland, and is not subject to the disqualification enumerated in Article 5, is eligible for election to the Senate. For the purpose of this article, residence, either in Ireland prior to the enactment of this Constitution, or outside Ireland in the service of Ireland, shall be treated as residence in Ireland.

IV – The Executive Council (An Choirle Ghniomhach)

Article 19

(1) The supreme executive authority is exercised, as hereinafter provided, by an Executive Council consisting of a President (Uachtaran), a Vice-President (Leas-Uachtaran), a Minister of External Affairs (Minister na nGnothai Eachtranach) and seven other Ministers. The members of the Executive Council are chosen for three years, they remain in office till their successors are appointed, and they are chosen anew after each election of the House of Representatives. (2) The House of Representatives shall from its own members elect in order the President, the Vice-President and the Minister of External Affairs. Any one or more of these three Ministers shall resign, if by an express formal vote, the House call upon him or them to do so. (3) The House shall elect the seven other Ministers by Proportional Representation, from among all the Irish citizens eligible to the House, who are not subject to any of the disqualifications enumerated in Article 5. If any one or more of these seven Ministers be a member of either Chamber, such membership shall forthwith be terminated. In electing these seven Ministers account is to be taken not only of personal fitness but also of the desirability of assuring the representation of the different regions and parties. (4) Vacancies which occur shall be filled at the next ensuing sitting of the House of Representatives for the remainder of the three years' term of office.

Article 20

The members of the Executive Council have the right to speak in the House of Representatives and also the right to make motions on the subject under consideration; if summoned by the House it shall be their duty to attend. But only the President, Vice-President, and Minister of External Affairs have the right to vote, such right being in virtue of their position as Representatives.

Article 21

The members of the Executive Council may not, during their term of office, occupy any other office or follow any other pursuit or exercise a profession. They shall receive an annual salary to be determined by Congress.

Article 22

The Executive Council is presided over by the President, or in his absence the Vice-President. For the purpose of facilitating administration, the business of the Executive Council is distributed by departments among its members. In external affairs the members of the Executive Council other than the President, Vice-President and Minister of External Affairs, have only a consultative voice. But all decisions emanate from the Executive Council as a single authority.

Article 23

The Executive Council shall have the power of appointment, control, supervision and dismissal of all officers and officials, save as otherwise prescribed by this Constitution or by legislation. It may call in the aid of experts for special matters.

Article 24

The Executive Council shall issue the general administrative instructions and executive decrees necessary for the carrying out of laws, so far as these decrees are authorised by, and not in contradiction with, legislation.

Article 25

The Executive Council shall make to Congress proposals for legislation, general reports at the opening of each ordinary session, and such special reports as may be demanded by Congress.

V – Legislation and Administration

Article 26

(1) All records, journals, and proceedings of Congress may be kept in the Irish or in the English language or in both; all Bills, Acts and notices of general public importance issued by the Government shall be in both languages. (2) The Irish and English language shall possess equal freedom, rights and privileges; without

prejudice to the attribution of a large measure of linguistic autonomy to uni-lingual minorities and areas, whether Irish or English speaking.

Article 27
The Irish Free State shall foster the ideal of decentralisation and regional autonomy within the unity Ireland. It shall therefore be within the competence of Congress to transmit to local representative assemblies such derivative author-ity in legislative, administrative, cultural and economic affairs, as is compatible with the unity and integrity of Ireland, without derogating from essential national services and rights. Congress may delegate to local parliaments the right to make ordinances within the ambit of the Constitution in relation to matters comprised in the following classes of subjects, local administration of justice and maintenance of order, direct taxation for local revenue, borrowing of money on local credit, education other than higher, local institutions and councils, works and undertak-ings not extending beyond the local borders.

Article 28
The declaration of war, the conclusion of peace and all alliances and treaties with other States, must be validated by Congress. The provisions of any such treaty shall not be incorporated as part of the Constitution of the Irish Free State; but effect shall be given thereto by appropriate legislation.

Article 29
(1) Eighty thousand voters may demand, in general terms, the passing of a law on a specified subject for a specified purpose. (2) If Congress approves of such a demand, it shall enact the legislation demanded. (3) If Congress does not approve of the proposal, then the question whether such a law shall be enacted or not, shall be submitted to the vote of the people. If a majority of citizens taking part in the vote, express themselves in the affirmative, the necessary legislation shall be passed by Congress in conformity with the people's decision.

Article 30
(1) Eighty thousand voters may present a demand in the form of a completely drafted Bill. (2) If Congress approves thereof, it shall pass the Bill in the ordinary way. (3) If the Bill is rejected by Congress, it shall nevertheless be referred to the people for acceptance or rejection. (4) If Congress drafts an alternative proposal, it may first submit its own proposal to the people. Should this be rejected by the people, then the Bill emanating from the popular initiative shall be submitted to the people for acceptance or rejection.

Article 31
(1) Laws are passed either by the People, or by the House of Representatives with the approval of the Senate. (2) Bills may be introduced into the House by the Executive Council or by individual members. Such Bills may, after preliminary

reading, be referred to the Senate prior to further consideration in the House. The Senate may also on its own initiative draft schemes of legislation and refer them to the House. (3) Bills appropriating revenue or imposing taxation must, however, be originated by the Executive Council or by the Finance Committee in the House of Representatives.

Article 32
(1) The promulgation of a law which has been passed by the House and approved by the Senate shall be deferred for seventy five days if one-third of the House of Representatives so demand; provided that the law is not the annual budget or has not been declared urgent by both House and Senate. (2) If within this interval fifty thousand voters express their will to have a referendum on the law, it shall be submitted to a vote of the people for acceptance or rejection.

Article 33
(1) All Bills passed by the House shall be presented to the Senate for approval. If, within one month – being the time of session – after such presentation, the Senate does not express disapproval, it shall be taken to have approved. (2) In case the Senate amends or rejects the Bill, it shall be brought before the House for further consideration. Should the House and Senate not arrive at an agreement within three months, being time of session, the Bill, if it appropriates revenue or imposes taxation, shall become law as finally passed by the House save as provided in the preceding article; if the Bill does not appropriate revenue or impose taxation, it shall become inoperative unless within that interval a referendum is demanded by fifty thousand voters or by a majority of the House or Senate, in which case the law as finally passed by the House shall be submitted to a vote of the people for acceptance or rejection. (3) If the House by a two-thirds majority declares that the measure is of extreme emergency, the period of three months provided in the preceding section shall be reduced to one month.

Article 34
(1) The annual budget shall be prepared by the Executive Council before the opening of the financial year, shall be examined and reported on by the Finance Committee of the House, and shall be presented to the House by the Executive Council. (2) Any Bill which appropriates revenue or moneys for the ordinary annual services of the government shall deal only with such appropriation. (3) All public expenditure shall be subject to annual vote unless, for definite and adequate reasons, specific enactment is otherwise made in special cases.

Article 35
(1) Only in virtue of law can the State (a) raise a loan or (b) alienate, exchange or mortgage State property, subject however to article 65; or (c) impose public contributions or taxes. (2) All public revenues, save as otherwise provided by legislation in the case of any undertaking to be administered as an independent

economic unit, shall be paid into and form one fund from which appropriations shall be made by the State Auditor only in virtue of law and under the regulations of the Ministry of Finance (Ministriocht an Airgid). (3) All public accounts, including those of local public bodies, shall be audited and reported on by the State Auditor (Cuntasoir an Stait) who shall be appointed by Congress and shall enjoy the independence assigned to Judges of the Supreme Court (article 40). The State Auditor shall be assisted by a staff consisting of (a) auditors, who are members of an incorporated society of auditors, to be appointed by Congress on the recommendation of the Finance Committee, and (b) civil servants appointed by competitive process. (4) The accounts of all departments shall show their total expenditure, capital and revenue, and, as far as possible, shall be reduced to units of cost.

Article 36

(1) It shall be the duty of the Finance Committee of the House to examine and report on all proposals of revenue and expenditure, including all clauses involving a charge on the public funds; to investigate the administration, expenditure and use of all sums voted by the House; to consider the annual statements of audited expenditure in all branches of the public service, and to supervise the application of comparative costing and statistical methods to the public estimates and accounts. (2) For this purpose the Finance Committee shall have the assistance of a special secretariat, shall have power to call in the aid of experts, to examine witnesses and officials and to order the production of documents except as provided in article 48; and it shall have authority to require the attendance of the State Auditor, the Minister and officials of the Department of Finance.

Article 37

(1) In addition to territorial autonomy legislation shall institute a measure of functional autonomy for the different branches of social service and economic life. In particular a Council of Education (Coirle an Oideachais), a Council of Agriculture (Coirle na Talamhaiochta), a Council of Transport (Coirle an Iumparachain), and a Council of Industry (Coirle an Oibreachais), shall, as soon as possible be established; and in each of these Councils the relevant occupational groups shall be represented according to their social and economic importance. Legislation shall determine the advisory, supervisory, and administrative capacity of such Councils. (2) Drafts of important Laws, involving social and economic policy, proposed by the Executive Council shall be submitted to the Council to which they appertain, for consideration and criticism, before they are introduced into the House of Representatives. Bills may also be referred by the House of Representatives to a Council. The Councils have the right of originating such Bills themselves. Should the Executive Council disapprove of them, it must nevertheless introduce them into the House of Representatives, with a statement of its own views.

Appendix 4

VI – The Judiciary

Article 38

(1) The judicial power of the Irish Free State shall be vested in and exercised by a Supreme Court (Ard-Chuirt), and such inferior courts as may be established by law. (2) The Supreme Court shall consist of a Chief Justice (PrimhBhreitheamh), the ordinary judges of appeal and the other judges of the several divisions. (3) Congress shall by law determine the original and appellate jurisdiction of the Supreme Court; and in particular may assign thereto original jurisdiction in matters relating to (a) this Constitution and its interpretation, (b) admiralty and maritime jurisdiction, (c) the competency of subordinate parliaments, (d) the validity of elections to the House of Representatives. (4) Judges shall in adjudicating have the right to inquire into the validity of an executive decree; but save as aforesaid they shall not be competent to question the validity of a duly promulgated law.

Article 39

(1) The Appellate Division of the Supreme Court shall consist of the Chief Justice, two ordinary judges of appeal, and two additional judges of appeal assigned by the Chief Justice to the Appellate Division from any of the divisions of the Supreme Court. These additional judges shall continue to perform their duties in their respective divisions when their attendance is not required in the Appellate Division. The Chief Justice may, if necessary, assign any other judge or judges of the Supreme Court to act temporarily in the Appellate Division. (2) The decisions of the Appellate Division of the Supreme Court shall in all cases be final and conclusive and shall not be subject to review by any other person, court, or tribunal whatsoever.

Article 40

(1) All judges shall be bound only by law and shall enjoy such privileges and immunities as are necessary for the independent exercise of their judicial functions. (2) All Judges of the Supreme Court shall be appointed by the Executive Council with the consent of the Senate. They shall receive such remuneration as is prescribed by law and this remuneration shall not be diminished during their continuance in office. They shall continue in office until the attainment of the age limit prescribed by law, unless previously removed from office, on the grounds of misbehaviour or incapacity, by the Executive Council with the approval of Congress. (3) Upon occurrence of a vacancy in any division of the Supreme Court, the Executive Council or Senate may, if a reduction in the number of judges in such court be considered to be in the public interest, postpone filling the vacancy until Congress determine whether such reduction shall take place. (4) In the case of any general rearrangement of the courts of justice or their circuits, the Executive Council may, with the consent of the Senate, order the compulsory transfer of a judge to another court or division, or his retirement, but only on

the condition of his retention of full salary. (5) All judges and magistrates, save Judges of the Supreme Court, shall be appointed by the Judges of the Supreme Court with the consent of the Executive Council.

Article 41

(1) Save as prescribed by law, the sittings of all courts shall be public. (2) No one shall be tried save in due course of law and in accordance with the forms prescribed by law. All exceptional or extraordinary courts are illegal. (3) Punishment for an offence shall occur only in virtue of a law promulgated prior to the commission of the offence. (4) Except in cases of summary jurisdiction prescribed by law for minor offences, no one shall be tried for any crime without a jury; and the trial shall be held at such place or places as shall be prescribed by law.

Article 42

(1) Proceedings may be instituted against the Irish Free State in such manner as may be determined by law. (2) Legislation shall provide that every citizen shall have the right to reparation or compensation for damage or loss caused by the civil or military organs of the State, acting officially without conforming to law. The responsibility lies in principle against the State in whose service the official acts without prejudice to a counter charge by the State against the official. Permission of the public authorities is not required for such charge, and the regular course of law cannot be excluded. Detailed provisions are left to legislation.

Article 43

(1) Limitations of liberty, personal or domiciliary, are admitted only in cases provided for by law, according to the form prescribed by law, and on the orders of a competent judicial authority. (2) Upon complaint made by or on behalf of any person that he is being unlawfully detained, the Supreme Court and every judge thereof shall forthwith inquire into the same and may make an order requiring the person in whose custody such person is detained to produce the body of the person so detained before such Court or Judge without delay and to certify in writing as to the cause of the detention and such Court or Judge shall thereupon order the release of such person unless satisfied that he is being detained in accordance with law.

VII – Individual Rights and Duties

Article 44

All persons, irrespective of sex, born or naturalised in Ireland, who are subject to the jurisdiction of the Irish Free State and are not citizens or subjects of any other State, are Irish citizens. Details and conditions relative to the acquisition and extinction of citizenship or nationality, or to the acquirement or loss of political and civic rights by Irish citizens, shall, subject to this Constitution, be determined by law.

Article 45
The enumeration, in this Constitution, of personal, social, economic and religious rights and duties, shall not be construed to deny or discharge other rights and duties. In so far as these enumerated rights do not merely express an ideal requiring to be elaborated, determined and applied by future legislation, they shall have immediate juridical effect from the date of enactment of this Constitution.

Article 46
All citizens are equal before the law, independently of birth, sex, status or rank. Hereditary titles of nobility may no longer be conferred or received. Legislation may determine a date after which such titles shall merely form part of the name. Non-hereditary titles may be received only with the approval of the Executive Council. Titles may be conferred only when they indicate office, function or academic qualifications.

Article 47
(1) Every citizen has the right, within the limits prescribed by law to express his opinion freely by word, writing, printed matter, or pictorial representation, or in any other matter. (2) Legal measures are admissible for regulating public entertainments in the interests of morality and public order, for suppressing obscene and indecent literature, and traffic or propaganda subversive of public morality.

Article 48
(1) The secrecy of correspondence, as well as of the postal, telegraph and telephone services, is guaranteed; and exceptions may be admitted only by law. (2) Professional confidence, as well as the right to refuse evidence, of clergymen, members of the medical profession, and others, shall be protected by law.

Article 49
All citizens have the right, without having to give notification or secure special permission, to assemble peacefully and without arms. Open-air meetings, however, may be made notifiable by law, and, to safeguard public order and convenience, may be forbidden.

Article 50
(1) All citizens have the right to form unions, associations, and societies, the objects of which do not contravene such penal legislation as is passed to secure public safety and morality. Every union is free to acquire legal rights or incorporation in accordance with general regulations prescribed by law. (2) Regulations may be imposed by law, in the interests of the community, on the formation and conduct of profit-making associations. Restrictions may also be imposed

on the participation of foreigners or non-citizens in political or profit-making associations.

Article 51

Legislation shall organise the military service and shall determine how far various rights must be restricted for the members of the armed forces in order to ensure the fulfilment of their duties and the maintenance of military discipline.

Article 52

(1) Armed forces shall be employed only on requisition of the civil authority on condition of strict observance of the laws in order to repress riot or to carry out the prescriptions of the law. Exceptions to this principle shall be admitted only in virtue of legislation dealing with civil disturbance or war, and in accordance with this article. (2) All proclamations of so-called martial-law shall be null and void. Suspension, in whole or part of the constitutional and legal rights and liberties of the civilian population, or of any section thereof, may be decreed by the Executive Council, only in case of necessity, in the interests of public order and security. This decree must be immediately submitted to Congress, which, if not sitting, may of full right assemble on the eighth day after the publication of the decree. If Congress refuses to give its consent, the decree shall forthwith become null and void. If the decree is issued while the House of Representatives stands dissolved and if the new House has not been elected before the eighth day after the publication of the decree, then it shall be competent for the Senate alone to act in this matter in the name of Congress. (3) Such suspension, even if approved by Congress, shall not validate the exercise of military jurisdiction over the civil population, except in so far as the civil courts are not capable of being held within an attainable area and within a reasonable time. (4) Until an impartial judicial investigation has been held into the acts committed in virtue of such a suspensory decree, no Act of Indemnity shall be passed by Congress.

VIII – Family, Education and Religion

Article 53

(1) Marriage, as the basis of family life and national well-being, is under the special protection of the State; and all attacks on the purity, health and sacredness of family life shall be forbidden. (2) The Irish State shall recognise, as heretofore, the inviolable sanctity of the marital bond. (3) The civil validity of religiously solemnised marriages shall be recognised, provided that the details of registration prescribed by legislation are duly complied with.

Article 54

(1) Parents have the right and duty of rearing and educating their children, so as to make them good citizens. The State has the right of supervision. Parents must

provide their children with education at least up to the completed fourteenth year of age. This obligation shall be determined in detail by law. (2) Children deprived of parental care have the right to the help and protection of the State in the limits fixed by law. A judicial decree is necessary to deprive parents of their right over the child.

Article 55
(1) Maternity shall be under the special protection of the law. (2) Young people shall be protected against exploitation and against moral, intellectual or bodily neglect. (3) The employment of children under fourteen in wage-earning occupations, work of adolescents in injurious trades, and industrial night work of women shall be forbidden by law.

Article 56
The entire public educational system is with the help of the Council of Education (Article 37), under State supervision, as regards equipment, efficiency, programme, co-ordination, provision or registration of educational establishments, training qualification and tenure of teachers. But there shall be no State monopoly of education, no infringement of the rights of parents to secure religious instruction for their children, and no executive interference with the academic autonomy of universities and learned bodies.

Article 57
In every educational establishment, engaged in the instruction of children under eighteen years of age, aided wholly or partly by the State or local public bodies, the teaching of religion is obligatory, except for those pupils whose parents or guardians express dissent therefrom. The direction and control of this religious teaching pertains to the religious association or body concerned, without prejudice to the general right of supervision reserved to the State educational authorities.

Article 58
No school shall be relatively penalised or suffer diminution of any rights or claims by reason of the fact that it is owned or controlled by a religious denomination, provided that such school satisfies the general conditions of educational efficiency and national service prescribed by law.

Article 59
(1) There is no established or State-endowed church. (2) Liberty of conscience and of religion is guaranteed to all citizens. No one may, by reason of his religious convictions, be limited in such rights as are exercised by other citizens. (3) All citizens have the right to practise their religion freely, in private or in public, in so far as public order or morality is not thereby affected.

Article 60

The State has the duty of making moral protection and religious ministrations available for citizens in public institutions such as educational establishments, barracks, hospitals, prisons, asylums. For such purpose ministers of religion have the right of access to their own co-religionists in such institutions.

IX – Economic Life

Article 61

(1) Every citizen is bound to make such use of his mental and physical powers as is for the welfare of the community, and to contribute according to his means to all public taxes imposed by law. (2) All citizens have an equal right, which must be determined by law, to a fair opportunity of providing, by labour of hand or brain, a decent livelihood for themselves and their families. (3) Every citizen has a right to the leisure and conditions necessary for his spiritual interests, social obligations and political rights. Sundays and holidays recognised by the State shall be under legal protection, as days of rest from work and for the promotion of spiritual and cultural purposes. (4) All transactions opposed to morality and all usurious contracts shall be regarded as null and void.

Article 62

(1) The right to hold private property is guaranteed; its extent and limits are defined by law. The right to hold private property, like other rights, implies a correlative duty, and it must not be exercised to the detriment of the community. (2) The right of alienation, bequest, and inheritance is guaranteed without prejudicing the fiscal claims of the State and its right to limit the alienability of the homestead, and to abolish entails and anti-social restrictions. (3) Expropriation of private property may be effected only by legislation, for the benefit of the community, and with compensation.

Article 63

(1) The natural resources of Ireland – including land, mineral deposits, fossil-fuels, water-power, harbours, fisheries – are for the maintenance of the people of the country, and are under the special supervision and control of the State. (2) Private property in such resources, or sectional monopoly of the credit necessary for their use and exploitation, must not be allowed to interfere with such conservation and development as is required for the well-being of the community. (3) All natural resources, which have not yet been effectively appropriated by private individuals or associations, are the property of the State.

Article 64

(1) Ownership, inheritance, distribution and use of land are superintended by the State, so as to ensure to every citizen a healthy residence, and to secure an

efficient exploitation of the soil and in the interests of the community. (2) The landholder is bound, in duty to the community, to secure a reasonably efficient working or utilisation of the land. (3) Increase in the value of the land, arising without expenditure of labour or capital thereon shall accrue to the community.

Article 65
The rights of the State in and to natural resources, the use of which is of national importance, shall not be alienated. Their exploitation by private individuals or associations shall be permitted only under State supervision, and in accordance with conditions and regulations approved by legislation.

Article 66
The transport system of Ireland – including railways, waterways for general traffic, roads and air-service – must be administered, worked, co-ordinated and developed so as to facilitate the agricultural and industrial needs of the community in time of peace and the defence of the country in time of war.

Article 67
It shall be the aim of social legislation to promote the association of employees with employers in the management and control of industry, to favour the diffusion of property, and to encourage co-operative ownership and organisation, and to facilitate the formation and functioning of professional guilds.

X – Amendment of the Constitution

Article 68
This Constitution may at any time be amended through the forms required for ordinary legislation. But, except as provided in the following article, every repeal or modification of, or addition to an article of the Constitution, or insertion of a new article therein, must be approved by a majority of the House and of the Senate and must be submitted separately to the decision of the people, voting yes or no, and must be accepted by a majority of those who take part in the vote thereon.

Article 69
(1) The question whether there ought to be a general revision of the Constitution shall be submitted to the people voting yes or no, when (a) both House and Senate pass a resolution in favour of such revision; or (b) the House, in spite of the dissent of the Senate, passes such a resolution by a two-thirds majority, at least two-thirds of the total number voting; or (c) one hundred thousand voters demand such a revision. (2) If the majority of those who vote in the referendum pronounce in the affirmative, there shall be a new election of the House for the purpose of preparing amendments. (3) In such constituent function the co-operation of the Senate shall

be by way of consultation without veto. (4) The Constitution as finally revised shall be submitted as a whole to the people for acceptance or rejection.

Article 70

(1) One hundred thousand voters may demand, in general terms, the addition of a new article or the repeal or modification of an existing article of the Constitution. (2) When Congress approves of such a demand, it shall draw up a partial revision in the sense of the petitioners and refer it to the people for acceptance or rejection. (3) If Congress does not approve of the proposal, then the question whether there shall be a partial revision or not, shall be submitted to the vote of the people. If a majority of the citizens taking part in the vote express themselves in the affirmative, the revision shall be undertaken by Congress, in conformity with the people's decision. The revised article shall then be submitted to the people in accordance with article 68.

Article 71

(1) One hundred thousand voters may present a demand for a partial revision of the Constitution, in the form of a completely drafted new article or modification of an existing article. (2) If Congress approves thereof, it shall be referred to the people for acceptance or rejection. (3) If Congress rejects the proposal, it shall nevertheless be referred to the people for acceptance or rejection; but it shall not be deemed to have been accepted unless carried by a majority of the electors or by a two-thirds majority of those who take part in the vote. (4) If Congress drafts an alternative proposal, it may first submit its own proposal to the people. Should the people reject this, then the demand emanating from the popular initiative shall be submitted to the people for acceptance or rejection as in the preceding section

Bibliography

Primary sources

Archives

Ireland

National Archives of Ireland, Dublin
    Department of the Taoiseach S Series files
    Provisional Government Cabinet Minutes
    Dáil Éireann papers
    1922 Constitution Committee files
Trinity College Dublin Archives
    E.M. Stephens Papers, 4234-41
University College Dublin Archives
    John A. Costello Papers, P190
    Eamon de Valera Papers, P150
    Desmond Fitzgerald Papers, P80
    George Gavan Duffy Papers, P152
    J.M. Kelly Papers, P147
    Hugh Kennedy Papers, P4
    Alfred O'Rahilly Papers, P178
University College Cork Archives
    Alfred O'Rahilly Papers, Special Collections
    A. O'Rahilly Articles, Special Collections
Personal papers
    Michael Rynne Papers (in the possession of Etienne Rynne, Galway, now deceased)

United Kingdom

British National Archives, Kew, London
    Cabinet Office files 1922

Bibliography

Published memoirs, autobiographies and speeches

Andrews, C.S., *Dublin Made Me: An Autobiography* (Mercier: Dublin, 1979).

Andrews, C.S., *Man of No Property: An Autobiography* (Mercier: Dublin, 1982).

Briscoe, R., *For the Life of Me* (Longmans: London, 1958).

Collins, M., *The Path to Freedom* (Welsh Academic Press: Cardiff, 1996) (First published by Talbot Press in 1922).

Ewart, W., *A Journey in Ireland* (University College Dublin Press, 2008) (First published in 1922 by G.P. Putnam & Sons: London & New York).

Figgis, D., *The Irish Constitution Explained by Darrell Figgis* (Mellifont Press: Dublin, 1922).

Gaughan, J.A. (ed.), *Memoirs of Senator James G. Douglas (1887–1954): Concerned Citizen* (University College Dublin Press, 1998).

Jones, T., *Whitehall Diary: Vol III Ireland 1918–1925* (Oxford University Press: London, 1971).

Kennedy, H., 'Character and Sources of the Constitution of the Irish Free State', An Address delivered at the meeting of the American Bar Association at Seattle, Washington, 25 July 1928, (1928) 14 (8) *American Bar Association Journal* 437.

O'Broin, L., *No Man's Man: A Biographical Memoir of Joseph Brennan, Civil Servant and First Governor of The Central Bank* (Institute of Public Administration: Dublin, 1982).

O'Sullivan, D., *The Irish Free State and Its Senate: A Study in Contemporary Politics* (Faber & Faber: London, 1940).

Pakenham, F., *Peace by Ordeal: An Account from First-Hand Sources of the Negotiation and Signature of the Anglo-Irish Treaty 1921* (3rd edn, Geoffrey Chapman: London, 1962).

Rynne, M., *Die volkerrechtliche Stellung Irlands* (Duncker & Humblot: Munich, 1930).

Secondary sources

Books

Augusteijn, J. (ed.), *The Irish Revolution 1913–1923* (Palgrave: New York, 2002).

Borden, R., *Canada in the Commonwealth: From Conflict to Co-operation* (Clarendon: Oxford, 1929).

Bradley, A.W. & Ewing, K.D., *Constitutional and Administrative Law* (13th edn, Longman: Harlow, 2007).

Buckley, D., *James Fintan Lalor: Radical* (Cork University Press, 1990).

Childers, E., *The Framework of Home Rule* (E. Arnold: London, 1911).

Clifford, A., *The Constitutional History of Éire / Ireland* (Athol Books: Belfast, 1985).

Coakley, J. & Gallagher, M. (eds), *Politics in the Republic of Ireland* (Folens: Dublin, 1993).

Coakley, J. & Gallagher, M. (eds), *Politics in the Republic of Ireland* (4th edn Routledge: London, 2005).

Colum, P., *Arthur Griffith* (Browne and Nolan: Dublin, 1959).

Coogan, T.P., *Ireland in the Twentieth Century* (Hutchinson: London, 2003).

Cosgrave, A. & McCartney, D. (eds), *Studies in Irish History* (University College Dublin, 1979).

Cree, N., *Direct Legislation by the People* (A.C.F. McClurg and Company: Chicago, 1892).

Cruise O'Brien, C., *Parnell and His Party 1880–1890* (Clarendon Press: Oxford, 1964).

Cruise O'Brien, C., *States of Ireland* (Hutchinson: London, 1972).

Curran, J.M., *The Birth of the Irish Free State 1921–1923* (University of Alabama Press: Alabama, 1980).

Davis, R.P., *Arthur Griffith and Non-Violent Sinn Féin* (Anvil: Dublin, 1974).

De Blacam, A., *Towards a Republic: A Study of New Ireland's Social and Political Aims* (Thomas Kiersey Palmerston Gardens: Dublin, 1919).

Dicey, A.V., *The Law of the Constitution* (8th edn, Macmillan: London, 1927).

Doherty, G. & Keogh, D. (eds), *1916: The Long Revolution* (Mercier Press: Cork, 2007).

Donaldson, A.G., *Some Comparative Aspects of Irish Law* (Cambridge University Press: London, 1957).

Doyle, O., *Constitutional Equality Law* (Thomson Round Hall: Dublin, 2004).

Dudley Edwards, O., *Eamon de Valera* (GPC: Cardiff, 1987).

Dudley Edwards, R., *Patrick Pearse: The Triumph of Failure* (Poolbeg: Dublin, 1990).

Dunne, T., *Theobald Wolfe Tone, Colonial Outsider: An Analysis of His Political Philosophy* (Tower: Cork, 1982).

Elwood, P.E. & Smith, H.A., *Canada and World Politics: A Study of the Constitutional and International Relations of the British Empire* (Faber & Gwyer, 1928).

Fanning, B., *The Quest for Modern Ireland: The Battle for Ideas, 1912–1986* (Irish Academic Press: Dublin, 2008).

Fanning, R. *Independent Ireland* (Helicon: Dublin, 1983).

Farrell, B., *The Founding of Dáil Éireann: Parliament and Nation Building* (Gill & Macmillan: Dublin, 1971).

Farrell, B. (ed.), *The Irish Parliamentary Tradition with Three Essays on the Treaty Debate* (Gill & Macmillan: Dublin, 1973).

Farrell, B. (ed.), *De Valera's Constitution and Ours* (Gill & Macmillan: Dublin, 1988).

Farrell, B. (ed.), *The Creation of the Dáil: A Volume of Essays from the Thomas Davis Lectures* (Blackwater Press: Dublin, 1994).

Figgis, D., *The Gaelic State in the Past and Future: The Crown of a Nation* (Maunsel: Dublin, 1917).

Fitzgerald, G., *Reflections on the Irish State* (Irish Academic Press: Dublin, 2003).

Fogarty, L., *James Fintan Lalor Patriot and Political Essayist (1807–1849)* (Talbot Press: Dublin, 1918).

Fossedal, G.A., *Direct Democracy in Switzerland* (Transaction Publishers: New Brunswick, 2002).

Foster, R.F., *Modern Ireland, 1600–1972* (Penguin: London, 1989).

Fraser, H., *The Representation of the People Act 1919 with Explanatory Notes* (Sweet & Maxwell Ltd: London, 1918).

Gallagher, F., *The Anglo-Irish Treaty* (Hutchinson: London, 1965).

Gallagher, M., *Political Parties in the Republic of Ireland* (Gill & Macmillan: Dublin, 1985).

Gallagher, M. (ed.), *Irish Elections 1922–44: Results and Analysis* (PSAI Press: Limerick, 1993).

Gallagher, M. (ed.), *Irish Elections 1948–77: Results and Analysis* (Routledge: London, 2009).

Garran, R., *The Making and Working of the Constitution* (New Century Press: Sydney, 1932).

Garvin, T., *The Irish Senate* (Institute of Public Administration: Dublin, 1969).

Garvin, T., *The Evolution of Irish Nationalist Politics* (Gill & Macmillan: Dublin, 1981).

Garvin, T., *Nationalist Revolutionaries in Ireland: 1858–1928* (Doubleday: New York, 1987).

Garvin, T., *1922: The Birth of Irish Democracy* (Gill & Macmillan: Dublin, 2005).

Gaughan, J.A., *Alfred O'Rahilly* (Kingdom Books: Dublin, 1986).

Griffith, A., *The Resurrection of Hungary: A Parallel for Ireland* (Whelan: Dublin, 1918).

Gwynn, D.R., *The Irish Free State 1922–1927* (Macmillan & Co.: London, 1928).

Gwynn, D.R., *The Life of John Redmond* (Harrap: London, 1932).

Hachey, T. & McCaffrey, L. (eds), *Perspectives on Irish Nationalism* (University Press of Kentucky: Lexington, 1989).

Hall, D.H., *The British Commonwealth of Nations: A Study of Its Past and Future Development* (Methuen: London, 1920).

Harkness, D.W., *The Restless Dominion: The Irish Free State and the British Commonwealth of Nations, 1921–31* (Gill & Macmillan: Dublin, 1969).

Headlam-Morley, A., *The New Democratic Constitutions of Europe: A Comparative Study of Post-War European Constitutions with Special Reference to Germany, Czechoslovakia, Poland, Finland, The Kingdom of the Serbs, Croats & Slovenes and the Baltic States* (Oxford University Press, 1928).

Hogan, G., *The Origins of the Irish Constitution 1928–1941* (Royal Irish Academy: Dublin, 2012).

Holdsworth, W., *History of English Law* (3rd edn, Methuen: London, 1923) (vol. 3).

Horgan, J.J., *Parnell to Pearse: Some Recollections and Reflections* (Browne & Nolan: Dublin, 1948).

Hughes, H., *National Sovereignty and Judicial Autonomy in the British Commonwealth of Nations* (P.S. King & Son Ltd: London, 1931).

Kee, R., *Ireland: A History* (Weidenfeld & Nicolson: London, 1980).

Keith, A.B., *The Sovereignty of the British Dominions* (Macmillan: London, 1929).

Keith, A.B., *The Constitutional Law of the British Dominions* (Macmillan: London, 1933).

Kelly, J.M., *Fundamental Rights in Irish Law* (Allen Figgis & Co. Ltd: Dublin, 1967).

Kelly, J.M., *The Irish Constitution*, eds G. Hogan and G. Whyte (Butterworth: Dublin, 2003).

Kennedy, W.P.M., *Essays in Constitutional Law* (Oxford University Press: London, 1934).

Kennedy, W.P.M. & Schlosberg, H.J., *The Law and Custom of the South African Constitution* (Oxford University Press: London, 1935).

Keogh, D., *The Vatican, the Bishops and Irish Politics: 1919–1939* (Cambridge University Press, 1986).

Keogh, D., *Ireland and the Vatican: The Politics and Diplomacy of Church–State Relations, 1922–1960* (Cork University Press, 1995).

Keogh, D. & McCarthy, A., *The Making of the Irish Constitution 1937* (Mercier Press: Cork, 2007).

Kissane, B., *Explaining Irish Democracy* (University College Dublin Press, 2002).

Kohn, L., *The Constitution of the Irish Free State* (George Allen & Unwin Ltd: London, 1932).

Kotsonouris, M., *Retreat from Revolution: The Dáil Courts, 1920–24* (Irish Academic Press: Dublin, 1994).

Lee, J.J., *Ireland 1912–1985: Politics and Society* (Cambridge University Press, 1989).

Lee, J.J. & O Tuathaigh, G., *The Age of de Valera* (Ward River Press in association with RTE: Dublin, 1982).

Litton, F. (ed.), *The Constitution of Ireland 1937–1987* (Institute of Public Administration: Dublin, 1988).

Lyons, F.S.L., *Ireland Since the Famine* (Fontana: London, 1973).

Macardle, D., *The Irish Republic* (Wolfhound Press: Dublin, 1999).

MacCarthaigh, M. & Manning, M., *Houses of the Oireachtas* (Institute of Public Administration: Dublin, 2010).

Mansergh, D. (ed.), *Nationalism and Independence: Selected Irish Papers by Nicholas Mansergh* (Cork University Press, 1997).

Mansergh, N., *The Irish Free State: Its Government and Politics* (Allen & Unwin: London, 1934).

Mansergh, N., *The Commonwealth Experience* (Macmillan: London, 1982).

Mansergh, N., *The Unresolved Question: The Anglo-Irish Settlement and Its Undoing 1912–72* (Yale University Press: New Haven, 1991).

May, T.E., ed. F. Holland, *The Constitutional History of England Since the Accession of George the Third 1860–1911 Vol III* (Read Books: London, 2007).

Meleady, D., *Redmond: The Parnellite* (Cork University Press, 2008).

Moran, D.P., ed. P. Maume, *The Philosophy of Irish Ireland* (University College Dublin Press: 2006).

Morgan, D.G., *A Judgment Too Far: Judicial Activism and the Constitution* (Cork University Press, 2001).

Morgan, J.H., *The New Irish Constitution: An Exposition and Some Arguments* (Hodder & Stoughton: London, 1912).

Morrissey, T.J., *Edward J. Byrne 1872–1941: The Forgotten Archbishop of Dublin* (Columbia Press: Dublin, 2010).

Moss, W., *Political Parties in the Irish Free State* (Columbia University Press: New York, 1933).

Mulvey, H., *Thomas Davis and Ireland: A Biographical Study* (Catholic University of America Press: Washington, DC, 2003).

Murphy, T. & Twomey, P. (eds), *Ireland's Evolving Constitution 1937–1997: Collected Essays* (Hart Publishing: Oxford, 1998).

Norman, E., *A History of Modern Ireland* (Allen Lane: London, 1971).

O'Briain, B., *The Irish Constitution* (Talbot: Dublin, 1929).

Ó Cearúil, M., *Bunreacht na hÉireann: A Study of the Irish Text* (Stationery Office: Dublin, 1999).

O'Farrell, P., *Who's Who in the Irish War of Independence 1916–1921* (Mercier: Dublin, 1980).

O'Leary, C., *Irish Elections 1918–1977: Parties, Voters and Proportional Representation* (Gill & Macmillan: Dublin, 1979).

O'Leary, D., *Vocationalism & Social Catholicism in Twentieth-Century Ireland: The Search for a Christian Social Order* (Irish Academic Press: Dublin, 2000).

O'Neill, D.J., *The Irish Revolution and the Cult of the Leader: Observations on Griffith, Moran, Pearse and Connolly* (Northeastern University Press: Boston, 1988).

O'Shiel, K., *The Making of a Republic* (Talbot: Dublin, 1920).

Oliver, P.C., *The Constitution of Independence: The Development of Constitutional Theory in Australia, Canada, and New Zealand* (Oxford University Press: London, 2005).

Parry, C., *Nationality and Citizenship Laws of the Commonwealth and of the Republic of Ireland* (Stevens & Sons Ltd: London, 1957).

Pearse, P., *Collected Works of Pádraic H. Pearse: Political Writings and Speeches* (Phoenix: Dublin, 1916).

Plunkett, H., *Ireland in the New Century* (Irish Academic Press: Dublin, 1982).

Quinn, J., *John Mitchel* (University College Dublin Press: 2008).

Regan, J.M., *The Irish Counter-Revolution 1921–1936: Treatyite Politics and Settlement in Independent Ireland* (Gill & Macmillan: Dublin, 1999).

Ruane, B., O'Callaghan, J. & Barniville, D., *Law and Government: A Tribute to Rory Brady* (Round Hall: Dublin, 2014).

Select Constitutions of the World (Stationery Office: Dublin, 1922).

Sexton, B., *Ireland and the Crown, 1922–1936: The Governor-Generalship of the Irish Free State* (Irish Academic Press: Dublin, 1989).

Shirer, W., *The Rise and Fall of the Third Reich* (Simon & Schuster: New York, 1960).

Shiva Rao, B. (ed.), *Select Constitutions of the World* (Madras Law Journal Press, 1934).

Sullivan, J.W., *Direct Legislation by the Citizenship through the Initiative and Referendum* (True Nationalist Publishing Company: New York, 1893).

Swift-MacNeill, J.G., *Studies in the Constitution of the Irish Free State* (Talbot: Dublin, 1925).

Ward, A.J., *The Irish Constitutional Tradition: Responsible Government and Modern Ireland, 1782–1992* (Irish Academic Press: Dublin, 1994).

Wells, W.B., *John Redmond: A Biography* (Nisbet: London, 1919).

Wheare, K.C., *The Statute of Westminster 1931* (Clarendon: Oxford, 1933).

Wheare, K.C., *Modern Constitutions* (Oxford University Press, 1966).

White, A., *The Irish Free State: Its Evolution and Possibilities* (Hutchinson & Co.: London, 1920).

Whyte, J.H., *Church and State in Modern Ireland 1923–1979* (Gill & Macmillan: Dublin, 1980).

Younger, C., *Arthur Griffith* (Gill & Macmillan: Dublin, 1981).

Chapters in edited collections

Farrell, B. 'The First Dáil and After' in Farrell, B. (ed.), *The Irish Parliamentary Tradition* (Gill & Macmillan: Dublin, 1973).

Fitzgerald, G., 'The Irish Constitution in its Historical Context' in Murphy, T. & Twomey, P. (eds), *Ireland's Evolving Constitution 1937–1997: Collected Essays* (Hart Publishing: Oxford, 1998).

Garvin, T., 'Cogadh na nCarad: The Creation of the Irish Political Elite' in Garvin, T., Manning, M. & Sinnott, R. (eds), *Dissecting Irish Politics*: *Essays in Honour of Brian Farrell* (University College Dublin: 2004).

Hogan, G., 'A Desert Island Case Set in the Silver Sea: The State (Ryan) v Lennon (1934)' in O'Dell, E (ed.), *Leading Cases of the Twentieth Century* (Round Hall Sweet & Maxwell: Dublin, 2000).

Bibliography

Kelly, J.M., 'The Constitution: Law and Manifesto' in Litton, F. (ed.), *The Constitution of Ireland 1937–1987* (Institute of Public Administration: Dublin, 1988).

Keogh, D., 'The Constitutional Revolution: An Analysis of the Making of the Constitution' in Litton, F (ed.) *The Constitution of Ireland 1937–1987* (Institute of Public Administration: Dublin, 1988).

Kissane, B., 'De Valera, the 1937 Constitution, and Proportional Representation' in Carolan, E. & Doyle, O. (eds), *The Irish Constitution: Governance and Values* (Thomson Round Hall: Dublin, 2008).

Larkin, E., 'The Irish Political Tradition' in Hachey, T. & McCaffrey, L. (eds), *Perspectives on Irish Nationalism* (University Press of Kentucky: Lexington, 1989).

Lee, J., 'Aspects of Corporatist Thought in Ireland: The Commission on Vocational Organisation, 1939–43' in Cosgrave, A. & McCarthy, D. (eds), *Studies in Irish History* (University College Dublin: 1979).

Maitland, F.W., 'Why the History of English Law Is Not Written' in Fisher, H.A.L. (ed.). *The Collected Papers of F. W. Maitland* (Cambridge University Press: 1911).

Murphy, B.P., 'Nationalism: The Framing of the Constitution of the Irish Free State, 1922 – The Defining Battle for the Irish Republic' in Augusteijn, J. (ed.), *The Irish Revolution 1913–1923* (Palgrave: New York, 2002).

O'Donnell, D., '"The Most Curious Forerunner" to the Fundamental Rights Provisions in the 1937 Constitution' in Ruane, B., O'Callaghan, J. & Barniville, D. (eds), *Law and Government: A Tribute to Rory Brady* (Round Hall: Dublin, 2014).

Weeks, L., 'Membership of the Houses' in MacCarthaigh, M. & Manning, M. (eds), *Houses of the Oireachtas* (Institute of Public Administration: Dublin, 2010).

Journal articles

Akenson, D.H. & Fallin, F.P., 'The Irish Civil War and the Drafting of the Irish Constitution' (1970) V (1) *Éire-Ireland* 10.

Akenson, D.H. & Fallin, F.P., 'The Irish Civil War and the Drafting of the Irish Constitution' (1970) V (2) *Éire-Ireland* 42.

Akenson, D.H. & Fallin, F.P., 'The Irish Civil War and the Drafting of the Irish Constitution' (1970) V (4) *Éire-Ireland* 28.

Barrington, D., 'Private Property under the Irish Constitution' (1973) 8 *Irish Jurist* 1.

Bendor, A.L. & Segal, Z., 'Constitutionalism and Trust in Britain: An Ancient Constitutional Culture, a New Judicial Review Model' (2002) 17 *American University International Law Review* 683.

Bromage, A.W., 'Constitutional Developments in Saorstát Éireann and the Constitution of Éire II, Internal Affairs' (1937) 31 (6) *The American Political Science Review* 1050.

Cahillane, L., 'Ireland's Forgotten Constitutions' (2009) 27 *Irish Law Times* 243.

Cahillane, L., 'The Prerogative and Its Survival in Ireland: Dusty Antique or Positively Useful?' (2010) 1 (2) *Irish Journal of Legal Studies* 1.

Cahillane, L., 'Anti-Party Politics and the Irish Free State Constitution' (2012) 35 *Dublin University Law Journal* 34.

Casey, J., 'Republican Courts in Ireland 1919–1922' (1970) 5 *Irish Jurist* 321.

Casper, G., 'Guardians of the Constitution' (1979–80) 53 *S Cal L Rev* 773.

Coakley, J., 'Ireland's Unique Electoral Experiment: The Senate Election of 1925' 2005 20 (3) *Irish Political Studies* 231.

Coakley, J., '"Irish Republic", "Eire" or "Ireland"? The Contested Name of John Bull's Other Island' (2009) 80 (1) *The Political Quarterly* 49.

Coquelin, O., 'Politics in the Irish Free State: The Legacy of a Conservative Revolution' (2005) 10 *The European Legacy* 29.

Costello, K., 'The Expulsion of Prerogative Doctrine from Irish Law: Quantifying and Remedying the Loss of the Royal Prerogatives' (1997) 32 *Irish Jurist* 145.

Daly, M., 'Irish Nationality and Citizenship Since 1922' (May 2001) 32 (127) *Irish Historical Studies* 377.

Deener, D., 'Judicial Review in Modern Constitutional Systems' (1952) 46 (4) *The American Political Science Review* 1079.

Delaney, V.T.H., 'The Constitution of Ireland: Its Origins and Development' (1957) 12 *University of Toronto Law Journal* 1.

Farrell, B., 'The Drafting of the Irish Free State Constitution I' (1970) 5 *Irish Jurist* 115.

Farrell, B., 'The Drafting of the Irish Free State Constitution II' (1970) 5 *Irish Jurist* 343.

Farrell, B., 'The Drafting of the Irish Free State Constitution III' (1971) 6 *Irish Jurist* 111.

Farrell, B., 'The Drafting of the Irish Free State Constitution IV' (1971) 6 *Irish Jurist* 345.

Farrell, B., 'A Note on the Dáil Constitution, 1919' (1969) 4 *Irish Jurist* 127.

Fay, P., 'The Amendments to the Constitution Committee 1926' (1978) 26 (3) *Administration* 331.

Foley, K.E., 'Australian Judicial Review' (2007) 6 *Wash U Global Studies Law Review* 281.

Garvin, L.F.C., 'The Constitutional Initiative' (1903) 177 (560) *The North American Review* 78.

Grant, J.A.C., 'Judicial Review of Legislation under the Austrian Constitution of 1920' (1934) 28 (4) *The American Political Science Review* 670.

Haines, C.G., 'Some Phases of the Theory and Practice of Judicial Review of Legislation in Foreign Countries' (1930) 24 (3) *The American Political Science Review* 583.

Hartman, B.J., 'The Arrival of Judicial Review in Germany under the Weimar Constitution of 1919' (2003–4) 18 *BYU J Pub L* 107.

Harvard Law Review Editorial Board, 'Decline of the Judicial Committee of the Privy Council; Current Status of Appeals from the British Dominions' (September 1947) 60 (7) *Harvard Law Review* 1138.

Hogan, G., 'Law and Religion: Church–State Relations in Ireland from Independence to the Present Day' (1987) 35 *AJCL* 47.

Humphreys, R., 'Review of Kelly: The Irish Constitution, Third Edition' (1994) 16 *Dublin University Law Journal* 222.

Keane, R., 'Judges as Lawmakers: The Irish Experience' (2004) *JSIJ* 1.

Keith, A.B., 'Notes on Imperial Constitutional Law' (1922) 4 (4) *Journal of Comparative Legislation and International Law*, Third Series, 233.

Kelly, J.M., 'Hidden Treasure and the Constitution' (1988) 10 *Dublin University Law Journal* 5.

Kissane, B., 'The Constitutional Revolution that Never Was' (2009) 104 *Radical History Review* 77.

Larkin, E., 'Church, State, and Nation in Modern Ireland' (1975) 80 (5) *American Historical Review* 1244.

Lenihan, N., 'Royal Prerogatives and the Constitution' (1989) 24 *Irish Jurist* 1.

Bibliography

Lowell, A.L., 'The Referendum, and Initiative: Their Relation to the Interests of Labor in Switzerland and in America' (1895) 6(1) *International Journal of Ethics* 51.

Malone, A.E., 'Party Government in the Irish Free State' (1929) 44 (3) *Political Science Quarterly* 363.

Mason, A., 'The Role of a Constitutional Court in a Federation: A Comparison of the Australian and the United States Experience' (1986) 16 *Federal Law Review* 1.

Mohr, T., 'Law without Loyalty – The Abolition of the Irish Appeal to the Privy Council' (2002) 37 *Irish Jurist* 187.

Mohr, T., 'The Foundations of Irish Extra-Territorial Legislation' (2005) 40 *Irish Jurist* 86.

Mohr, T., 'The Rights of Women under the Constitution of the Irish Free State' (2006) 41 *Irish Jurist* 20.

Mohr, T., 'British Involvement in the Creation of the Constitution of the Irish Free State' (2008) 30 (1) *Dublin University Law Journal* 166.

Mohr, T., 'The Colonial Laws Validity Act and the Irish Free State' (2008) 43 *Irish Jurist* 21.

Mohr, T., 'British Imperial Statutes and Irish Sovereignty: Statutes Passed after the Creation of the Irish Free State' (2011) 32 (1) *Journal of Legal History* 61.

Morgan, D.G., 'Constitutional Interpretation: Three Cautionary Tales' (1988) 10 *Dublin University Law Journal* 24.

Nagel, H., 'Judicial Review in Germany' (1954) 3 (2) *American Journal of Comparative Law* 233.

O'Dowd, J., 'Knowing How Way Leads on to Way: Some Reflections on the Abbylara Decision' (2003) 38 *Irish Jurist* 162.

O'Grady, J.P., 'The Irish Free State Passport and the Question of Citizenship, 1921–4' (November 1989) 26 (104) *Irish Historical Studies* 396.

O'Tuama, S., 'Judicial Review under the Irish Constitution: More American than Commonwealth' (2008) 12 (2) *Electronic Journal of Comparative Law* 1.

Paulson, S.L., 'Constitutional Review in the United States and Austria: Notes on the Beginnings' (2003) 16 (2) *Ratio Juris* 223.

Phelan, E.J., 'The Sovereignty of the Irish Free State' (1927) 3 *The Review of Nations* 35.

Prest, W., 'Law for Historians: William Blackstone on Wives, Colonies and Slaves' (2007) 11 *Legal History* 105.

Reinsch, P.S., 'The Initiative and Referendum' (1913) 3 (2) *Proceedings of the Academy of Political Science in the City of New York* 155.

Sircar, I. & Hoyland, B., 'Get the Party Started: Development of Political Party Legislative Dynamics in the Irish Free State Seanad (1922–36)' (2010) 16 *Party Politics* 89.

Stolleis, M., 'Judicial Review, Administrative Review, and Constitutional Review in the Weimar Republic' (2003) 16 (2) *Ratio Juris* 266.

Towey, T., 'Hugh Kennedy and the Constitutional Development of the Irish Free State, 1922–1923' (1977) 12 *Irish Jurist* 354.

Townshend, C., 'The Meaning of Irish Freedom Constitutionalism in the Free State' (1998) 6 (8) *Transactions of the Royal History Society* 45.

Ward, A. J., 'Challenging the British Constitution: The Irish Free State Constitution and the External Minister' (1990) 9 *Parliamentary History* 116.

Wilson, L., 'The Brehon Laws' *Hedgemaster – Periodical of the Irish Cultural Society of the City Garden Area* (New York 1989).

Bibliography

Theses

Corcoran, D., *The Irish Free State 1922–32: Government and Administration* (UCC Thesis 2009).

Hogan, G., *Development of Judicial Review of Legislation and Irish Constitutional Law 1929–1941* (TCD Thesis 2001).

Mohr, T., *The Irish Free State and the Legal Implications of Dominion Status* (UCD Thesis 2007).

Online publications

Kelly, J.M., 'Statements on the 70th Anniversary of the Constitution in Seanad Éireann', available at www.inis.gov.ie/en/JELR/Pages/Statements%20on%20the%2070th%20 Anniversary%20of%20the%20Constitution%20in%20Seanad%20%C3%89ireann.

Mac Aonghusa, P., 'Proportional Representation in Ireland' (1959), available at http:// proinsias.net/publications/pr_in_ireland/.

Ó Corráin, D. & O'Riordan, T., 'Arthur Griffith', Multitext Project on Irish History, available at http://multitext.ucc.ie/d/Arthur_Griffith.

Whyte, N. 'The Irish Senate Elections of 1925: An Exceedingly Severe Test' (17 February 2002), available on the Northern Ireland Social and Political Archive 'Ark' at www.ark. ac.uk/elections/h1925.htm.

Index